NOTHING GREATER, NOTHING BETTER

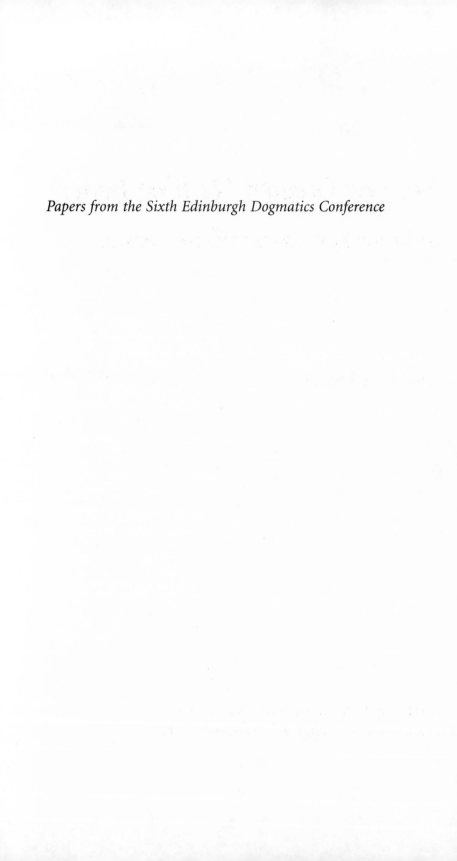

Papers from the Sixth Edinburgh Dogmatics Conference

Nothing Greater, Nothing Better

THEOLOGICAL ESSAYS ON THE LOVE OF GOD

Edited by

Kevin J. Vanhoozer

WILLIAM B. EERDMANS PUBLISHING COMPANY
GRAND RAPIDS, MICHIGAN / CAMBRIDGE, U.K.

Wm. B. Eerdmans Publishing Co.
255 Jefferson Ave. S.E., Grand Rapids, Michigan 49503 /
P.O. Box 163, Cambridge CB3 9PU U.K.

Printed in the United States of America

06 05 04 03 02 01   7 6 5 4 3 2 1

Library of Congress Cataloging-in-Publication Data

Nothing greater, nothing better: theological essays on the love of God /
edited by Kevin J. Vanhoozer.
          p.   cm.
     Includes bibliographical references.
     ISBN 0-8028-4902-4 (pbk.: alk. paper)
     1. God — Love.   I. Vanhoozer, Kevin J.

   BT140.N68   2001
   231'.6 — dc21

                                        2001040382

www.eerdmans.com

Contents

CHAPTER 1

Introduction: The Love of God — Its Place, Meaning, and Function in Systematic Theology

KEVIN J. VANHOOZER

I. THE DOCTRINE OF GOD: A PARADIGM REVOLUTION?

The opposite of love, it has been said, is not hate but indifference. The God of the Christian gospel is anything but indifferent toward humanity. Humanity, of course, has not always returned the compliment. Yet it is exceedingly odd that Christian theologians have themselves been somewhat indifferent — inattentive, neutral — with regard to the concept of the love of God, if we are to judge from their often oblique, indistinct, or awkward treatments of the subject. On the one hand, it is no exaggeration to say that defining and situating the notion of the love of God is the perennial task, and standing challenge, of Christian dogmatics. On the other hand, however, there is at present little consensus as to where the topic of the love of God belongs. Is the love of God an aspect of God's being, or should it be treated under some other heading: the Trinity, providence, or atonement perhaps? Further, what do the various headings under which the love of God is treated tell us about its meaning and function?

Though what it means to predicate "love" of God remains something of a mystery, this has not impeded its use in human affairs. "Love" has been the subject of poems, ballads, and philosophical treatises down through the ages. It has been a prominent theme in ethics and in theologi-

1

cal discussions of the appropriate human response to God's gracious initiative. The mere frequency of the term's use, however, stands in inverse proportion to its meaningfulness. In his 1936 film "Modern Times," a biting satire on industrial life, Charlie Chaplin sings "It's Love," a song that repeats the term "love" at breakneck speed dozens of times: "It's love — love, love — love, love, love, love, love, love. Love, love, love, love, love, love, love," etc. A mere repetition of the term leads inexorably to its devaluation. Hence the predicament of our modern, or postmodern times: to say what love is and how it may be affirmed of God.[1] It is not at all obvious, moreover, that contemporary thinkers have a distinct advantage in this effort over those of antiquity.

A growing number of Christian theologians nevertheless maintain that a major advance in understanding the love of God has been made, a step so significant as to entail a paradigm revolution in all of Christian theology. I refer to the suggestion that God's love is to be viewed in terms of interpersonal relations rather than in terms of substantival attributes.[2] As early as 1962, John McIntyre identified the prime difficulty in giving full value to the concept of the love of God as "an unduly narrow equation of the term with an attribute."[3] More recently, Vincent Brümmer has observed that, in the Christian tradition, "Love has generally been taken to be an attitude of one person toward another, rather than as a relation between persons."[4]

According to Sallie McFague, the essential core of Christianity is the transformative event of new life, grounded in the life and death of Jesus of Nazareth: "the event of God's transforming love."[5] This new paradigm for

---

1. The love of God, as perhaps no other theological topic, is particularly vulnerable to Feuerbach's suspicion that doctrines are projections of human ideals.
2. See, for instance, Philip Clayton, "The Case for Christian Panentheism," *Dialog* 37 (1998): 201-8. Cf. Vincent Brümmer's comment: "Since Aristotle our intellectual tradition has been infected by the ontological prejudice that there are only two sorts of reality: substances and attributes" (*The Model of Love: A Study in Philosophical Theology* [Cambridge: Cambridge University Press, 1993], p. 33).
3. John McIntyre, *On the Love of God* (London: Collins, 1962), p. 34.
4. Brümmer, *The Model of Love*, p. 33.
5. Sallie McFague, "An Epilogue: The Christian Paradigm," in *Christian Theology: An Introduction to Its Traditions and Tasks*, ed. Peter Hodgson and Robert King, 2nd ed. (Philadelphia: Fortress, 1985), p. 382. Note that for McFague, Christianity is itself a paradigm inasmuch as it constitutes a comprehensive interpretation (though only one; others are available) of God's relation with the world.

construing the love of God entails nothing less than a revision of the God-world relationship itself, which is to say, a revision of the whole of theology. To be precise, the revolution McFague has in mind involves the change from a view that sees the God-world relation in terms of unilateral sovereignty to a view that emphasizes bilateral fellowship. McFague, for instance, sees the world as God's "body" and world history as the process of "inclusive love for all."[6]

On a more popular level, the authors of *The Openness of God: A Biblical Challenge to the Traditional Understanding of God* similarly maintain that a new understanding of the love of God leads to a shaking of the foundations of traditional theism. "A new way of critical reappraisal and competent reconstruction of the doctrine of God is sweeping over the intellectual landscape."[7] Clearly, any concept such as the love of God that lies at the heart of such revolutionary change of theological paradigm merits serious consideration. Is it indeed the case that the concept of the love of God leads to the deconstruction of traditional Christian theism?

II. HISTORICAL REVIEW: WHERE WE ARE

Revolutions in paradigm are only visible against a background of "normal science," or in the case of theology, against the backdrop of Christian tradition.[8] How, then, did early theologians understand the love of God?

---

6. Sallie McFague, *The Body of God: An Ecological Theology* (London: SCM, 1993), p. 160. McFague acknowledges that, in speaking of the world as the "body" of God, she no longer considers the body of Jesus to carry exclusive significance. Her paradigm change requires considerable revision, not only of classical theism but of classical Christology too: "the first [move] is to relativize the incarnation in relation to Jesus of Nazareth and the second is to maximize it in relation to the cosmos. In other words, the proposal is to consider Jesus as paradigmatic of what we find everywhere: everything that is is the sacrament of God" (p. 162). As we shall see, a number of the essays in this volume find it difficult to speak of the love of God apart from the doctrine of the incarnation.

7. Clark Pinnock, Richard Rice, John Sanders, William Hasker, and David Bassinger, *The Openness of God: A Biblical Challenge to the Traditional Understanding of God* (Downers Grove, Ill.: InterVarsity Press, 1994), p. 9.

8. The language and idea of "normal science," "paradigms," and "scientific revolutions" go back to an influential work by Thomas S. Kuhn, *The Structure of Scientific Revolutions*, 2nd ed. (Chicago: University of Chicago, 1970).

The Love of God as Attribute and Action

Classical theism — the classic model for understanding the God-world relation — has a double origin: the Bible and ancient philosophy. Theology was to a large degree the attempt to reconcile the story of God's acts in Israel's history and in the history of Jesus Christ — essentially a love story of the Creator for his creation, his community, his child — with ancient Greek notions of perfect being.

According to Plato, love is either the desire (eros) for something I do not have or the desire never to lose what I now have in the future. Love is "always poor," always needy. Augustine agrees with Plato that love is essentially the desire for ultimate happiness. For Augustine, however, only one's love for God will not disappoint. Only God, that is, should be loved for his own sake and not for the sake of something else. How, then, can God love us? The gods, according to Plato, cannot love, for they lack nothing.[9] It is not as though God *needs* the human creature, for it follows from the notion of perfect being that nothing can add to God's own enjoyment of himself. Yet it is clear from Scripture that God loves us. Augustine's solution to the paradox of God's love is to posit a properly divine kind of love, a gift love: *agape.*

Nicholas Wolterstorff doubts that there is much of the Stoical rather than the scriptural about Augustine's position. For the Stoics, and the whole eudaemonist tradition of antiquity, happiness is a matter of uninterrupted bliss. The wise person is one who learns how not to be disturbed by changes in the world. The wise person lacks *pathos:* he or she is without passion, impervious to changes that would overturn the rule of reason. Wolterstorff observes that "Augustine stood in the Platonic tradition of seeing happiness as lying in the satisfaction of *eros* while the Stoics saw happiness as lying in the elimination of *eros.*"[10]

The implication for the concept of the love of God is clear: God's life is one of bliss and beneficence, or as Wolterstorff paraphrases it, a life of "non-suffering apathy."[11] Augustine's God "turns out to be remarkably like the Stoic sage: devoid of passions, unfamiliar with longing, foreign to suf-

9. See Brümmer's discussion of Plato's dialogue the *Symposium* in *The Model of Love,* pp. 110-20.

10. Nicholas Wolterstorff, "Suffering Love," in *Philosophy and the Christian Life,* ed. Thomas Morris (Notre Dame: University of Notre Dame Press, 1988), pp. 205-6.

11. Wolterstorff, "Suffering Love," p. 198.

fering."[12] In the Christian tradition, God was widely held to be "impassible": not able to suffer. In the classic theological paradigm, the Bible and classical philosophy are seen to agree: a perfect being who has life in himself cannot suffer. Where the Bible appears to ascribe emotion or suffering to God, the tradition quickly concludes that such language must be figurative. Classical theism thus functions as a theological hermeneutic for construing what Scripture says about the love of God.

How, then, does God "process" the suffering of the innocent, or the suffering of his Son? God is all-knowing, to be sure, but how should we characterize God's knowledge of those occurrences that involve loss (e.g., grief, injury, pain, death)? Wolterstorff believes that the root assumption behind the notion of divine impassibility is that God is unconditioned by anything not himself. If, as John of Damascus puts it, passion is "a movement in one thing caused by another," then God must, if he is unconditioned, have no passions. The question Wolterstorff presses home is simply this: if God cannot be affected by anything other than himself, then how are we to understand God's knowledge of human suffering and human loss? Is this something that God can know or not? Can a God who does not experience suffering, in some sense, be said to "know" particular instances of suffering in our world? More pointedly, can a God who is unable to sympathize be said to love?

Many of the same classical emphases that characterize Augustine may be found almost a thousand years later in Thomas Aquinas. God's being and God's will are unconditioned. God cannot change, for he is perfect (the doctrine of divine immutability). God's will is the final explanation for everything that happens (the doctrine of divine sovereignty). Is it correct to infer from these constants, however, as proponents of the new paradigm are prone to do, that "God's relation to the world [in the classical paradigm] is thus one of mastery and control"?[13]

What precisely is the love of God according to Aquinas? Question 20 of the *Summa Theologiae* treats *de amore Dei* and, significantly enough, follows question 19 on "will in God." The love of God for Aquinas is God's willing the good. God is benevolent (*bene volere* = "good willing"). To love someone is to will that person good. Does God love the whole world? Yes, for God wills some good to each existing thing. However, God loves some

---

12. Wolterstorff, "Suffering Love," p. 210.
13. Richard Rice, "Biblical Support for a New Perspective," in *The Openness of God,* p. 11.

things more than others, "for since his love is the cause of things . . . one thing would not be better than another but for God willing it more good."[14] Importantly, Aquinas does not believe that God *responds* to the good in a thing by loving it, but rather that God's love for a thing is the *cause* of its goodness.

On the traditional view, then, God metes out good but takes neither joy nor delight in the good he brings about (for this would make God's joy conditional on something in the world). That in which God takes delight turns out to be his own exercise of benevolence. Classical theism pictures God, not as a utilitarian or pragmatist who delights in results, but rather as a Kantian — a modern Stoic — who takes pleasure simply in his good will: good for goodness' sake. Wolterstorff admits that such a picture is coherent, but he denies that it is biblical.[15]

For Aquinas (and here he follows Aristotle), God moves the world but is not moved by the world. This is simply another way of stating what it means for God to be immutable and impassible. God, says Aquinas, is like a stone column to which humans stand in relation. The column may be on our left or our right, in front of or behind us, but our relation to the column is in us, not in the column. Similarly, we may experience God's mercy or his wrath, but it is not God who changes, only our relation to him. "What changes is the way we experience the will of God."[16] With regard to God's will, it is his goodness alone that can move it. The concepts of immutability and impassibility here converge: God's will cannot be affected or changed by anything outside himself. God is, to use Richard Creel's fine phrase, "unsusceptible to causation."[17] This is a most important analytic point: impassibility no more means impassive than immutable means immobile. God may be unmoved (e.g., transcendent — unsusceptible to

14. Thomas Aquinas, *Summa Theologiae*, vol. 5, ed. Thomas Gilby (London: Eyre & Spottiswoode, 1963), p. 65.

15. It would appear that both the traditional and the revisionist views work with a combination of natural and revealed theology, that is, with a concept of divine perfection and with the biblical storyline. As to the notion of God's valuing his own good will, this is not entirely without biblical support, as the language of Ephesians 1 attests: "according to the purpose of his will" (1:5, 11); "for the praise of his glory" (1:12, 14).

16. Richard E. Creel, "Immutability and Impassibility," in *A Companion to Philosophy of Religion*, ed. Philip L. Quinn and Charles Taliaferro (Oxford: Blackwell, 1997), p. 317. See also Creel's earlier, more comprehensive work: *Divine Impassibility* (Cambridge: Cambridge University Press, 1986).

17. Creel, "Immutability and Impassibility," p. 314.

worldly causes), but he is nevertheless a mover (e.g., immanent — active and present in the world). On the contrary, the original intent of both concepts is to insist that no creature can move or affect or change God by dint of its own will.[18]

Twentieth-Century Developments: Responsiveness and Relation

A number of twentieth-century developments have led to the demise of the classical paradigm that saw God's love in terms of divine sovereignty, that is, in terms of God's ability unilaterally to will and to do good. The problem is not *that* God loves, but rather *what* God's love is. What, then, is the effect of what Langdon Gilkey calls contemporary theology's "war with the Greeks" upon the notion of the love of God?[19]

Metaphysical Developments: Process Philosophy

Process philosophy stands out in the twentieth century for its resolute commitment to the metaphysical project — constructing a comprehensive account of the categories by which to understand all of reality, from the amoeba to the Absolute — and for its critique of the classical theistic model of conceiving the God-world relation. From a process perspective, the classical picture of a universe filled with various kinds of individual substances fails to capture the dynamic and interrelated nature of the physical world, not to mention the other, nonphysical orders of reality. Classical theism, process philosophers suggest, pictures God as a spiritual, personal substance of infinite perfection that exists over ("transcends") the world order.

18. Thomas Gilby, editor of the English translation of the *Summa Theologiae*, argues that the entire structure of the *Summa* can be seen as creation's "going forth" and "returning home" (vol. 1, p. 43); this is something akin to Barth's two-part reading of Christology in terms of the parable of the Prodigal Son: the "way into the far country" and "the homecoming"). Gilby suggests that the love of God is essentially a matter of friendship, a sharing wherein one wills to communicate good to others.

19. Langdon Gilkey, "God," in Hodgson and King, eds., *Christian Theology: An Introduction*, p. 105.

George Newlands rightly comments that "Faith has been a central theological motif particularly in the tradition of Luther and of modern existential thought. Hope has appeared as the new promise of a future oriented theology. . . . Love has come to the fore particularly in process thought in America."[20] Charles Hartshorne, a theologian who draws chiefly on the process philosophy of Alfred North Whitehead, sought to rethink the nature of divine perfection. God, says Hartshorne, must be thought of not as "above it all" but as "in touch with it all." The universe is not a collection of discrete entities, each complete in itself, but rather a vast organic network where each entity is what it is thanks to its relation to other entities. God is God, says Hartshorne, not because he is above this social network but rather because he is at the heart of it. God, in short, is God because he relates to everything that happens. It is in this sense that we may affirm that "God is love" (1 John 4:8): "To love is to rejoice with the joys and sorrow with the sorrow of others. Thus it is to be influenced by those who are loved."[21]

Process theologians conceive of God in terms of their newer metaphysical categories: temporality, development, change, relatedness, and interdependence. They see no reason to apologize for this (after all, classical theists had their metaphysical categories too), for many of these qualities are, they would argue, essential if we would understand the love of God. Love in a process world is no longer a matter of unilateral benevolence.[22] On the contrary, love means entering into a relationship in which one is willing to undergo — to suffer — change. As Paul Fiddes puts it: "To love is to be in a relationship where what the loved one does alters one's own experience."[23]

---

20. George Newlands, *Theology of the Love of God* (Atlanta: John Knox Press, 1980), p. 37.

21. Charles Hartshorne, *A Natural Theology for Our Time* (LaSalle, Ill.: Open Court, 1967), p. 75. Hartshorne called his view "panentheism" to signal that "all," while not the same as God, was nevertheless "in" God. See also his *The Divine Relativity: A Social Conception of God* (New Haven: Yale University Press, 1948).

22. For a critique of the traditional model of a sovereign God, see John Cobb and David Ray Griffin, *Process Theology: An Introductory Exposition* (Philadelphia: Westminster Press, 1976).

23. Paul S. Fiddes, *The Creative Suffering of God* (Oxford: Clarendon Press, 1988), p. 50. On a process view, love seems to be a metaphysical as much as ethical phenomenon, inasmuch as relatedness is an essential aspect of a being's constitution.

Theological Developments

Classical theism has also been criticized by theologians proper. The twentieth century saw a renaissance of sorts in Trinitarian theology. This has had a twofold effect with regard to our topic of the love of God. In the first place, Trinitarian theology challenges approaches to the doctrine of God that begin with the notion of "perfect being" — "the one" — rather than with the economy of salvation. In the second place, the renewed interest in Eastern Orthodox approaches to the Trinity has led some to redefine God's being itself in terms of its Trinitarian relations. As John Zizoulas has argued, the Cappadocians made *person* rather than substance the prime ontological category.[24] Love for another is thus more basic — that is, more fundamental to reality — than self-sufficiency. Thus the same theme — relationality — comes to the fore as in process thought, but for reasons wholly internal to Christian theology.

Karl Barth's theology reflects a similar tendency to begin with the concrete acts of God rather than with abstract speculation on the nature of perfect being. For Barth, God is knowable only because he reveals himself through himself, that is, in Jesus Christ. Indeed, all that can be known of God is known only on the basis of his revelation through Jesus Christ. Hence, one can discuss God's being only on the basis of his "act" in Jesus Christ, an all-encompassing act that embraces both revelation and reconciliation. In rigorously refusing to think about God except on the basis of Jesus' life, death, and resurrection, Barth comes to the conclusion that God essentially is the one who goes out of himself for the sake of another. God is "the one who loves in freedom," and these two qualities "love" and "freedom" define for Barth the whole range of divine attributes.[25]

Intriguingly for our purposes, Newlands suggests that the whole of the *Church Dogmatics* might be described as a theology of the love of God, since it is concerned with the act of God in Christ on humanity's behalf.[26] Perhaps the most startling thesis to emerge from a focus on the act of God in Jesus Christ, however, is Jürgen Moltmann's thesis that God himself suffered and "died." If the cross of Christ is the prime criterion for correct

---

24. John Zizoulas, *Being and Communion: Studies in Personhood and the Church* (London: Darton, Longman and Todd, 1985).

25. See Karl Barth, *Church Dogmatics* II/1 (Edinburgh: T & T Clark, 1957).

26. Newlands, *Theology of the Love of God*, p. 46.

speech about God, then we must assert that God, somehow, suffers because he loved the world. A God who cannot suffer, Moltmann states, "is poorer than any human . . . he is also a loveless being."[27]

Three other twentieth-century theological developments have lent support to Moltmann's criticism of divine immutability and impassibility. Alister McGrath mentions "protest atheism" (where was God during Auschwitz?), the rediscovery of Luther's theology of the cross, and the growing impact of the "history of dogma" movement that sought to prise the gospel apart from its formulation in terms of Greek thought.[28] In light of this combined attack, it is becoming increasingly difficult for classical theists to defend the intelligibility of the love of God as an apathetic and unilateral benevolence.

Sociopolitical Developments

We should not ignore the significance of sociopolitical developments in the surrounding culture as we attempt to trace the genesis of the current paradigm revolution in theology. The following movements are arguably as much sociopolitical as they are theological.

(1) Liberation Theology: Solidarity with the Oppressed

Marxism and other social theories have raised our collective consciousness regarding the plight of the oppressed. The power of ideas such as justice and solidarity can be seen in the social upheavals that have followed in their wake. In highlighting the social dimensions of sin and reconciliation, liberation theologians have raised searching questions concerning the complicity of the classical theological paradigm with certain forms of institutional oppression. The upshot for the doctrine of God has been a new emphasis on God's solidarity and identification with the poor and oppressed. The God of liberation theology, unlike his classical theistic counterpart, is not far off, but active and present wherever there is liberating activity.

---

27. Jürgen Moltmann, *The Crucified God* (London: SCM Press, 1974), p. 222.

28. Alister McGrath, *Christian Theology: An Introduction*, 2nd ed. (Oxford: Blackwell, 1997), p. 251. Fiddes lists similar factors as explanations for the trend toward speaking of a suffering God (see *The Creative Suffering of God*, pp. 12-15).

(2) Feminist Theology: Against "Male Love"

Feminist theologies are united by the shared belief that women's concerns have been systematically repressed in traditional systematic theology. Could it be that the classical view of the love of God was similarly distorted, male-authored, and male-centered? The God of classical theism is a God of "royal love" — a monarchical "provide and protect" kind of love that is in fact an exercise in control (albeit benevolent). Yet a benevolent dictator is still a dictator. For many feminist theologians, the God of classical theism is a God who loves while remaining distant and unaffected — in short, a *male* projection.

Catherine LaCugna reclaims the doctrine of the Trinity on behalf of feminist theology and argues that God's being as communion excludes any suggestion that persons can be subordinate to one another. From her perspective, the basic problem with Western Trinitarian theology is that it begins with a substance ontology that tries to think "being" before "person" or "relation." LaCugna believes that substantival metaphysics and patriarchal politics mutually reinforce one another: "The subordination of woman to man is but a symptom of the conceptualization of personhood deep at work in patriarchy: a perfect person is self-sufficient."[29] The point of Trinitarian theology, however, is that it is the essence of God to be in relationship to other persons.

And not to persons only. Sallie McFague claims that God is related to the world as spirit is to body. What the secular scientist calls evolutionary development is for McFague, from a theological perspective, the story of God's inclusive, nonhierarchical love for all. McFague proposes a number of models for imagining God's relation to the world, among them God as "lover." The love she has in mind is not *agape*, however. For many feminists, it is culpably misleading to suggest that women *qua* women are more beholden to the ideal of love as self-sacrifice than are men. Indeed, some feminists believe that women can give *too much* of themselves, to the point of becoming virtual non-entities.[30] Feminist theologians and ethicists have sought new ways of defining love so that it retains the aspect of self-giving

29. Catherine Mowry LaCugna, "God in Communion With Us," in *Freeing Theology: The Essentials of Theology in Feminist Perspective,* ed. LaCugna (San Francisco: Harper-Collins, 1993), p. 91.

30. Lisa Sowle Cahill, "Feminism and Christian Ethics," in *Freeing Theology,* ed. La-Cugna, p. 217.

while at the same time giving "new emphasis to a mutuality or reciprocity that makes possible and completes the genuinely interpersonal and relational dimensions of love."[31]

According to McFague, love is about finding a person valuable (and being found valuable) just because of who one is. It is also about the desire to be united with the beloved. A God who simply wills good to others is not yet a lover.[32] That God loves the world means, for McFague, that God finds the world valuable and wants to reunite with it. The love of God thus implies a certain need in God for the world — for the world's loving response, for the world's wholeness, both of which are necessary to make God whole.[33] In particular, the response that God the loved needs from his beloved world is cooperation: "The model of God as lover, then, implies that God needs us to help save the world!"[34]

The Love of God in Postmodernity

I have been tracing the contours of a nascent revolution in theological paradigms. The notion of the love of God in the wake of the critique of theism is, as we have seen, more up to date. The themes of relatedness, mutuality, and inclusiveness have appeared, quite independently, in process, Trinitarian, liberation, and feminist theology. Twenty-first-century theologians exegete the love of God in terms that are familiar to modern culture: sympathy, compassion, mutuality, solidarity, inclusiveness. Culture, together with the history of ideas, however, marches on — and so does the story of the love of God.

The authors of *Christian Theology: An Introduction to Its Traditions and Tasks* assume that the Enlightenment was the watershed for paradigm

---

31. Cahill, "Feminism and Christian Ethics," p. 217. According to William Madges, whereas Catholics stress God's self-love (i.e., Trinitarian unity and community) and Protestants stress other-love (e.g., self-sacrifice), feminists have championed an alternative definition of love as mutuality ("Love," in *A New Handbook of Christian Theology*, ed. Donald W. Musser and Joseph L. Price [Nashville: Abingdon Press, 1992], p. 300).

32. Sallie McFague, *Models of God: Theology for an Ecological, Nuclear Age* (Philadelphia: Fortress Press, 1987), p. 130.

33. McFague argues that we should see "change" as a divine attribute (*Models of God*, p. 134).

34. McFague, *Models of God*, p. 135.

change. And so it has proved for modern theology. Yet the paradigm change in Christian thinking about the love of God intersects in complex fashion with another paradigm change: from the modern to the postmodern. The meaning of love has undergone another permutation in postmodern writing, acquiring the sense of "excess" and "self-abandonment." Jean-Luc Marion, for example, suggests that because God, as love, gives himself, theology must abandon all metaphysical attempts to conceive God, for love is precisely that which does not have to "be." God's self-communication is pure gift, excess, and cannot be correlated with Being.[35] David Tracy, in his foreword to Marion's book, concludes that the task for contemporary theology is to think the excessive reality of an "*agape* beyond Being."[36] Tracy interprets this postmodern theme of love as excess as a retrieval of the neo-Platonist metaphor of God's love as "overflow."[37] "Love enters postmodernity first as transgression, then as excess, and finally as transgressive excess of sheer gift."[38] It is not yet clear what the love of God in postmodernity will become. One thing, however, is certain: the love of God in postmodern theology surpasses both its medieval and its modern predecessors, inasmuch as it is "beyond being" and "beyond relationality."[39]

III. CENTRAL ISSUES

The concept of the love of God is both fundamental to the doctrine of God and, oddly, disruptive of it. There seems to be no one place in a systematics in which the notion of the love of God neatly fits. What, therefore, is the significance of the place of the love of God in systematic theology for its meaning and function?

---

35. It would be interesting to compare and contrast Nygren's sense of *agape* or "gift love" with the postmodern treatment of love as "gift."

36. David Tracy, "Foreword," in Jean-Luc Marion, *God without Being*, trans. Thomas A. Carlson (Chicago: University of Chicago Press, 1991), p. xv.

37. David Tracy, *On Naming the Present: God, Hermeneutics, and Church* (Maryknoll, N.Y.: Orbis, 1994), p. 56.

38. Tracy, *On Naming the Present*, p. 44.

39. Tracy, *On Naming the Present*, p. 44.

Structure

With regard to the structure of systematic theology, the love of God functions either as a discrete doctrinal topic (e.g., one of the *loci*) or as the structuring principle that provides a point of integration or thematic unity between individual doctrines. Somewhat surprisingly, few theologians have chosen the latter option. Instead, most medieval and post-Reformation systematic theologies discuss the love of God, when they discuss it at all, as one subheading under the attributes of God.

Most discussions of the love of God in the classical paradigm take place under the heading of "God's being." This location perhaps reflects an underlying substantival metaphysics in which beings of different kinds have different essences and properties (attributes). The prior issue is whether one discusses the being of God from the starting point of the notion of "perfect being" or from the biblical story of salvation. It may transpire, of course, that the God of infinite perfection simply is the God of Abraham, Isaac, and Jacob, and the classical paradigm assumes as much at the outset. As we have seen, however, the notion of "perfect being" is not absolute but subject to the vagaries of multiculturalism (cf. the different views of perfection held by Aristotle in antiquity and Hartshorne in modernity).

The structure of Aquinas's *Summa Theologiae* shows that he conceives of God first as he is in himself and only then as he is in relation to his creatures. Aquinas limits himself in questions 2 to 26 to examining attributes of God's unitive being ("the one God"). And, as we have seen, he defines the love of God in terms of will: benevolence. The Trinity does not receive serious attention before question 27, only after the divine ontology has largely been mapped out. Not only is God's love discussed under the heading of the will of the one God, but the Trinity is presented as a self-sufficient divine community, unrelated to the world.

According to John McIntyre, the love of God should not only be the controlling category of Christian theology, but should be *seen* to be so.[40] The question for the classical paradigm is whether the love of God can structure theology in this manner if it is only one of several divine attributes of an infinite, personal (though single) being. It comes closer to doing so in Barth's *Church Dogmatics,* for Barth defines God's being not in terms

---

40. John McIntyre, *On the Love of God* (London: Collins, 1962), pp. 32-33.

of substantival metaphysics but in terms of God's revelation in Christ. On the basis of God's being-in-act (e.g., incarnation), Barth concludes that God is essentially the one who goes out of himself for the sake of fellowship with another, or simply, as "the one who loves in freedom." In Barth's *Church Dogmatics*, love operates as a kind of "control attribute" that regulates the other divine perfections. And, with regard to the structure of his theology, Barth reserves his discussion of the divine attributes to volume II. In other words, the discussion of God's being and attributes follows Barth's treatment of God's self-revelation and the doctrine of the Trinity.[41]

Meaning: Attribute, Attitude, Action, Relation?

To this point, we have considered how the love of God has been implicated in a paradigm revolution in contemporary theology. What now needs to be added is that the paradigm revolution is in fact a revolution in models for understanding love.

Love as Model and Models of Love

According to McFague, all theological language is metaphorical, and its purpose is to articulate the nature of the God-world relation.[42] "God loves the world." The love of God intersects with models and metaphors on two levels — first, as a general characterization of the way in which God and the world should be thought. The love of God is thus a metaphor of the God-world relation. Indeed, to a large extent, the model of love functions as a control metaphor that determines much else in one's doctrine of God. However, this is not the end of the story. For what is the meaning of the love of God? Here too contemporary theologians have seen fit to use metaphors. Understanding the love of God depends upon our ability to formulate multiple images (e.g., benevolence, mutuality, etc.) of a root metaphor

---

41. Barth thus devotes the first volume of his *Church Dogmatics* to the doctrine of the Word of God.

42. In his contribution to the present volume, Trevor Hart points out that McFague's metaphors are adverbial: they express ways of relating to God rather than something about God's nature.

(namely, love).[43] The claws of metaphor dig deeply indeed into Christian doctrine.

McIntyre argues that no one metaphor can give full value to the concept of God's love. Accordingly, he examines six different models for viewing God's love: concern, commitment, communication, community, involvement, and identification. For her part, McFague believes that there are an open-ended number of relatively adequate metaphors for depicting the God-world relationship. Among the many options, she chooses three in particular that best convey the nature of this relationship to a "nuclear, ecological age" such as ours: mother, lover, friend.[44] Brümmer examines a number of models of human love — romantic, mystic, courtly, neighborly — but ultimately opts for a literal definition: "Love must by its very nature be a relationship of free mutual give and take, otherwise it cannot be love at all."[45] In so saying, however, Brümmer is doing no more than stating his preference for one definition of love over another. Insofar as he assumes this definition without further argumentation, moreover, his treatment of the love of God risks begging what is arguably the main question: what does it mean to predicate love of God?

Love as Sovereign Will

The classic model of traditional theism conceives the love of God in terms of sovereign will: benevolence, the intent and the ability to will and to act for a person's good. Brümmer complains that the tradition conceives of the love of God as something "attitudinal rather than relational." Western thought, he opines, "has suffered from a systematic blind spot for relations."[46] His basic criticism of the traditional picture of benevolence is that such love is *impersonal*. Willing someone good, he reasons, hardly qualifies as an instance of a genuine personal relation; indeed, it would be more accurate to describe it as manipulative rather than mutual.[47]

---

43. Whereas McFague treats the love of God as a metaphor, Brümmer treats it alternately as a model and a concept, McIntyre as a complex concept.

44. See McFague, *Models of God*, chs. 4-6.

45. Brümmer, *The Model of Love*, p. 161.

46. Brümmer, *The Model of Love*, p. 33.

47. Brümmer, *The Model of Love*, pp. 156-63. Fiddes agrees, adding that the notion of a personal, loving God also entails the suffering of God. Traditional theology escapes this con-

Traditional theologians, however, are unhappy with the suggestion that the conception of God's love as sovereign will is "impersonal." Augustus Strong, for instance, states that "By love we mean that attribute of the divine nature in virtue of which God is eternally moved to self-communication."[48] This self-communication originates from God (e.g., incarnation) and counts as an initiative of love even if its objects fail to respond: "He came unto his own, and his own received him not" (John 1:11). Note too that, for Strong, and perhaps for much of the Christian tradition besides, love is not the all-inclusive divine attribute. True, "God is love" (1 John 4:8); but 1 John also tells us that "God is light" (1:5). Strong sees "light" — that is, divine holiness — as the broader of the attributes, for love does not include God's holiness, whereas holiness includes God's love.[49] While the concept of the love of God does indeed tend to underline God's relatedness, the accent of holiness is on God's separation from, not relation to, the world of human beings. It remains an open question whether this emphasis on holiness makes God's transcendence (e.g., his otherness, his set-apartness) more fundamental to his being than his immanence.[50]

That God is both "love" and "light" recalls McIntyre's caution not to let any one definition of love exclude all others. Such a monologic approach to love is bound to be reductionistic. Does the classical model of the love of God stress divine transcendence at the expense of divine immanence and so fall prey to reductionism? Of McIntyre's six models, two — concern and involvement — when taken together, best correspond to the classic view. God's love for the world means that his concern passes into action, his compassion into passion — a self-communication and an identification that culminate in the incarnation and the cross. McIntyre's discussion of these aspects of the love of God is useful in dismissing some of the caricatures of the classic model. Immutability, for instance, does not mean immobility, only that God is thoroughly self-consistent and reliable.

---

clusion only "by regarding love as an attitude and action of *goodwill* towards another person" (*The Creative Suffering of God*, p. 17).

48. Augustus H. Strong, *Systematic Theology* (Valley Forge, Penn.: Judson Press, 1907), p. 268.

49. Strong, *Systematic Theology*, p. 268.

50. It is perhaps preferable, however, to see the love of God as itself both transcendent and immanent, rather than classing love on one side rather than the other.

Self-consistency, moreover, "is compatible with a whole variety of reactions to different situations."[51]

Love as Reciprocal Relation

Vincent Brümmer speaks for many today when he questions the intelligibility of the classic model of the love of God as benevolence or "gift love." If there is no desire in God, then presumably God does not need or desire us to return his love. But if love is not only communication but communion, then it seems wholly inadequate to suggest that God's love is a "one way" phenomenon, a giving without a receiving.[52] As we have seen, Brümmer himself defines love as a relationship in which the traffic flows in both directions.

By itself, of course, the term "relation" is not very illuminating. There are many kinds of relations in the world. Causality, for example, covers a whole family of relations.[53] Impersonal causal relations, however, have nothing to do with loving relations, for the latter are interpersonal. Yet here too we need considerably more precision, for there are many types of interpersonal relationships (e.g., parent/child; friend/friend; friend/enemy, etc.), and some of these resemble their causal counterparts (e.g., master/slave). How do we know which of these interpersonal relationships are genuinely loving and thus apt metaphors for the love of God?

Proponents of the relational view usually qualify such love with adjectives such as "mutual," "reciprocal," or "inclusive," though it is arguable whether these categories ever get beyond the notion of justice ("light"?). As we have seen, Brümmer offers the following stipulative definition: "Love must by its very nature be a relationship of free mutual give and take, otherwise it cannot be love at all."[54] I confess to finding this definition rather puzzling. In the first instance, Brümmer seems to have transgressed his own methodological boundaries by giving us love's "very na-

---

51. McIntyre, *On the Love of God,* p. 57. On divine impassibility, McIntyre leaves us with the intriguing suggestion that God suffers in the manner "appropriate to his nature," though he does not tell us just what this manner might be (p. 56).

52. See John Burnaby, *Amor Dei: A Study of the Religion of St Augustine* (London: Hodder & Stoughton, 1938), p. 307.

53. Aquinas followed Aristotle in distinguishing four distinct types of causality.

54. Brümmer, *The Model of Love,* p. 161.

ture" rather than a metaphor or model. More seriously, it is not clear that his definition is coherent. If love *is* the relationship, then it follows that the notion of unrequited love is impossible. For if love's overture is unrequited, then there is no reciprocity, and where there is no reciprocity there is no free mutual giving and taking, no relationship — no love. If Brümmer is correct, then it becomes difficult in the extreme to know how to love one's enemies. How can one love those who refuse to enter into relations of mutuality if love just *is* that mutual relation? Clearly, Brümmer's model on its own will not do. If, on the other hand, there is such a thing as unrequited love, then love cannot merely be identified with the relationship. The only alternative would be to argue that God's love is of such a nature that it unilaterally *creates* relationships that invariably elicit a genuine response on the part of the beloved. But that is another theological controversy.[55]

These conceptual problems lead us back to Brümmer's basic assumption, namely, that all genuinely loving personal relations must be characterized by mutuality and reciprocity. Is it indeed the case that all genuinely loving interpersonal relations must be symmetrical? Must they be *exactly* symmetrical (and how does one determine this)? A mother may indeed be desirous of a response on the part of her infant, but the quality of the infant's response may not be such as could be described in terms of "mutuality" or "reciprocity." Furthermore, it is hardly self-evident that the peculiar relation that characterizes the God-world relation — namely, the relation of Creator to creature — should be thought of in terms of mutuality and reciprocity. Again, even were one to accept these qualifications, do mutuality and reciprocity alone take us beyond justice ("light") to love?

Function: Critical vs. Constructive

It has become a virtual given in much contemporary theology that one should interpret the Bible in such a way as to maximize the love of God. This is not quite Augustine's famous hermeneutical rule. Whereas Augustine said, "Choose the interpretation that most fosters the love of God," the

---

55. I refer, of course, to the notion of irresistible grace. It may also be the heart of the issue. As we have seen, Brümmer's fundamental problem with the notion of unilateral love is that it *depersonalizes* us by rendering us the "objects" of divine manipulation (pp. 136-37).

contemporary equivalent might be, "Choose the interpretation that most fosters the understanding of God as love." As we have seen, however, (1) "love" is not the only model for how God relates to the world, and (2) there are at least two significant proposals as to how one should understand the love of God. Before introducing the essays of this book, it may prove useful to look at two concrete examples that show how theologians use the concept of the love of God in debates about other doctrinal topics. The love of God functions in contemporary theology both as a critical and as a constructive principle.

The Scripture Principle: Divine Control or Divine Love?

Edward Farley, in his *Ecclesial Reflection* — a masterful deconstruction of the Scripture principle — appeals to the love of God at a critical point in his argument against the theological method of classic orthodoxy, which he dismisses as "argument by citation."[56] To be precise, Farley undermines the logic of the Scripture principle by challenging the presupposition of salvation history on which it rests, namely, the notion that God sovereignly intervenes in human history.

The notion that God can direct salvation history — including the composition of the biblical canon — implies that God controls either all of history or only a part of it. If we say that God's sovereign will applies only to a portion of history, we must conclude that he does not will the good for, that is, love and save, the rest of it. If, on the other hand, we say that God's sovereign will is universal, then the horrors of history have the same relation to God as the saving events. In either case, Farley reasons, classical theism founders on the problem of evil: either God is involved with only part of the world in a loving way, or everything that happens is a result of God's will, in which case we cannot say that God is love.

Farley presents us, in other words, with the following dilemma: either God is sovereign or God is love. If God is love, the implication is that God is not in control of history (nor of the process of Scripture's composition). Farley expects his readers to agree with him: faced with deciding for God's

56. Edward Farley, *Ecclesial Reflection: An Anatomy of Theological Method* (Philadelphia: Fortress Press, 1982). Similar points are made in Farley and Hodgson, "Scripture and Tradition," in Hodgson and King, eds., *Christian Theology: An Introduction*, pp. 61-87.

control or God's love, "there is really no choice."[57] What the world needs now is love. What, however, does Farley assume to be the meaning of the love of God? Is there really a contradiction between the love and the sovereignty of God? Not according to Thomas Aquinas. For the tradition, as we have seen, God's love means God's settled determination to will *and to effect* the good. This is precisely what Farley's God cannot do. Farley's God may want the good, but he cannot will it. Farley's God, in essence the God of process theology, can invite cooperation but cannot unilaterally intervene in human history, for good or for ill. The question for Farley is what we mean when we affirm that God is love, if God *cannot* act unilaterally for the good of humankind. For if the traditional model preserves a valid insight, God can be *love* only if he is also *Lord* (e.g., free, sovereign).

Divine Impassibility: Divine Love and Divine Suffering

We have already hinted at the second way in which the love of God has been applied as a critical fulcrum in order to revise Christian tradition. Divine passibility may strike us at first glance as a somewhat marginal topic in the doctrine of God, an unlikely beachhead for a paradigm revolution in theology. As we have seen, however, the basic issue comes down to this: can God be affected — in his being, will, nature, or emotions — by something external to himself? Can not-God condition God? If God is love, and if love means sympathy ("suffering with"), then it would indeed appear that God is affected by what happens in the world — that God "suffers change." Paul Fiddes, in agreement with Hartshorne, argues that, because love is "the sharing of experience," God's love for the suffering must include God's real participation in that suffering. However, while God may sorrow and suffer because of his people's unbelief and disobedience, he nevertheless remains God. Note, however, that suffering entails change: "To love is to be in a relationship where what the loved one does alters one's own experience."[58]

---

57. Farley, *Ecclesial Reflection*, p. 156.

58. Fiddes, *The Creative Suffering of God*, p. 50. The nature of theological language, and in particular analogy, is an issue for many of the essays in this book. The challenge is to speak intelligibly of God without succumbing to anthropomorphism. Fiddes' comment provides an interesting test case: how are we to understand the notion of God's having experiences? or suffering in a manner appropriate to his nature?

It is noteworthy that Fiddes sees fit to build certain bridges in the direction of process theology. Love is "essentially mutuality."[59] God and the world are, on this view of love, *partners* — a suggestion that would doubtless have horrified most classical theists. This way of stating the implications of relational theism also clarifies the outstanding challenge: if God's love is seen in terms of God's suffering change by that which is not God, then can God love in this sense and remain *God?*

Between Theism and Panentheism

These two examples pale in comparison to the larger paradigm revolution, from theism to panentheism, that is currently under way. In large part, the theme of God's love has served as the impetus for the growing tendency to abandon theistic models of the God-world relation for panentheistic models. Again, the basic point of contention concerns whether God suffers change because of what his creatures will and do, and if so, in what respects.

The authors of *The Openness of God* argue that there is "genuine interaction" and "genuine dialogue" between God and human creatures. God is "open" to receiving creaturely input. The course of history is not the product of divine action alone, but of humans cooperating (or not) with God. God does not merely act, but also *reacts.*

Clark Pinnock sounds familiar themes when he declares that his aim "is to do greater justice to mutuality and relationality in both the triune God and the God-human covenant."[60]

For Pinnock, God is sovereign in the sense that he is free and able to create beings with free wills who are able to make a difference to his life. If God is no longer unconditioned, unaffected by everything outside himself, it is only because he has willed to be so. God, in other words, wills to be "open" to the effects of human history.[61]

Are these categories not part of a cultural hermeneutic every bit as much as "substance" and "immutability" were categories of antiquity's in-

---

59. Fiddes, *The Creative Suffering of God,* p. 173.

60. Clark Pinnock, "Systematic Theology," in *The Openness of God,* p. 101.

61. In Pinnock's words: "God is unchanging in nature and essence but not in experience, knowledge and action" ("Systematic Theology," p. 118); "The open view of God stresses qualities of generosity, sensitivity and vulnerability more than power and control" (p. 125).

terpretative framework? Is the panentheistic way — the open view — of thinking about the love of God a correction of philosophical notions in the light of the biblical witness or an interpretation of the biblical witness in the light of contemporary thought forms? Is the open view a return to biblical sources or merely the substitution of one conceptuality of love for another? Is it indeed necessary, with regard to classical theism, to abandon ship?

McIntyre was prompted to write *On the Love of God* in response to an overly exclusivistic understanding of the love of God (the book begins with an account of a Highland communion service in which only the "worthy" — a fraction of the congregation — dare partake). Some thirty years on, the cultural context has altered dramatically. For the love of God is now seen as something thoroughly *inclusive* (e.g., "open"). There is no fence around the communion table, no cultural, ethnic, or class (or moral?) barrier to the love of God. Indeed, to paraphrase McIntyre, the prime difficulty in giving full value to the concept of the love of God in the new paradigm may be its unduly narrow equation of the term with a *relation*.

The above review may lead us to conclude that it is inadvisable to define the concept of the love of God univocally. As with so many other doctrines, the concept falls short of the narrative that generates it. If this is so, then perhaps McIntyre's method of combining six models is to be preferred to Brümmer's overarching relational model. It would seem that we must say at least three things: the love of God is something that God has, something that God does, and something that God is. And perhaps, in a manner that we cannot yet conceive, the love of God transcends the categories currently on offer in theism and panentheism alike.

IV. THE PLAN OF THE BOOK: AN OVERVIEW

The purpose of this introductory essay is to explore the larger context and its significance for the properly dogmatic questions to be addressed in the rest of this volume. I have concentrated in particular on the potential for paradigm change that accompanies an examination of the concept of the love of God. The following essays, while not indifferent to the question of paradigm change in theology, do not for the most part address it directly. These essays offer no one definitive response to the above questions, either as to the place of the love of God in systematic theology or as to its implications for the broader doctrine of God, namely, the choice between theism and panentheism. (They do not take sides.) However, in examining various aspects of the love of God they do deal indirectly with what is arguably the prime critical and constructive principle of this revolution. If there is a single theme in the following essays, it is perhaps that it is not human love per se, but rather the love of the man Jesus — representative both of God and of an authentic humanity — that is the ultimate criterion for thinking about the love of God.

In his wide-ranging essay on the concept of love, Gary Badcock revisits Anders Nygren's famous distinction between *agape* and *eros* and subjects his concomitant thesis — that the Christian concept of *agape* or "gift love" is the polar opposite of its Platonic counterpart *eros* or "need love" — to searching critique. Badcock argues that it is incorrect to define *eros* in terms of egoism only. Plato is concerned with wholeness, not selfishness. Badcock offers an alternative that goes beyond the well-worn debate between Nygren and Plato by suggesting, on the basis of God's act in Christ, that the response of love to the divine initiative of love may be something that it is *appropriate* for God to "need."

The Bible is obviously an indispensable resource for Christian theology. To speak of a "biblical theology" of the love of God, however, is to invite a number of methodological questions. Brümmer, for example, warns against simply looking at the way words for "love" are used in the Bible. To do so is to overlook other ways in which the Bible speaks about the love of God. He also challenges the assumption that there is one unambiguous concept of love in the Bible.[62] Geoffrey Grogan's chapter reviews the diversity of the biblical evidence, fully aware of these risks. In particular, he calls attention to the various objects of God's love: Israel, the needy and oppressed, creation per se, and above all his Son, Jesus Christ. Whereas Badcock raises conceptual issues, Grogan presents the exegetical issues that a dogmatic reflection on the love of God ignores only at its own peril.

Lewis Ayres turns to the third strand of theological reflection, the historical, examining Augustine's understanding of the love of God as it is expressed in his commentary on 1 John and in his great work on the Trinity. Ayres locates the heart of Augustine's reflections within an incarnational Trinitarianism: God shares our nature so that we may share his. The incarnation — God's act of love toward humanity — is the fulfillment of a Trinitarian mission, a sending out in order to bring back. God's love has been

---

62. Brümmer, *The Model of Love*, pp. 30-33.

poured into human hearts through the Spirit. In being given the Spirit, humans have a share in the Father-Son relationship too. Ayres helpfully draws out the intimate connections in Augustine's thought between knowing and loving: we can know the love of God only as we come to participate in it.

Emil Brunner once called the assertion "God is love" the "most daring statement that has ever been made in human language." It is perhaps just as dangerous to embark on an attempt to say just what it means, yet this is the task that Trevor Hart undertakes in his chapter. Before turning to the concept of the love of God, however, he raises a more fundamental question: how can we say *anything* about God? The "vertical" problem of referring to God is that a univocal use of terms effectively denies God's transcendence. Hart contends, with Barth, that the possibility of human speech about God rests entirely upon the incarnation: God makes himself known — in flesh, in word. Yet even this revelation is veiled; even the analogy of faith implies both likeness and unlikeness when predicating love of God. Strictly speaking, defining God is not a human prerogative. What we have in the incarnation is a God-given analogy, a fleshly representation, of the reality of the love of God.

Alan Torrance takes up a number of the above themes — analogical language, the incarnation, the Trinity — in an attempt to understand the great Johannine assertion "God is love" (1 John 4:8). He argues that we cannot adequately separate questions about how to define God (language) from the nature of God's being (Logos). To predicate anything of God apart from God's self-revelation invariably runs the risk of anthropomorphic projection. We cannot assume that humans and God each have love in proportion to their respective "being." This is the way of natural theology, which neither begins from nor leads to the cross of Christ. What we need, says Torrance, is an ontology that grounds analogy. He finds it in Athanasius's notion of the *homoousios* — the oneness of being of the Son and Spirit with God the Father. God's being — and the concept of love itself? — is defined by Christ. Of course, only those who fellowship with Christ will be willing to let their minds, and their language, be transformed by him. Only those who participate in God's Trinitarian life can therefore speak of God's love in a way that refers truly. Torrance concludes, perhaps surprisingly, that it is ultimately God's love that is the condition for God-talk in general!

In the wake of these epistemological and ontological discussions, Tony

Lane addresses the first of three specific questions concerning the love of God: can we think of God's wrath and God's love together, and if so, how? He begins with a critique of the contemporary cultural horizon, which is all too inclined to accept a sentimental view of God's love as indiscriminate inclusiveness. In opposition to this popular picture, Lane argues that wrath, far from being a rival attribute, is actually a dimension of God's love. God's love, that is, is "inclusive" of a hatred of evil. Indeed, a failure to hate evil implies a deficiency of love (understood here, perhaps, in the traditional sense of willing the good). Lane is concerned to avoid the Marcionite error of positing a "kinder, gentler" New Testament God who forbids sin — but only in writing. At the same time, one must not affirm wrath as of the essence of God as is love, for wrath is the divine response to what is contingent only, and it has no part in the Trinitarian divine life itself.

Paul Helm addresses the second of the three questions: can God love the world? Intriguingly, he embarks on his investigation via natural theology rather than by a contemplation of the cross of Christ. His chapter is a good example of how classical theism can benefit from "analytic cleansing." In the first instance, it is important to clarify the question: does it mean the world as a collective, as Augustine thought, or the world as inclusive of every individual? Helm's ultimate aim is to explore what it means to say that God's love could be equally distributed, and whether or not this is logically possible in the face of what appears to be empirical evidence to the contrary. He submits claims that God does treat all people equally to careful scrutiny and concludes that God *could not* be equally benevolent to all human beings. This conclusion, from natural theology, yields a hermeneutic for revealed theology and leads Helm to interpret biblical passages about God loving the world as referring to the world as an organic unity, rather than to each element or entity in the world. At the same time, he acknowledges that there is nothing to prevent us from concluding that God loves all men and women *unequally*.

David Fergusson's chapter tackles the final question: will the love of God ultimately triumph? Eschatology presents a peculiar problem for those who construe the love of God in terms of an "open relation," for if God's future is genuinely open — indeed, at risk — then divine triumph is by no means a foregone conclusion. Yet eschatology also presents a challenge to the theological tradition, insofar as it was able to secure the triumph of the love of God only by limiting its scope (e.g., to the elect). The tendency of twentieth-century theology has been toward eschatological inclusivism, that is, universalism. On this view, God's offer of love will eventually solicit a positive response from every person, because God is infinitely patient and infinitely persuasive. However, the fact that his creatures are allowed to affect the Creator excludes any form of universalism that holds that the love of God *must* triumph in the end. In the words of John Burnaby: dogmatic universalism "contradicts the very nature of love, by claiming for it the kind of omnipotence which it refuses."[63] Fergusson argues that both those who affirm double predestination and those who affirm universalism ultimately remove human freedom by construing God's love as something that constrains human choice. By way of contrast, he concludes that God's love triumphs precisely by according freedom to the human creature in the first place. There is nevertheless no symmetry between acceptance and rejection, for grace alone suffices to explain our redemption.

The final chapter, a sermon on Hosea 11 by Roy Clements, moves from dogmatics proper to doxology, yet without ignoring the theological issues discussed in previous chapters. It thus represents a paradigm of how theology may be brought to bear upon the preaching of the Word (and vice versa). Clements begins with an analysis of Western culture, a piece of cultural exegesis that not only serves to highlight the problem of using analogical language to speak of God but also makes the further point that a society that no longer understands love will have a harder time believing in, or understanding, God. He then turns to Hosea 11 in a profound meditation on its featured model of love: that of a husband for a harlot. Hosea 11 contains, *in nuce*, the whole gamut of theological issues concerning the love of God, including striking evidence to which both classical theists and contemporary panentheists could appeal. On the one hand, we read, "I am God not man"; but on the other hand we also read, "My heart is changed within me." Hosea 11 strains the language of the love of God to the breaking point and points forward, says Clements, to a resolution that is neither linguistic nor conceptual but historical: the cross of Jesus Christ. Ultimately, it is not enough to talk about the love of God (or to have conferences about it); if the world is to recover the meaning of love, and the credibility of God, it is up to the church to render this reality through its witness: a practice of costly love. If we are to articulate the love of God to a love-illiterate world, we must be prepared to love to the limit.

---

63. John Burnaby, *Amor Dei*, p. 318.

V. CONCLUSION: BETWEEN
METAPHOR AND METAPHYSICS

Brümmer and McFague agree that metaphors describe the way we relate to God, not the nature of God himself.[64] The model of love is no exception. Does not such an approach necessarily elide the distinction between the way we love God and the way God loves us? Does not thinking of God as "lover" or "mother" (or "father") risk confusing the way we love one another with the way God loves us? Anthropomorphism is an ever-present danger, even in theology according to the new paradigm.

If, however, the Word of God is the final criterion and control for God-talk, then Christian theology must attend to the biblical witness. Scripture consistently directs our attention to a God who pours himself out — in creation, in Jesus Christ, on the cross, through the Holy Spirit — on behalf of those who do not merit such attention. If this gospel, this story of salvation — a story of God's costly love for creation and, above all, for the covenant creature — is the control story for Christian life and thought, then we have a precious touchstone for what divine reality is like. Christian theologians must therefore be prepared to put their preconceived notions of perfect being — whether stemming from antiquity, modernity, or postmodernity — to the critical test of the biblical text. Not just any model or metaphor will do.

Can we ever get beyond metaphor to metaphysics, beyond language to reality? Can love describe not merely the God-world relation but the being of God himself? I believe it can and does. As Janet Martin Soskice points out, scientific models and metaphors may refer to reality truly, though not exhaustively. Religious metaphors are similarly "reality depicting."[65] The metaphor of love adequately describes God's being, but only when biblical narrative — that is, the storied history of Jesus Christ — is allowed to regulate the use of the term "love." When the narratives of the gospel of Jesus Christ do discipline theological thought, we may find ourselves cheering Richard of St. Victor's correction of Anselm's famous definition of God as the being "greater than which none can be conceived." Richard, focusing

64. Brümmer states: "The metaphors and models employed in God-talk are primarily relational: they are intended to indicate the ways in which we are to relate to God" (*Model of Love*, p. 19).

65. Janet Martin Soskice, *Metaphor and Religious Language* (Oxford: Oxford University Press, 1984).

on the interpersonal, intra-Trinitarian relations, argued that such a God loves with a love "so great that nothing greater can exist and . . . of such a kind that nothing better can exist."[66]

What, then, is the place of the love of God in systematic theology? Will it serve as a linchpin to maintain the status quo, or will it provide critical leverage for a paradigm revolution? It is too soon to tell. Perhaps the moral of this introduction is that the love of God should occupy no one place in a theological system, but every place. Instead of trying to situate the love of God under one doctrinal locus, the theologian's task is rather to witness to its inexhaustibility. To write on the love of God is the Christian theologian's supreme privilege and supreme responsibility. In the final analysis, of course, the love of God belongs not only in systematic theology, but in the praise of those who know God's love and who cannot help but witness to it by their lives and loves.

---

66. Richard of St. Victor, *On the Trinity* III.2, in *Richard of St. Victor*, trans. Grover A. Zinn (New York: Paulist Press, 1979), p. 375.

CHAPTER 2

The Concept of Love: Divine and Human

GARY D. BADCOCK

I

> One of the scribes came near and heard them disputing with one another, and seeing that he answered them well, he asked him, "Which commandment is the first of all?" Jesus answered, "The first is, 'Hear, O Israel: the Lord our God, the Lord is one; you shall love the Lord your God with all your heart, and with all your soul, and with all your mind, and with all your strength.' The second is this, 'You shall love your neighbor as yourself.' There is no other commandment greater than these."
>
> MARK 12:28-31, NRSV

And so it is that with love, we are at the center of everything in the teaching of Jesus — and all the more to the extent that we stress the truth of the unity of the Old and New Testaments and the idea that Jesus came not to abolish, but to fulfill the law and the prophets. When taken together with such Johannine statements as "God is love" and "God so loved the world," such texts rightly lead us to conclude that we have in the concept of love a kind of symbol of the whole of the Christian message, both in its foundations in the being and acts of God and in its application in the spiritual life. Theologically, everything is to be located and found here; everything is to be organically developed in relation to this one concrete concept.

But what is love? More specifically, in what does the love of God consist — the love that demands a commitment of the whole self to God, the love of neighbor that Jesus demands, the love that God in some sense is, and the love that God has for the world? Although it might rightly be said that the basic theological problem that we face in life is one of actually loving rather than of merely thinking about loving, there are, in fact, good reasons for entering upon such an exploration. First, and most obviously, the meaning of the concept of love has become so widely debased in our time that we simply cannot assume that the idea of the love of God or of the answering love of human beings has a self-evident meaning for our culture. Second, it is fair to say that love can legitimately mean many things, some lofty and some not so lofty. It is said that the peoples of the Arctic, the Inuit, have a multitude of words for snow, corresponding to the multitude of varieties of snow that they might conceivably encounter in their world. The word "love" can similarly be taken to express in the English language anything from sex to a natural affection for a pet, to a liking for some food or other, to an interest in some hobby or pastime, right on up the scale to friendship, parental love, married commitment, and selfless sacrifice. To which of these does the love of God properly correspond? Third and finally, as we shall see, an exploration of the content of the concept of love opens up wide theological questions relating to the being of God and the nature of human being in relation to God — questions that are obviously more than narrowly intellectual in character, but rather lie right at the heart of Christian theology.

Let me begin, therefore, by citing two definitions of love that have come to be accepted as paradigmatic in much of the literature: the first from the philosopher Plato, and the second from the Lutheran scholar Anders Nygren. Plato discusses the nature of love in a variety of places, the most important of which are the discussion of *philia* in the *Lysis* and of *eros* in the *Symposium*. In both cases, Plato makes the point that love in its differing forms of *philia* and *eros* is born of need, in the sense that it is a lack of the good in a man or a woman that drives him or her to desire something more, to desire the completion of the self, whether through some natural good such as food or drink, through another person, or, for that matter, through some intellectual or moral good such as wisdom or justice. One loves such things out of one's need, in the precise sense that one can be human in the complete sense only by seeking such things and finding them. In the *Lysis*, this leads Plato to the paradoxical affirmation that a *perfectly* good person could never, by definition, be a lover of the good, since the love of the good derives from one's need of it. Thus, with reference to his own primary love, the love of wisdom or *philosophia* which dominates his own personal project and way in life, Plato concludes that "those already wise are not friends to wisdom, whether they are gods or human beings," since only the foolish can be in need of wisdom (*Lysis* 218a, my trans.).

In the *Symposium*, Plato amplifies this by further consideration of a point already present in the *Lysis* passage, to the effect that those who desire wisdom in this way can be neither completely wise, for then they would have no need, nor completely foolish, for then they would not know their need, but somewhere in between. They must, in short, be "on the way" from lack to fulfillment, so that love becomes, in Plato's definition, something that comes between the two extremes: "So love is neither in nor out of need, but stands midway between wisdom and foolishness" (*Symp.* 203e, my trans.). In the brilliant philosophical and psychological analysis of the dialogue, Plato argues that love is a feature of the human being as a divided self, yearning for integration. It is well known that the perception of human fragmentation is basic to Plato's philosophy, but less well known is the fact that it is none other than love that makes integration possible, for love is that which impels us to draw together our fragmented selves and our own existence with that of others in families and societies, and ultimately, for Plato, to seek the absolutely Good and the absolutely Beautiful in the theological sense, since it is these, supremely, that the human mind and soul desire.

This is hardly an ignoble vision of the human lot in the world, and certainly not one that we should dismiss lightly. Plato is not advocating a doctrine of love with the self at its center, as if all love were merely a form of egoism. His view is much more subtle than that, and a great deal more convincing. To do it justice in a contemporary philosophical or theological vocabulary one would have to express his position in some such terms as these. Human being is by nature partial and fragmented, but it is also by nature oriented toward the other in such a way that otherness, whether in the form of the human other or in the form of the divine Other which is the ultimate ground and goal of human selfhood, is paradoxically a permanent feature of the self. In other words, human being is inherently *ekstatic* and relational, which is simply to say that it is not self-constituted or self-sufficient. It exists in relation, and is what it is only in relation, in the sense that the individual is only an individual in a community of relations, both earthly and transcendent. The basic metaphysical reality that Plato attempts haltingly to describe in this way — for one must always be careful not to take his always rather tentative suggestions as if they amounted to hard and fast definitions — is not that of an isolated self whose love is a form of egoistical self-service, but rather that of human being as something existing within a great cosmic scheme, in relation to which the destiny of the individual is naturally and necessarily to be worked at and worked out.

Against this Platonic conception, however, one must set the view of Anders Nygren, for Nygren argues precisely against the Platonic doctrine of love in his now-classic *Agape and Eros.*[1] Nygren's thesis is that the Christian doctrine of *agape* is, as it were, the *totaliter aliter* of the Platonic conception, its polar opposite, there being between the two a difference none greater than which can be conceived. The New Testament ideal of *agape* represents a direct and, in Nygren's view, an entirely *conscious* reversal of the Platonic ideal; Paul in particular, according to Nygren, presents the way of *agape* as opposed to the religious *eros* of the ancient world. The distinction is summed up under a series of antitheses: "Eros is a desire of good for the self"; "Agape is self-giving." "Eros is man's way to God"; "Agape is God's way to man." "Eros is determined by and dependent on the quality of its object, its beauty and value"; "Agape is sovereign and independent with regard to its object, and is poured out on the evil and the good."[2] The two thus represent opposing attitudes to life and to the divine.

Nygren's more positive description of *agape* itself is also important and instructive. He sums the concept up under four headings,[3] the first of which is that *agape* is *"spontaneous and 'uncaused.'"* That is to say, it is not called out of anything but itself: "when it is said that God loves man, this is not a judgment on what man is like, but on what God is like." The corollary to this is found in the second heading, that *agape* is *"indifferent to human merit."* When Jesus calls the righteous together with the sinner to the kingdom of God, the idea of merit vanishes from the religious scene. God no more loves the righteous because of his or her righteousness than he

---

1. Anders Nygren, *Agape and Eros,* trans. A. G. Hebert et al., 2 vols. (London: SPCK, 1932, 1938).
2. Nygren, *Agape and Eros,* 1:165.
3. Nygren, *Agape and Eros,* 1:52ff.

loves the sinner because of his or her sin. Human worth must therefore be left entirely out of account in our reckoning with the love of God. Third, Nygren argues that *"agape is creative."* Rather than resting on a recognition of the intrinsic worth of the object of love, *agape* can be said actually to create the worth of the object of love. "The man whom God loves has not any value in himself. His value consists simply in the fact that God loves him." Anything other or less than this would imply that God's love is not uncaused and that human merit does indeed "cut some ice" with God. Finally, according to Nygren, *agape "opens the way of fellowship with God."* That is to say, no human righteousness or striving can lead to God, but only God's own act in bestowing value on the unrighteous. Any other way than the way of *agape,* therefore, is a false way that does not and cannot lead us to God.

In summary, therefore, we may say that two forms of love have been identified thus far. The first can be designated as "need love," in that it is geared to the satisfaction of some physical, mental, or spiritual desire within the self. I love my corn flakes because of their taste and because I am hungry at breakfast; I love my friend because he spins an entertaining yarn; I love God because to do so is my highest good. On the other hand, there is something that we might call "gift love," which is characteristically centered on the other rather than on the fulfillment of some need in the self. Someone who runs into a burning building at great personal risk to rescue trapped children, even though they are perfect strangers, shows such love. Even if we might like to add that being made a hero in the tabloid press or in the evening news oftentimes follows such acts of bravery, the split-second decisions that people make to do such things without reference to any kind of personal profit is evidence that there is such a thing as real selflessness in human life. Although the literature subsequent to Nygren has tended to be critical of his tendency to antithesize the concepts of human love and divine love, there is no doubt that egoism and altruism can both be present in such ways in the concept of love generally and that the basic distinction between "need love" and "gift love" can be sustained.[4]

In the end, however, I find that I must take exception to Nygren's version of this position. I do so on a number of grounds. First, as we have

---

4. Cf. M. C. D'Arcy, *The Mind and Heart of Love,* 2nd ed. (London and Glasgow: Collins, 1954); Alan Soble, *The Structure of Love* (New Haven and London: Yale University Press, 1990).

seen, the assertion that the Platonic idea of love is fundamentally *selfish* involves a misunderstanding of the Platonic position. It is true that Plato's understanding of love rests on the presupposition that those who love are desiring something that will fulfill and complete the self, but it must also be recognized that the Platonic conception is part of a whole metaphysical framework that is much larger than the self in question. In fact, a similar framework of understanding is present just underneath the surface of the whole of Nygren's theology, for when all is said and done, Nygren too wants to be the object of God's love, since only this can justify. It is for this reason that he writes his book, and it is idle nonsense to deny that this is the case.

Second, however, and more importantly, Nygren's view that God loves specific human beings, not because of any good in them, but purely because that is what he chooses to do, represents, if not a denial of the doctrine of creation, at least an unhelpful disjunction between it and the doctrine of redemption. In patristic theology, for example, the notion that created human being bears the image of God is of such central importance that even the doctrine of redemption is geared to it and understood in terms of it: the purpose of the whole of the saving economy can be said to be to restore that image, to stamp it again upon human nature, or to clear away the springs of life within human nature so that the waters of divine life can again flow freely. Nygren himself, of course, disagrees with the patristic sources, regarding them as having distorted the primitive evangelical conception of *agape* and as having confused it with the pagan notion of *eros*. But he himself is able to argue in this way only by denying that the goodness of the original creation has any relation to God's re-creative intention in reaching out to the world throughout history.

The same point might be put another way, in relation to the doctrine of sin. So all-consuming is Nygren's doctrine of sin, we might say, that he is unable to see any good remaining within human nature after the fall. But this represents an unduly pessimistic view of human nature and an inadequate doctrine of sin. On the pastoral level, for example, Nygren's view is nothing short of disastrous. Let us take the case of depression, for it is the depressed person above all who needs to recognize that the truth about himself or herself is not that of worthlessness and unloveliness; rather, such persons must recognize that the one absolute estimate of their being, that made by God, is that they are of intrinsic worth and goodness. Without wishing to trivialize the matter, I would suggest that the affirmation that "God loves me," understood in this sense, is the one thing that can bring healing to some people in life. Nygren's theology, however, appears to entail that the depressed and those who work with them are bound to agree that there is nothing good in them or in their lives, nothing in them that shines with the light of God's creative glory and goodness, no worth or value that can call out an absolute affirmation of their dignity and at- tractiveness. God does not love *them*, after all, for who they are and what they are, nor could he, for God's love is uncaused and human worth is of no interest to him. On Nygren's view, even God, it seems, agrees with the pathological self-image of the depressed person. To say to the depressed that God loves them despite who they are, in Nygren's fashion, thus by- passing the actual existence of the human being in question, his or her his- tory and experience and potential for good, is oftentimes actually to court suicide, since it merely confirms the perception of an intrinsic valueless- ness in the sufferer. In such a situation, surely, it is the love of God for the person that is all-important, the divine love that recognizes the goodness or the potential for goodness buried deep beneath the mound of perceived unloveliness. This is what needs to be highlighted, and not to recognize it is merely to drive the sufferer deeper down, thus making the journey to- ward the light and health, when it comes, that much more difficult and dangerous.

It is thus in fact hugely questionable that *agape,* or gift love, whether in its divinely pure form or in its partial human expressions, is disinterested in the goodness of its object. The hero who runs into the burning house at great risk to life and limb can hardly be said to have less love for the chil- dren in the flames because he recognizes them to be human beings, with family and friends and a future, with all that this implies. Similarly, the selfless acts of gift love frequently undertaken by parents, such as sitting up at night with a sick, sleeping child when the child could just as well go to sleep on its own after a spell of crying, or the continuing commitment a mother or father daily makes to the rebellious teenager, or the frequent spending of parental love on a drunkard — all of these gift loves are funda- mentally unselfish, but they are not for that reason disinterested in the in- trinsic value of the object of love. In fact, sometimes only the moral imper- ative that instructs us to care for the needy because they are of value gives us the strength to do such things. On the human level, therefore, *agape* is not something disinterested; nor, I have suggested, can this be said to be true of God.

A third reason why I find Nygren's position unacceptable — and much of the popular Christian piety that coincides with it, particularly in the Protestant tradition — is that the Bible itself does not actually make the rigid distinction that Nygren presupposes between Christian love, *agape,* and other forms of human love. To begin with, the historical fact is that the Greek word *agape* appears in the New Testament because it had earlier been used to refer to the love of God in the Septuagint, and it was used in the Septuagint because already in secular Greek usage the word carried connotations of the rational in love, of ethical commitment, of making a definite choice for the good of another, rather than of being compelled to love through irrational impulse or external necessity. It was a word connected more with the sometimes tedious and troublesome virtues of duty than with the exciting experiences of ecstasy, but it was for that very reason a more appropriate word than any other available for expressing in Greek the Old Testament idea of covenant love, which involves a definite, fixed determination on the part of God to show favor to his people, to care for them, to love them *almost* despite themselves. Through its use in the Septuagint, as the writers of the article on *agape* in Kittel's *Theologische Wörterbuch zum Neuen Testament* rightly note, a deeper range of meaning was given to the word, derived from the richness of the Old Testament concepts of God's love.

It was because of this Old Testament background and linguistic precedent that the word *agape* came to be used in the New Testament. However, though *agape* is exalted in the New Testament, above all in the so-called hymn to love in 1 Corinthians 13, the New Testament usage, on the whole, simply does not support the notion of an utterly distinctive concept of "gift love," as opposed to "need love," as defining *agape.* Although, for example, "God is *agape*" according to the Johannine witness (1 John 4:8), the very same source can just as easily say, "Do not love the world or the things in the world. The love of the Father is not in those who love the world; for all that is in the world — the desire of the flesh, the desire of the eyes, the pride in riches — comes not from the Father but from the world" (1 John 2:15-16, NRSV).[5] The verbal forms of *agape* that are uniformly used in this text give the lie to the idea that *agape* always refers to a special gift love,

5. Μὴ ἀγαπᾶτε τὸν κόσμον μηδὲ τὰ ἐν τῷ κόσμῳ. ἐάν τις ἀγαπᾷ τὸν κόσμον, οὐκ ἔστιν ἡ ἀγάπη τοῦ πατρὸς ἐν αὐτῷ. ὅτι πᾶν τὸ ἐν τῷ κόσμῳ, ἡ ἐπιθυμία τῆς σαρκὸς καὶ ἡ ἀλαζονεία τοῦ βίου, οὐκ ἔστιν ἐκ τοῦ πατρὸς ἀλλ᾽ ἐκ τοῦ κόσμου ἐστίν.

whether in the form of a love that is disinterested in the value of its object or in the form of a love that does not seek its own value. In fact, quite the opposite is directly in view here: one can love the world with *agape* and fall into divine disfavor, precisely because in so loving one is lustful, proud, and selfish.

To sum up, therefore, it is difficult to sustain the idea that *agape* as divine love and Christian love is to be totally distinguished from other forms of human love. Although the Christian doctrine of love speaks distinctively of the love of the enemy, and not merely of the neighbor, and though it involves the utterly crucial duty of forgiveness — according to the teaching of Jesus in the synoptic Gospels in particular — it is too much to say that it bears no relation to the ordinary range of human affection generally.

II

Having in this way torn down much of the edifice of piety on which I was myself reared, it remains for me to attempt to say something more positive concerning the concept of love. There is much here that I would like to be able to say. For example, following my own father's death, and some words that I spoke at his funeral concerning his character, an old friend of his came to visit the family. I had spoken of my father as a man of love, as a man who was capable of great self-sacrifice and devotion to whom and what he loved. His friend told me that I was right. He had worked with my father closely for over twenty years, he said, and yet he had never once heard him say a bad word about anyone. My father was not an overtly religious man, and he had very little time for anyone who made great religious claims, but I am given to wonder what a text such as "God is love, and those who abide in love abide in God, and God abides in them" (1 John 4:16b, NRSV) means in relation to him. Are the love of neighbor and the love of God so closely related as to suggest that human forgiveness and peaceableness are not only parables of the divine favor but also evidence of it and the gate of entry to it? Is the showing of love in what we might call the "ecology of human relationships" something more than just a private phenomenon?

Again, I am intrigued by another question that I would have liked to explore, which concerns what the implications for theology might be of seeing love as the center of everything truly theological. Theology is the *logos* of *theos,* as we have all been told and probably said again too in our turn — or is it? If the knowledge of God, rightly conceived, is centered in its foundations and implications in the concept of love, then is it really rightly conceived as the *knowledge* of God? Might it not rather best be seen and enacted as the *love* of God, to the extent that theology as conventionally practiced in the church and in the academy would have to be acknowledged as at best a mere spectator on the edge of the arena of human life under grace in which the real events that constitute its subject matter take place? What then would be the role of knowledge, and how might it be related to love in our theologies?

But I will leave these questions aside for the present. Instead, I would like to explore a rather different *kind* of question, but one that, at the end of the day, is no less theologically pressing. It relates to an unexamined presupposition in the understanding of love in both Plato and Nygren. According to Plato, for example, love is possible only on the basis of need; as perfectly good, wise, and so on, God cannot be said to love, since to love is evidence of imperfection. What we have here is an interesting variation on the doctrine of divine impassibility. Since to love is to be in process — in progress, as it were, toward the good — God cannot be said to love in the strict sense, even though God is axiomatically good, indeed *is* the Good in the absolute sense. This conviction underlies the sense in practically all Greek thought that God cannot, by definition, be bothered in himself about the existence or the woes of the world, for anything else would militate against the divine perfection.

Of course, the Christian doctrine of God from the earliest times, relying on its Hebraic presuppositions, has always tried to understand God to be personal in character, and thus to have the capacity to love, both in himself and in his activities toward what he is not. Even where this conviction is qualified by an apophatic reticence concerning the limitations of theological language, the fact remains that, on Old and particularly New Testament authority, we know love to be a divine perfection. But now note what Nygren's position is. According to Nygren, God's love is unconditional and spontaneous. Deriving from God's own being and decision alone, the love of God for you and me and for the world in general bears no intrinsic relation to either human worth or human need and is, indeed, totally unconditioned by anything in our existence. It cannot change, for example; and indeed its constancy, thus conceived, is its prin-

cipal attraction for Nygren: God's love cannot fail, because it is unconditioned by human obedience or sin, by faith or faithlessness; even where
faith and obedience are found, they are themselves the product of divine
love at work in the world in history and in the personal lives of men and
women.

We might respond that, conceived in this way, the love of God for the
world is made possible, but that this love does not really conflict with the
Platonic prohibition against divine love just cited. God himself is able to
love only, according to Nygren's conception, because in so doing he is actually unaffected by the act of love or by its object. All the biblical expressions regarding divine jealousy or anger or even the pain of rejection, as
for example in the book of Hosea, are on this view merely crude
anthropomorphisms. The fact that God loves the world derives solely from
God himself, who is in himself unchanging, so that the love of God for the
world is a function of the unchanging being and life of God. Rather like
the late Platonism of the early Christian centuries, in fact, according to
which God reaches out to the world in *agape* (for so Plotinus teaches) by a
kind of internal necessity as the Good, so the Christian God impassively
radiates a divine energy of love, which in some cases, at least, itself creates
an answering response of love — a response that Nygren prefers to desig-
nate as "faith" — among men and women. But nothing new happens for
God in and through all of this, for his love is by definition unconditioned
by anything other than itself. Only in this way, according to Nygren, is it
the love of God.

I am not necessarily suggesting that *all* of this is to be rejected, but it is
by now clear that I am profoundly unsympathetic to Nygren's position as
it stands, and to the general theological outlook to which it corresponds.
First of all, I do not regard the doctrine of love as oriented toward the good
or the potential good in its object as inconsistent with divine or human
agape. Second, however, a more radical implication of this is emerging, an
alternative position on the nature of God's love. In the remainder of this
essay I would like to undertake a kind of thought experiment, in order to
attempt to discern whether another concept of love is possible, one that
comes somewhere between the positions of Plato and Nygren and at one
crucial point bypasses both of them. Thus far, I have explored the possibility that God's love for the world is of the sort that *is*, in fact, conditioned in
some sense by the actions of his creatures. Human beings do have worth in
God's eyes. A further step is now necessary. If in fact God does care about

the world for what it is in itself, if his love for me, in short, can be affronted by my disobedience or confirmed and even deepened by my obedience and faithfulness, then it becomes necessary to say that God's love, like ours in the Platonic conception, is based on a kind of need. If this is correct, then it naturally follows that the old doctrine of divine impassibility, which is, after all, of Greek origin, is incompatible with the Old and New Testament conception of the God who loves.

I have myself never been so drawn to the tendency to reject the doctrine of divine impassibility that characterizes so much of contemporary theology as I am at this moment, having followed this line of reasoning. It has always seemed to me that the burden of theological tradition is not to be lightly rejected, and I would certainly continue even now to insist that it is not to be rejected on the grounds of presuppositions drawn from a narrow attachment to some contemporary philosophical position. As most contemporary philosophical positions are at root anti-theological, their adoption by the contemporary theologian must always be something fraught with danger, if not something peculiar and even perverse. I do not intend, therefore, to enter into a long excursus on the advisability or applicability to the matter in hand of the recent theme of the "atheistic doctrine of God" that so many of our German friends, and not a few of our British and North American contemporaries, have been so strongly advocating. I personally believe this to be both a lost cause in the long term and a waste of time in the present, since only a philosophy involving a metaphysics actually compatible with belief in God ought to be entertained in one's theology. Otherwise, one runs the risk of ending up in a kind of anti-theological pseudo-theology — something, in my view, not so very remote from the current "atheistic doctrine of God," and any number of other contemporary theological and even ecclesiastical positions that spring all too readily to mind.

On the other hand, if it is really the case that the doctrine of divine impassibility makes it difficult or even impossible to make sense of the biblical witness, and in this instance of such a central conception as God's love for the world, then it surely makes perfect sense to probe the matter further. At this point, without, I trust, appearing to be overly selective in my use of sources, I would appeal to one of the basic principles of the theology of Karl Barth. One of Barth's most characteristic and seminal themes is that God is known and knowable only in his acts, in the precise sense that there is from beginning to end no other criterion of the content of the name of God than who and what God shows himself to be in his revelation. We do not, according to Barth, know that God is infinitely loving on the grounds of the philosophical idea of God as the highest essence, as possessing in himself the sum of all possible perfection, such that he possesses also the perfection of loving to the utmost possible degree. Rather, we know that God is infinitely loving purely because of the fact that he is so revealed.

My one scruple in citing Barth's theology in this way is that for him, the act of God in revelation is a synonym for the name "Jesus Christ," whereas I would prefer to insist on a broader definition of the acts of God, including creation, the history of Israel, and perhaps at certain points even one's own experience of God — for I take it that such a thing is possible and even normative. Nevertheless, the basic point is absolutely sound: without God's outreach, we would have no idea of him, for not only would there be no access to him, and not so much as a whisper about him, but we would not ourselves even exist. The fact is, however, that the world as God's creature and his activity in history in individual lives, in the corporate history of Israel, and in the incarnation and all that flows from it are structured in such a way, by divine goodness, as to make God, implicitly or explicitly, the real theme of human life and existence, and God's will the real goal of creatureliness as such. The world in its essential being is dependent and derivative and in this sense looks and points to its source, apart from which it is not and cannot be even what it is.

Once this is acknowledged, the Barthian principle, however much transformed, assumes for me a kind of fortress-like, unassailable quality. The question we now need to ask with reference to the love of God is whether there are any grounds for the notion that God's love is the sort of thing that Nygren suggests it is, a pure self-gift, a bestowal of commitment and acceptance that is actually disinterested in its object and that is simply bestowed because it is what it is as an *unconditional* love. As I have argued, I do not find such a concept of love to be coherent or convincing, but were there grounds for such a conception that could be pointed to in the acts of God, I would, given the broadly Barthian principle enunciated, be obliged to accept it as the case and to amend my thoughts accordingly.

The most obvious place where one might find evidence of such unconditional divine love as pure self-gift and selflessness is, of course, the cross of Jesus. A remarkable passage in C. S. Lewis's *The Four Loves* speaks precisely in this way and is worth quoting in full:

God, who needs nothing, loves into existence wholly superfluous creatures in order that He may love and perfect them. He creates the universe, already foreseeing . . . the buzzing cloud of flies about the cross, the flayed back against the uneven stake, the nails driven through the mesial nerves, the repeated incipient suffocation as the body droops, the repeated torture of back and arms as it is time after time, for breath's sake, hitched up. If I may dare the biological image, God is a "host" who deliberately creates His own parasites; causes us to be that we may exploit and "take advantage of" Him. Herein is love. This is the diagram of Love Himself, the inventor of all loves.[6]

Lewis's position appears to rest on a number of presuppositions: the doctrine of *creatio ex nihilo* is there, the foreknowledge of human sinfulness too, together with the notion that God in the crucified Christ is bearing the pain that human beings inflict upon him. There is an undeniable piety in such a vision, something corresponding to much else in the Christian world, and particularly in the late medieval world. But something is missing from Lewis's vision, something of such crucial significance that the whole thing falls to the ground without its support. And what is missing is love, for though Lewis claims that the God who tolerates the parasite is the norm and criterion of all real love, that the act of such a sacrifice is "the diagram of Love Himself," it is extremely difficult to recognize in it anything remotely corresponding to what love is. For unless we can see in the act of God in submitting himself to such a fate some higher goal, some purpose for which all of this is done, what we have in the cross is not the paradigm of love but the paradigm of something merely pathetic, something disagreeable in the extreme, such that God is not so much loving as merely a simple fool, or worse again, a masochist. Who or what, after all, in all the universe gives itself up for nothing?

Lewis does not, I say, present us with a tenable or true picture of the love of God. For what we know of the cross is not that it represents for us the God who wills to suffer from the hostile acts of his own creation, as if he enjoyed suffering for its own sake, but rather a God who bears with it all in order to bring salvation to the world, and it is the lack of any reference to this latter dimension that I find so surprising and disagreeable in what Lewis has to say. It makes no difference in this respect whether we adopt

---

6. C. S. Lewis, *The Four Loves* (Glasgow: Collins, 1960), p. 116.

what is sometimes called a "subjective" or an "objective" view of the atonement, for whether God is revealing his deep love for the world so that it will be drawn to return to him or dealing with the predicament of human sinfulness and corruption, with death and the devil, at its root, the basic fact remains the same, that God does this so that the world can be saved. He has a purpose for the world, it seems, that can be achieved, or that he wills to be achieved, in this way and no other. God has never yet dealt with the world as if it were a parasite or as if it were superfluous, and the greatest measure of the fact that he has not and that he does not is the cross of Christ itself, which indeed is the diagram of love, not in the sense that it shows God to be Lewis's "host," but in the sense that it reveals what the world is to God. That "God so loved the world" in this way needs, quite simply, to be taken seriously in our theology, regardless of all our secondary definitions of *agape*-love as necessarily and by definition unconditioned by its object.

This significance of the world and of human beings to God is confirmed by the fact that we have to conclude, from all the evidence we possess, whether from Scripture, tradition, or experience, that the involvement of God in history that is the sign and seal of his love for the world is of a sort that constantly requires a real human response. The human response is, in short, part and parcel of the saving work of God, just as it is of the existence of the human creature as such. Even if we were to say that the one and only *adequate* response that God has received was in the life of Jesus, and thus that it came into being as a direct result of the divine personal initiative and presence, nevertheless even here a *human* response was needed in order for God's purpose in the world to succeed, and a real *human* response was given: *vere deus, vere homo* runs the old formula. Had this human response *not* been given, there would have been no Christ-event, no gospel, and not even a cross for us to speak of as full of theological significance.

In the end, I suspect that Lewis himself would have agreed that his analogy of God's love as his willingness to be the host for a swarm of parasites cannot be defended. Among other things, it implies that everything good in human existence is also merely parasitic: the birth of a child and the joy of its parents, the first kiss of a couple, and even the great acts of sacrifice of the martyrs would all alike be, not acts of love that are of value as such, but rather merely acts just as superfluous to God's interests as everything else. If such is really the case, then why did God pronounce at the beginning, "Behold, it was very good," or again, why is there joy in heaven over the repentant sinner? So much of Lewis's writings elsewhere relies on the natural analogy between the earthly and the heavenly that I find it impossible to accept the passage quoted as his final word on the subject.

If God is love, then does he really need nothing? I do accept, of course, that the language of "need" is, strictly speaking, inappropriate for God, and yet we have no other words to use here, or anywhere else in our theology, than our own human language. Both Plato and Nygren have resisted the idea that God has need of anything and that need of any sort can, in principle, be at the heart of God's love. Their resistance to this idea, however, leads to the distortion of the love of God in both systems of thought: according to Plato, God cannot love; according to Nygren, God loves but somehow does not love *us*. Could it be the case, however, that both are wrong, and that in fact God does "need" the world?

The God of Christian revelation wills the world into being and cares enough for what he has made to redeem it when it goes astray. The sheer fact of its freedom to sin is evidence that God is not the sort of character who considers his creation merely superfluous. The evidence suggests that God wants a response of love, and that in this sense — because he is love, perhaps — the response of love is something that it is appropriate for God to need. We cannot ultimately penetrate the heavens to speak of what God is from eternity to eternity, but in the world of God's outreach and of human response it seems to this extent entirely appropriate to speak of God's "need" of the world. Without its response of obedience, of faith, of love, his own purpose does not triumph. And in this way, if what happens in time is any kind of guide at all to what is true of eternity, we can speak of God only as needing us in some way, since we know of no God to whom our existence is superfluous and who bears us as parasites.

To speak of God as "needing" the world, or as "needing" the response of men and women in order to achieve his purposes, is obviously fraught with difficulties, but such language is, I have argued, the language of love and of all relationality properly and consistently conceived, and so also of any language of the love of God. I would suggest that the sense in which God has need of the world must be understood fundamentally in terms of the act of creation, by which God calls into being out of nothing something that he is not himself. God, in other words, has a genuine "other" in the world, to the extent that each individual act that takes place in it, even though it has its origins in God the creator, is nevertheless something possessing the relative freedom of creatureliness and thus the relative independence from God, which gives it the potential to be either good or evil. In the existence of human being, God has an other that is capable, in principle, of love; in this way, God has an other that images his own capacity to love, to adopt a course of action for the good of the other, and thus to find himself in relation to it. This also implies, however, that the act of creation is a much greater mystery, and of much more profound theological significance, than is often perceived to be the case. For in giving life to the other, God has clearly made himself vulnerable; he has exposed his heart of love in a way that he could not otherwise have done, in a way that is absolutely universal, and to an extent that is comparable only to the great singular act of compassion that we have before us in the cross of Jesus Christ.

At the beginning of this section, I suggested that the understanding of the concept of divine and human love that I wished to develop would steer a middle course between the positions of Plato and Nygren with which the essay began. It now remains only for me to specify how this has been achieved. First of all, both positions err in not recognizing that the existence of the world adds something to God's experience, in the sense that it calls into being an other that matters to him. His actions in relation to it — whether in the initial creation of the world or above all in the history of Jesus, where the personal involvement of God becomes definitive — and its actions in relation to him both involve something new, even for God himself. Our doctrine of God must be expansive enough to accommodate such paradoxical insights. Second, however, I wish to suggest that it is only when Nygren's doctrine of *agape* is tempered with the Platonic understanding of love as grounded in need that the love of God for the world makes theological sense. God *is* affected by the world — or at the very least he chooses to be so — which is no more than to say that it matters to him, that he loves it. Were it true to say that God is simply indifferent to its goodness or its rebellion, or that his beneficence in relation to the world takes no account of the events that take place in it, then it would not be possible to say of him that he loves the world. God's charity does not, and cannot, overlook the actual condition of its object. It is precisely who and what we are that has been taken up, justified, and so affirmed in God's self-giving love in Jesus Christ.

CHAPTER 3

A Biblical Theology of the Love of God

GEOFFREY GROGAN

I. METHODOLOGICAL CONSIDERATIONS

The possible scope of this study is very great, as is shown in the varied terminology, in the many passages and indeed whole books (e.g., Hosea and 1 John) that are relevant to the theme, and of course in the central importance of the theme itself, which binds together so many diverse elements of biblical thought.

Because the legitimacy of biblical theology as a discipline is a matter of continuing dispute and because there is difference of opinion even among its practitioners as to what it is,[1] we must first look briefly at the various factors that need to be borne in mind in any exercise in biblical theology.

The Unity Factor

The term "biblical theology," in the singular, implies an underlying unity in the biblical teaching. This immediately raises, of course, the question of a possible Divine Mind as the cause of this unity. C. H. Dodd, in his book

---

1. See the helpful discussion in C. H. H. Scobie, "The Challenge of Biblical Theology," in *Tyndale Bulletin* 42, no. 1 (1991): 31-61, and also in his "The Structure of Biblical Theology," in *Tyndale Bulletin* 42, no. 2 (1991): 163-94.

According to the Scriptures, argued from the unity of the New Testament writers in the way they handled the Old Testament to its cause in the interpretative teaching given by Christ to the apostles.[2] Biblical theology of course goes further still and assumes a biblical and not simply a New Testament unity.

The Diversity Factor

Plurality of authors means that differences in experience and in styles of expression are to be expected and truth presented in a wide variety of literary forms. Clearly we must allow for the possibility of antinomies not easily resolved. It is important that we do not force unity on the material in a way that is exegetically unsound. It is better to leave loose ends untied in the meantime than to do violence to the given material.

The Terminological Factor

Clearly there are important terms to be considered, and the approach taken by works like Norman Snaith, *Distinctive Ideas of the Old Testament,*[3] and Leon Morris, *The Apostolic Preaching of the Cross*[4] (both containing material highly relevant to our topic), is largely that of studies in leading biblical terms.

There is a great wealth of material even at the purely terminological level. Clearly, to do a study of the subject covering only the Hebrew and Greek words normally translated "love" would be totally inadequate. Even at this level there are surprises — when we discover, for instance, that despite the overall impression we get that divine love is expressed by *agapan,* the love of God or of Jesus for people is *philia/philein* in John 11:3, 36; 16:27; and 20:2, and that *philein* is used even for the Father's love of the Son in John 5:20.

2. C. H. Dodd, *According to the Scriptures* (London: Collins, 1965), pp. 109, 110.

3. N. H. Snaith, *The Distinctive Ideas of the Old Testament* (London: Epworth, 1983).

4. L. Morris, *The Apostolic Preaching of the Cross* (Grand Rapids: Eerdmans, 1956).

The Conceptual Factor

James Barr in *The Semantics of Biblical Language* criticized the word-study approach as inadequate and argued that attention should be directed instead to concepts, which are often present in a passage when the words most frequently associated with them are not.[5] So, for example, the Synoptic Gospels nowhere state clearly that God loves human beings, yet the concept is everywhere in them.

D. H. Palmer says,

> Jesus is not recorded in the Synoptic Gospels as using *agapao* or *phileo* to express God's love for men. Rather he revealed it by his countless acts of compassionate healing (Mk. 1:41; Lk. 7:13), his teaching about God's acceptance of the sinner (Lk. 15:11ff.; 18:10ff.), his grief-stricken attitude to human disobedience (Mt. 23:37; Lk. 19:41f.), and by being himself a friend *(philos)* of tax-collectors and outcasts (Lk. 7:34). This saving activity is declared in John to be a demonstration of the love of God, imparting an eternal reality of life to men (Jn. 3:16; 1 Jn. 4:9f.).[6]

One difficulty with concept rather than simply word study is the danger of wrongly identifying the presence of a concept in a passage. Should we, for instance, assume automatically that actions that have beneficial results for some party are actually motivated by love in the one who does them? If we were dealing with human actions we could not assume this, but the biblical teaching about God is a special case, as in him action and motivation are clearly linked and there can be no question of consequences unforeseen by the one who acts.

The Historical Factor

In the Bible, theology is grounded in history. Eternal truths are taught, not in abstraction from historical events, but as demonstrated in and through those events.

Moreover, because the material is historically grounded, there is a chronological factor. Biblical theology cannot ignore altogether the histor-

---

5. J. Barr, *The Semantics of Biblical Language* (Oxford: Oxford University Press, 1961).
6. D. H. Palmer, "Love, Beloved," in *The Interpreters' Bible Dictionary*, vol. 2, p. 197.

ical development or disclosure of truth. Certain parts of the material actually highlight this factor as theologically important.[7] So chronological considerations need to be taken into account when they are conceived to be relevant.

The Normative and Dogmatic Factors

Here we reach the heart of the problem of biblical theology. Is biblical theology simply historical or is it also normative?

The historical form is patent for all to see. Recognition of it as normative may be regarded as traditional or it may be based on assertions within the material itself or due to the internal witness of the Spirit. For evangelical Christians the text itself and the leading of the Spirit are important as complementary to and as confirming each other, and they respect tradition insofar as it reflects the importance of these witnesses.

If in fact we view the material as normative, we note in passing that this prevents us from accepting either Bultmann's demythologizing approach or the way Tillich denies the ontological status of the biblical language, treating it all as simply symbolic. It means that, for us, biblical truth is ultimate truth. There may be truths not yet revealed, but their existence does not call into question the ultimacy of what has been unfolded to us.

The fact that biblical theology is historical prevents us from treating it as simply furnishing a dogmatic system for us, because theological truth for us clearly owes something of its shaping to the questions we ask of the material and also to the theological debates we have inherited as well as those we face in our vocation as the church of Christ today. Biblical theology is highly relevant to dogmatic theology but is not identical with it.

It is therefore important for us, in seeking to do biblical theology, to recognize our own dogmatic conditioning and to seek an interpretation and a shaping of the material that arise from that material itself. The fact that this is not easy is no reason for not attempting it, but it is a reason for the biblical theologian to be constantly self-critical and to be willing to face the criticism of others.

7. E.g., Gal. 3; Heb. 3, 4.

The Structure of This Essay

We will now turn to a consideration of the main theme of this essay, a biblical theology of the love of God. We will deal first with God's love for his people, then for the world as a whole, then for his Son, and finally we will consider love in relation to the nature of God by exegeting the important material in 1 John.

II. GOD'S LOVE FOR HIS PEOPLE

Most of Scripture focuses on the people of God, whether in the Old Testament or the New, and it is therefore best for us to start here.

God's love toward his people assumes many different forms. The richness of the terminology makes us aware of this, and much, although not all, of this rich terminology is special to his relations with the people with whom he comes into covenant relationship. A number of forms or expressions of God's love to his people are particularly important.

God's Love Is Expressed in His Goodness in Simply Giving to His Creatures

This is an expression of his love to his people simply as his creatures, but it is often linked with his steadfast love, his *chesed,* as in Psalm 136, and it embraces his works both in nature and in the history of his people. All is for them and all is the product of his goodness. *Chesed* goes beyond *tob* ("goodness"), but the two are so much linked together that when God's people think about his goodness they particularly focus on his covenant-keeping.

God's Love Is Expressed in His Compassion or Pity for the Needy

There is need, and, in his love, God meets it. The nature of the need varies somewhat. God was compassionately concerned about the suffering of his people in Egypt and so he came down to rescue them through Moses

(Exod. 3:7-10). Ezekiel says that God had pity on infant Jerusalem when none had compassion on her, and so he said to her, "Live!" (Ezek. 16:4-6).

There is a tenderness in compassion or pity, and an element of tenderness, along with grace, certainly appears in Hosea's presentation of God's attitude to Israel, especially in the picture of the father and child in Hosea 11:1-4, God loving Israel, leading his people with cords of human kindness, and bending down to feed them.

Christ was moved with compassion and demonstrated it to the needy, whether these were the hungry, the sick, or the bereaved (e.g., Matt. 15:32; 20:34; Mark 1:41; Luke 7:13) or shepherdless sheep who needed to be taught (Matt. 9:36-37).

God's Love Is Expressed in His Concern
to Liberate the Poor and Oppressed

Clearly there is a link here with his compassion, but his saving righteousness also comes into operation. The poor are oppressed by the rich, and this is fundamentally unjust, so that God expresses his justice as well as his love in liberating the poor (Ps. 35:10; 140:12).

In Isaiah 40–55, God's people are in Babylon. It is true that they are there as a judgment on their sin, but, at the human level, their foes have no right to treat them as they have. This means, therefore, that God is dealing with that injustice as well as acting in compassion (and indeed also in grace) when he liberates them (Isa. 46:11-13). This is his saving righteousness.

In this connection, and in other acts of deliverance, whether corporate or individual, God is said to save or redeem his people, so that acts of salvation and redemption are functions of his love for them. These concepts of course develop, especially in the New Testament, beyond application to purely physical acts of deliverance, and thus they come to have overtones of grace and atonement.

God's Love Is Expressed in His
Unmerited Favor toward His People

God's attitude to Israel is never represented in terms of Israel's merits. Even when there are conditions to his promises of blessing and Israel meets those conditions, there must always be the assumption that the very offer of acceptance and blessing is an expression of God's character, not Israel's.

God's proclamation on Mount Sinai expresses this very clearly: "The LORD, the LORD, the compassionate and gracious God, slow to anger, abounding in love and faithfulness, maintaining love to thousands, and forgiving wickedness, rebellion and sin" (Exod. 34:6). This was the confidence expressed in the prayer recorded in Nehemiah 9:17.

This expression of God's love is strongly emphasized in the New Testament. Luke uses *charis* in Acts in connection with the gospel of Christ (e.g., Acts 14:3; 20:24) and, by extension, with the working of God in bringing people to himself through that gospel (Acts 11:23; 15:11; 18:27).

Paul, of course, uses it extensively in both ways, but perhaps most characteristically in connection with justification (Rom. 3:24; 4:16; 5:12-21). In Ephesians 2:4-5, grace is an expression of God's great love and of his mercy.[8]

God's Love Is Expressed in His Gracious Election of His People

The Old Testament shows God's love being focused especially on the patriarchs and on Israel after them.

Deuteronomy takes up the theme of God's special love for Israel. God delighted in the fathers and loved them (Deut. 10:15; cf. 4:37), and he loved Israel after them and for the sake of their fathers (Deut. 7:8; 23:5; 33:3). It is clear that God's love can find no explanation within the people themselves (that is, of course, because it is completely undeserved by them); rather, his love is due to what he is and not what they are (Deut. 7:8ff.).

God's special love for Israel is also clear in Isaiah 43:3-4, where God says that he will give various peoples and nations in return for Israel because of his love for his people. The Queen of Sheba recognized this special love (1 Kings 10:9; cf. 2 Chron. 2:11).[9]

---

8. One of the literary characteristics of Ephesians is the tendency to use superlatives and to link together many synonyms and near-synonyms to express the greatness of the gospel.

9. We should note, though, that God also loves the stranger *(ger)*, the resident alien in Israel's land (Deut. 10:18).

It is interesting to note that Malachi stresses that electing love operated even within the covenant family, when he declares, "'Was not Esau Jacob's brother?' the Lord says. 'Yet I have loved Jacob, but Esau I have hated'" (Mal. 1:2-3; cf. Ps. 47:4).

There is further selectivity within the descendants of Jacob, especially in relation to Judah, in preference to other tribes, and most especially the city of Jerusalem (Ps. 78:67, 68). God loves the gates of Zion more than all the dwellings of Jacob (Ps. 87:2).

There are references, too, to God's special love for particular persons: for God's chosen servant (Isa. 42:1), for the king (Ps. 89:24-29), and for Solomon (2 Sam. 12:24; Neh. 13:26).

It should come, then, as no surprise that Paul should take up this theme of an election within an election in Romans 9–11, since the ground for this had been laid in the Old Testament itself.

The Gospel of John has much to say about the love of God and of Christ for the disciples (e.g., John 14:21; 15:9; 16:27; 17:23, 26). The church, which was the product of their witness, in turn becomes the focus of divine love (Gal. 6:16; Eph. 5:25).

Some expressions may or may not have election implications, such as "Christ loved the church and gave himself up for her" (Eph. 5:25), but the election or predestination of the members of Christ's church is clearly expressed in passages like Ephesians 1:4, 5, 11, and 2 Thessalonians 2:13, 14, 16.

We might also note that the concept of adoption, employed by Paul, may well have implications of election, depending on the extent to which its significance depends on its social background, for it is obvious that at the social level adoption implies choice on the part of the adopting parent.

The Gospels refer to Christ's compassion not only for the multitudes but also for particular persons, such as the rich young ruler (Mark 10:21) and, of course, in particular "the disciple whom Jesus loved" (John 13:23; 19:26). B. F. Westcott's comment here is surely apt: "It marks an acknowledgement of love and not an exclusive enjoyment of love."[10] Paul, too, writes of Christ's personal sacrificial love for him in Galatians 2:20.

---

10. B. F. Westcott, *The Gospel according to St. John* (London, 1908), on John 13:23, *ad loc.*

God's Love Is Expressed in His Initiation
of a Covenant Relationship with His People

In Abraham we see God's electing love taking the form of a divinely initiated covenant with a family, so that the grace of God finds expression in a form that is structured and pledged. Here then the love of God is seen as a commitment by him to his people.

The covenant appears at first in the Old Testament to have the treaty as its model; from Hosea onward it is modeled on the marriage covenant, which, of course, has special overtones of love.[11]

There are also covenants within the Abrahamic/Mosaic covenant structure, with David for the kingship (Ps. 89) and with Levi for the priesthood (Mal. 2:4-6).

Jeremiah wrote of a new covenant (Jer. 31:31-34), and this covenant language, applied to the relationship between Christ and his disciples, is expressed in Christ's teaching at the Last Supper (Mark 14:24). Such language is also applied to the church in passages like 2 Corinthians 3:6-18; Galatians 3:15-25; 4:24-27; and Hebrews 7:11–10:39. Questions are raised in these passages about the relationship between the various covenants, but consideration of this matter would take us too far from our main subject.

God's Love Is Expressed in the Faithfulness That
Maintains the Covenant, When Once It Has Been Established

Jacob was aware of his unworthiness and of God's continued acceptance of him despite this (Gen. 32:10). Jeremiah was deeply aware of his people's sinfulness, yet he records God as saying, "I have loved you with an everlasting love and with everlasting mercies have I drawn you" (Jer. 31:3).

The most important word used in this connection, of course, is *chesed,* "covenant love" or "steadfast love," so characteristic of the Old Testament. This word is used particularly frequently in the Psalms. God's love is allied to his faithfulness, to the fact that he keeps his promises. We note, for example, how God's faithful love is expressed in relation to the covenant of kingship with David, for instance in Psalms 89 and 132.

---

11. D. I. Brewer has demonstrated this in "Three Weddings and a Divorce: God's Covenant with Israel, Judah and the Church," in *Tyndale Bulletin* 47, no. 1 (May 1996): 1-25.

God's covenant love, unlike that of Israel,[12] is not transitory. He maintains it even in the face of Israel's sin and flagrant breaches of the covenant. Although this passage does not employ *chesed*, Hosea 11:8-9 is a particularly moving expression of God's covenant love, with its striking assertion as to the reason for God's persistent love for Israel, when Yahweh says, "For I am God and not man."

Such passages concerning God's love certainly have implications regarding his nature. God's love, demonstrated in his relations with Israel, is no incidental expression of what he is; rather, it is integral to his whole character. Can this perhaps be an important part of the Old Testament background to the great New Testament statement, "God is love"?

Some passages suggest that God will no longer love Israel because of her sin, but in some cases these are balanced by assertions within the same context that God will again love her. Such passages presumably are to be understood as speaking of Israel's conscious experience of God's love. If, objectively speaking, God's love did not continue during Israel's rebellion, he would have taken no steps (e.g., through the ministry of the prophets) to restore Israel to himself.

Christoph Barth says, "When the OT portrays God as 'submitting' to the legal agreement that he has set up, it is speaking figuratively. After all, the covenant is simply God's Word to Abraham when he promised him his blessing. . . . The covenant is not a legal precedent. It is not a document that has authority apart from God himself."[13] But, of course, God's word is a most reliable basis for confidence, for it clearly reflects what God is. In the New Testament, Romans 8:31-39 gives a particularly strong expression of the persistence of God's love for his people in Christ.

God's Love Is Expressed within the Fatherly Relationship of God with His People

God is rarely described as "Father" in the Old Testament (Exod. 4:22; Deut. 14:1; Isa. 63:16). In Hosea 11, God's love for his son Israel is clearly expressed.

In the New Testament, of course, the term "Father" is frequently used

---

12. See Hosea 6:4 (the NIV renders *chesed* as "love").
13. C. Barth, *God with Us* (Grand Rapids: Eerdmans, 1991), p. 52.

in reference to God's relationship with his people. We might say, in fact, that if in the Old Testament the relation is like a treaty or a marriage, in the New Testament God's relation to his people is paternal. Within that relationship is to be found a love that expresses itself in forgiveness, protection, guidance, and both material and spiritual blessings.

In the Synoptic Gospels, when Jesus is speaking to his disciples, he often refers to God as "your heavenly Father." John uses terms like *pais* and *teknon,* but Paul makes fairly extensive use of *huios.* It is quite tempting to place all the blessings of membership of the church of Christ under the rubric of fatherhood and sonship, and this could be done fairly easily with passages like Ephesians 1:3-14 and 1 Peter 1. But this description alone may be too simplistic for all the New Testament material relating to the blessings God has bestowed on Christian believers.

God's Love Is Expressed in the Gift of Atoning Sacrifice

In the Old Testament, the sacrifices, including those within the Levitical system, are divinely ordained. A striking expression of this divine origin is the assertion that Yahweh has given the sacrifices to the Israelites to make atonement for their lives upon the altar (Lev. 17:11). The people brought the sacrifices to God, but he had first given the sacrifices to them.

God's love is singularly expressed in the atoning work of Christ. It hardly needs demonstration that the New Testament uses rich vocabulary of love quite prodigally in relation to the cross; the language of grace, compassion, justification, adoption, blessing, and the amount of relevant material are too vast to be presented here with any fullness. The cross was the expression of the love of God (Rom. 5:8; 1 John 4:10) and of the love of Christ (Eph. 5:2, 25; Rev. 1:5). The cross was in fact the supreme expression of God's love, as Revelation 1:5 and, even more clearly, 1 John 4:10 imply. The great repeated assertion "God is love" (1 John 4:8, 16) comes in a context that sees the atonement not only as the manifestation of God's love but virtually as definitive of it. It should be noted, too, that Christ's resurrection, as his vindication by the Father, forever validates the cross and therefore establishes that it is the authentic expression of the love of God.

God's Love Is Expressed in His Determination
to Make the Object of His Love Holy

The Psalms declare that God loves righteousness and justice (Ps. 11:7; 33:5; 99:4), and so it is not surprising to find it asserted that he loves the righteous (Ps. 37:28; 146:8). Similarly, Paul says that God loves a cheerful giver (2 Cor. 9:7).

Loving acceptance does not necessarily imply satisfaction with the object of divine love. To achieve his sanctifying purpose, God rebukes and chastens his people (Prov. 3:12; Rev. 3:19). In Hebrews 12:6, God's chastisement is explicitly connected with his love. The blessings bestowed on the beloved are intended to minister to God's purposes: the holiness of the beloved and thus the glory of God's own name (Eph. 1:3-6). Christ's love for the church was expressed in his death, the purpose of which was to sanctify the church as his bride (Eph. 5:25-27).

God's Love Is Expressed in the Consummation
of His Purpose for His People

This, too, needs little exposition, for the eschatological nature of New Testament salvation clearly implies that the love which took the initiative of grace and which sustains that relationship will consummate it at the second advent of Christ. Ephesians 2:7 spells out the assurance that in the ages to come God will show the incomparable riches of his grace in his kindness toward us in Christ Jesus.

God's Love Is Expressed through His People's
Love, Which Is Created by Him

Christian love is a responsive love, for "we love, because he first loved us" (1 John 4:19). The first epistle of John insists on the outgoing of love from the believer as proof of the genuineness of Christian profession (e.g., 1 John 4:20-21).

There is a close connection between the new birth and our love for others (1 Pet. 1:22-25), for Christian love, like peace and faith, is the gift of God (Eph. 6:23). It is, of course, his love in us, and the great description of love in 1 Corinthians 13 looks very much like a description of the character of God incarnate in Christ.

God's Love Is Not Inconsistent with Acts of Judgment Even in Relation to His Beloved

God's judgment on Israel is declared with great frequency and in book after book of the Old Testament. Moreover, it seems as if God's love and anger can coexist toward the same people.

J. Goldingay says,

> The tension between judgment and mercy is particularly clear in the prophecies of Hosea. Hosea emphasizes the inexplicable and paradoxical character of God's love, which is portrayed in terms of the wooing of a wanton, and which is capable of coexisting with anger. "I will love them no more" (9:15) and "I will love them freely" (14:4) . . . are allowed to stand side by side with no attempt at reconciliation, signifying that on the basis of the prophetic faith at any rate there is no method of reconciling them. The only answer is to flee from the wrathful to the loving God.[14]

We may note several points concerning God's judgment.

(1) These acts of judgment are often said to be the product of God's anger or wrath or even of his hatred. Sometimes, of course, this hatred is simply a strong expression of preference. It appears to be so in Deuteronomy 21:15 (cf. Luke 14:26). It is also true that most often God is said to hate particular deeds or aspects of character, as in such passages as Proverbs 8:13; Amos 5:21; Zechariah 8:17; and Revelation 2:6.

Occasionally he is said to hate even his people, as in Hosea 9:15 and Jeremiah 12:8. They are his own people, whom elsewhere, and most markedly in the same Old Testament books (as we have already seen), he is said to love with an everlasting love, for he is God and not man. This hatred would then seem, although real, to be temporary until his people have returned to him.

(2) These acts are sometimes related specifically to the special status of

---

14. J. Goldingay, *Theological Diversity and the Authority of the Old Testament* (Grand Rapids: Eerdmans, 1987), pp. 193, 194.

his people. There is a striking expression of this in Amos 3:2: "You only have I chosen of all the families of the earth; therefore I will punish you for all your sins."

(3) These acts may result in the destruction of part of the beloved group, but not the whole. In Exodus 32–34 and Numbers 13–14, as Goldingay points out, "Yahweh speaks of utterly destroying Israel because of their sin, but tempers his decision to a punishment of the present generation."[15] It is also true that a local church may have its lampstand removed (Rev. 2:5) without the existence of the Christian church as a whole being under threat.

(4) These acts are called "God's strange work." God's love for Israel is everlasting (Jer. 31:3). In Isaiah 28:21, God's work of judgment against Israel is described as his strange or alien work, as if, somehow, it is foreign to his deepest desires. In this case, as the context shows, the work, unpalatable as it may be, is decreed and will be performed. In Hosea 11, however, in a prophetic book that has much to say about God's judgment on Israel, there is an oracle in which mercy appears to triumph over judgment. This reminds us, perhaps, of passages where God is said to relent and not to bring threatened judgment on his people after all (Exod. 32:14; cf. 2 Sam. 24:16).

It is true, of course, that God's mercy is sometimes linked quite explicitly with Israel's own repentance (Jer. 18:8), but what is to be noted is the apparently deep reluctance of God to judge his people.

(5) The true and strange works of God find reconciliation at the cross of Christ. The cross is an expression of both the love and the judgment of God. We have already seen the cross as the expression of God's love, but it is also clear that it is an act of judgment. Sacrificial language is frequently employed of the cross in the New Testament, and the frequent language of blood sacrifice and of propitiation, which Leon Morris has ably defended as the proper translation in passages like Romans 3:25 and 1 John 2:2 and 4:10, comes out of an Old Testament background where sacrifice is provided by God for the averting of his wrath against sin.[16]

---

15. Goldingay, *Theological Diversity and the Authority of the Old Testament*, p. 194.
16. Goldingay, *Theological Diversity and the Authority of the Old Testament*, chs. 5 and 6.

III. GOD'S LOVE FOR THE WORLD

God's love for the world is manifest in a variety of ways, from creation, to covenant, to the cross. Again we may note a number of points.

(1) If God's love means the imparting of himself, this is shown on a grand scale in the creation of the universe. This is not an essay in systematic theology, so we can hardly discuss the incommunicable and communicable attributes of God, but some basis for recognition of the latter is found in the biblical doctrine of creation.

God gives himself in a most diverse creative work, in which many sentient creatures are brought into being and provision is made for their physical needs (Gen. 1; Ps. 104). His self-giving to human beings would appear to be greater still, for he creates them in his image; and Genesis 3:8 perhaps implies a relationship of fellowship with human beings before the fall.

(2) The Bible gives clear indications and suggestions that God's love goes beyond Israel. The Old Testament has in it both particularism and universalism. In Psalm 145, God's love for his people and for the world seem to be interwoven, and the psalmist declares God's compassion to be over all that he has made (Psalm 145:9, 13).

We note evidence, some of it most striking, of God's love for other nations in passages like Psalm 87; Isaiah 15:5; 16:9, 11; 19:19-25; 42:6-7; 49:6; the book of Jonah; and perhaps Amos 9:7. God is also said to be concerned for the sins of one nation against another, even when neither of them is Israel (Amos 2:1-3).

In Acts, Paul's sermons to pagan Gentiles enunciate a simple doctrine of creation and of history. In Acts 14:17, Paul says that God showed his kindness by giving good gifts in every season, providing them with food, and filling their hearts with joy. In Acts 17:25-26, Paul says that God gives life, breath, and all things (cf. 1 Tim. 6:17).

(3) This goodness must include an element of grace, what the dogmaticians would call "common grace," because it is bestowed on all of humankind, despite its sinful nature. As we have seen, this general goodness of God may be seen in Psalm 145:9, 13.

(4) God's love for the world has taken covenant form. After the flood, God made a covenant with Noah as the representative of all the human race; this covenant included pledges by God for the provision of regular seasons and of food, as well as the promise not to destroy the earth again with a flood (Gen. 8:20–9:17).

(5) Some expressions of the New Testament doctrine of the atonement are universal in form, although these require interpretation in their contexts. Such expressions occur in the Johannine tradition in passages like John 3:16 and, particularly, 1 John 2:2, but such expressions also occur in Romans 5:18 and 1 Timothy 2:6. It is said of heretics, in 2 Peter 2:1, that they deny the sovereign Lord who bought them but also that they bring swift destruction on themselves. However the dogmatician relates such passages to the particularism of election and also to references to the atonement that are more particularist in form (e.g., Eph. 5:2, 25), the biblical theologian must highlight their need of serious treatment.

Most theological arguments against particular redemption are also arguments against unconditional election, which the New Testament appears to teach quite clearly. The main exception is the exegetical argument, and not only is it vitally important that this argument be faced, but it brings the issue properly into the sphere of biblical theology.

Consideration of the issue in detail is impossible within the limits of this essay, but we will look briefly at two passages often considered the most difficult to square with particular redemption.

The first of these is 1 John 2:2. However, the style of 1 John is broad, and it would be consistent with this style if 1 John 2:2 were to be understood as having ethnic or geographical rather than strictly numerical bearing, so that "the whole world" in this case would mean "people of every nation" or "people in every part of the world."

The second passage is 2 Peter 2:1, but even this passage (which I long considered the strongest exegetical argument against particular redemption) loses much of its difficulty once we recognize that the heresy referred to appears from the context to be ethical rather than Christological. The words "denying even the Master who bought them" probably refer to the spurious profession of the people in question, involving their professed subscription to a doctrine of the person and work of Christ in line with the authentic gospel and their profession of true personal faith, and an obedient faith at that. This last is strongly suggested by the use of *despotes*, unique in the New Testament in Christological contexts, except for the somewhat parallel reference in Jude 4.

I am not asserting that such passages must be interpreted in a particularist fashion, but rather that such interpretation does not do violence to their meaning in terms of their literary context.

(6) In the New Testament, the gospel of God's love and grace in Christ

is to be proclaimed in all the world. This note is sounded in various versions of the Great Commission (Matt. 28:18-20; Mark 16:15; Luke 24:46-49; Acts 1:8), and it is presupposed in the account of the missionary expansion of the church given in the Acts of the Apostles.

IV. GOD'S LOVE FOR CHRIST

This might appear to be a largely Johannine concept, but in the Synoptics Jesus is designated by the Father's voice as *ho agapetos* in certain events of obviously great importance: his baptism (Matt. 3:17; Mark 1:11; Luke 3:22) and transfiguration (Matt. 17:5; Mark 9:7; Luke 9:35; cf. 2 Pet. 1:17).

These statements may have some Old Testament basis in expressions of God's paternal love for Israel (e.g., Hos. 11:1) and for Israel's king (Ps. 89:24-28) as, especially in Matthew (2:6, 15), Jesus Christ is Israel and its expected king. In Matthew Jesus is also the beloved servant of God (12:17, 18; cf. Isa. 42:1).

In the Synoptic Gospels, Jesus calls God "my heavenly Father," while to the disciples he is "your heavenly Father." Never is God called "our heavenly Father," and the post-resurrection expression "My Father and your Father" (John 20:17) seems particularly significant. God is the Father of his disciples, but he is the Father of Jesus in some special sense.

In the Gospel of John, Jesus teaches the love of the Father for him and explains that God has given everything into his hands (John 3:35; 5:20; 15:9). He also asserts that there is a mutuality about this love (John 17:26). Now this would not have appeared to have special significance were it not for the fact that the Father's love of the Son is said to have been a reality before the foundation of the world (John 17:24), and so it is an eternal fact. If this is so, every use by Christ of the language of Fatherhood and Sonship has implications of love. This then would greatly extend the range of material related to our theme.

Paul tends to use the phrase "Son of God" for Christ rather sparingly, but some of his uses are significant for our theme. Romans 8:32 uses the expression, *tou idiou huiou* (cf. 8:3, *ton heautou huion*) in connection with the verbal form *epheisato* employed of Abraham and Isaac in Genesis 22:16, where Abraham's love for his son is emphasized (cf. 22:2). Ephesians 1:6 refers to "the One he [i.e., God] loves."

V. LOVE AND THE NATURE OF GOD

The assertion of 1 John 4:8, repeated in verse 16, that "God is love" may well be the most quoted affirmation in the Bible. A great deal is inferred from it. It is therefore of particular importance that its exegesis is accurate.

1 John is a brief book, and therefore it is wise for us to seek to interpret this statement in its total literary context.

Light and Love in God's Nature

The epistle's purpose is clearly indicated in 5:13: "I write these things to you who believe in the name of the Son of God, so that you may know that you have eternal life." The opening of the epistle states that eternal life is a person, the incarnate Son of God.

The message conveyed through that historical revelation in Christ is that "God is light." Here is a statement identical in its syntactical form to "God is love." Both are, at least on the face of it, ontological affirmations. An examination of the context suggests that both revelation and holiness, particularly the latter, are in view in the statement that God is light.

This message, however, can also be summarized in terms of love, for in 3:11 the writer says, "This is the message you heard from the beginning. We should love one another." This is surely the old, yet new, command of 2:7-8 (cf. John 13:34-35), and it is significant that these verses are followed immediately by references to light. In fact, in 2:7-11, light and love are constantly and intimately related to each other.

It is true that love here is the love shown by Christians, but elsewhere, as we shall see, John sees Christian love as resulting from the communication of God's love.

God's Love and Earlier Revelation of Him

The word "God" in the statement comes to us, of course, out of earlier revelation, on which this epistle, like the whole New Testament, rests.

The Old Testament is never quoted explicitly here, but many passages remind us of it. The references to propitiation, to blood, the implicit reference to Genesis 3 (2:16) and to the devil as sinning from the beginning

(3:8), the reference to Cain and his brother (3:12), the concern to distinguish between true and false prophecy (4:1-6), and the warning against idolatry (5:21) are the most obvious examples.

It is important to note that most of these references remind us of light, of truth, and of judgment. The writer takes all this seriously, and it forms part of the context of his statement, "God is love."

He does not, however, explicitly relate his statement, "God is love," to anything in the Old Testament, not even to Hosea 11, which is perhaps the nearest Old Testament passage, although of course we must not forget the brevity of the letter.

The revelation in Christ, particularly as conveyed through the Johannine tradition, constantly influences the teaching of this epistle. As we have seen, the epistle commences with a major statement about the incarnation and its foundational character for John's message. Much of the vocabulary of the epistle is to be found in the Gospel of John, and this is especially the case as far as references to God are concerned, with the word "Father" having great prominence.

God's Love and the Cross

The close link between light and love is also seen in the fact that God's love is revealed at the cross, and it is clear that the atoning work of Christ there had propitiatory meaning. In fact, the two uses of the term *hilasmos* appear in the context of God as light and God as love, respectively. This is surely most significant and provides us with an important link between them. It is at the cross that they meet.

We should note, too, that the two occurrences of our basic statement are both to be found in contexts, or in one combined context, in which the activity of God, especially at Calvary, is much to the fore.

Does this mean then that "God is love" is simply an alternative to "God acts lovingly"? Certainly it means at least this, but it must mean more, for the activity of God is said to be God showing his love. What is shown in fact exists before it is shown. So love must be a quality in the character, the nature of God, which is then revealed in God's loving deeds, and especially in the atoning work of Christ.

The Status of "Love" in Relation to God

Does love then, for 1 John, exhaustively define God? This has sometimes been claimed, but the claim is open to question. The epistle's teaching about God in fact begins with light, and love first emerges in the context of light. Moreover, the writer's method of expounding Christian truth involves the intertwining of various concepts, such as life, light, truth, love, and righteousness. The best explanation of this is that all of these are really attributes of God, and that because they meet in God, they need to meet also in those who belong to God's family and who share God's nature by new birth and so by indwelling and by fellowship. Here is a well-rounded concept of family applied to the Christian relationship with God.

Not only may all these qualities be intertwined, but they must be if we are to be shown to be members of God's family. Moral attributes that find their point of union in his character must also find this union in ours. These qualities may be distinguishable, but they are certainly not divisible.

And this is why John can argue in both directions. We know that we love God because we love his children, and we know that we love his children because we love God. The Christian life is a seamless whole made up of many moral attributes, and it is such because it reflects the many-sided and yet seamless character of God.

The fact that love is a central moral attribute of God is clear in 1 John, but love's very definition depends on its relation to other qualities, of which light is the most important. To use P. T. Forsyth's phrase, it is always "holy love."[17]

---

17. This term occurs with such frequency in his writings as to render documentation superfluous.

CHAPTER 4

Augustine, Christology, and God as Love: An Introduction to the Homilies on 1 John

LEWIS AYRES

I. INTRODUCTION

In some ways talking of God as love can seem intensely speculative. Love is a term whose significance, perhaps more than any other of those which Christians apply to God, is learnt only in the context of a personal relationship with another. To put the matter directly, love is most commonly understood in terms of the love of *a person* for something else. Hence, to say that "God loves" has always come easily to the lips of Christians, and yet perhaps too easily if such statements result in a failure to think through the implications of what it means for the Triune mystery of God to "love" (both "Triune" and "mystery" here being of great importance). However, these difficulties do not mean that we should stop talking of God as love, and, in fact, in the light of its biblical and traditional warrant, "love" is one

A shorter version of this article appeared as "Augustine on God as Love and Love as God," *Pro Ecclesia* 5 (1996): 470-87. All abbreviations for Augustine's works are from C. P. Mayer, ed., *Augustinus Lexicon* (Stuttgart & Basle: Schwabe & Co., 1986-). The main abbreviations used here are: *ep.* (letter); *ep. Io. tr.* (Tractates on 1 John); *Io. ev. tr.* (Tractates on John's Gospel); *trin.* (On the Trinity); *div. qu.* (Diverse Questions to Simplicianus); *serm.* (sermon).

of the most important, theologically potent, and suggestive terms that Christians apply to God.

However, the complexity involved in calling God "love" and in talking of God "loving" should perhaps mean that when we try to construct a theology of God's love we can best proceed with a simultaneous discussion of the means by which we learn about that love, including, centrally, discussion of how and on what basis our love may or may not be compared with God's. Going further, the methodological discussion indicated in the last sentence should itself be understood as part of a wider exercise in Christology, theological analogy, ecclesiology, and, centrally, Trinitarian theology. My intention in this essay is to offer an introductory account of one key, but often controversial, resource in the theological task of talking about God's love, the work of St. Augustine of Hippo (A.D. 356-430).

A great deal of modern systematic theology has tended to offer a very clear story of theological history in which Augustine is the originator of much subsequent thought in the West, and in particular the originator of many things taken to be bad in that tradition. I think especially of his Trinitarian and Christological views, areas of special relevance to the theology of God's love. Recent scholarship has shown that these accounts of Augustine are far too simplified: many of the later positions supposedly taken from him bear little relation to his actual thought; many of the things he is taken to have originated are the commonplace of his day and can be found in many of the writings of his contemporaries and near contemporaries, which recent theologians have treated much more generously.[1] I have not devoted any time in this essay to arguing against these critics in any detail. Rather, I have attempted to provide an exposition of one key text in which Augustine discusses God as love. My intention in so doing is to show that

---

1. For an attempt to describe some of the problems of such readings of Augustine in the area of Trinitarian theology, see M. R. Barnes, "Augustine in Contemporary Trinitarian Theology," *Theological Studies* 56 (1995): 237-50; for the origins of the twentieth century's accounts of differences between Eastern and Western Trinitarianism (with special reference to Augustine) see Barnes's "De Régnon Reconsidered," *Augustinian Studies* 26 (1995): 51-79. For recent and closely related reconsiderations of Augustine's Trinitarian theology see M. R. Barnes, "Re-reading Augustine's Theology of the Trinity," in *The Trinity: An Interdisciplinary Symposium on the Doctrine of the Trinity,* ed. S. T. Davis, D. Kendall, and G. O'Collins (Oxford and New York: Oxford University Press, 1999), and my own "The Grammar of Augustine's Trinitarian Theology," in *Augustine and His Critics,* ed. R. Dodaro and G. Lawless (London and New York: Routledge, 1999), pp. 56-71.

Augustine shaped his theology of God as love in a clearly Christological and Trinitarian context; indeed, the two are so interwoven that an introduction to Augustine's theology of God as love may serve also as an introduction to some aspects of Augustine's Christology.[2]

The central text with which I will be concerned in this paper is Augustine's series of ten homilies or tractates on 1 John, probably delivered in the year 407.[3] I will also use Augustine's *Tractates on the Gospel of John* as corroboration at some points; the tractates on 1 John were preached during the Easter octave, interrupting his series of sermons on John, and we find in these two works many similar themes and very close mirroring of phraseology at a number of points. Not only does the text on which Augustine comments include the most famous biblical material on God as love, but once we are also aware that the 1 John series was preached at the time of baptizing catechumens and celebrating the mystery of Easter, it is no surprise that Augustine focuses this work on the nature of faith, community, and the love that *is* God.

Three sections of the homilies on 1 John will be considered here: in the first half of the essay I concentrate on the first tractate in the series, which does not deal directly with God as love, but which to some extent can be read as a microcosm of the whole series. My aim is to follow the argument of this sermon, sequentially setting out the interconnection of

2. A brief introduction is provided in B. Daley's excellent article "A Humble Mediator: The Distinctive Elements in Saint Augustine's Christology," *Word and Spirit* 11 (1987): 100-117. Daley's article concentrates on questions pertaining to the union of divine and human in Christ in a way that this essay does not. See also the appropriate chapter in B. Studer, *Trinity and Incarnation: The Faith of the Early Church* (Edinburgh: T. & T. Clark, 1994). Literature on other aspects of Augustine's Christology is provided in notes throughout this essay.

3. The literature on these homilies is still rather thin, despite the frequency with which Augustine's treatment of God as love is referred to. A key introduction to Augustine's incarnational theology now available in English is to be found in Studer, *Trinity and Incarnation*. On the homilies themselves see D. Dideberg, *Saint Augustin et la première épître de s. Jean* (Paris: Beauchesne, 1975); for a brief introduction in English see E. G. Cassidy, "Augustine's Exegesis of the First Epistle of John," in *Scriptural Interpretation in the Fathers*, ed. V. Twomey and T. Finan (Dublin: Four Courts Press, 1995), pp. 201-20. More generally on the subject of love in Augustine see R. Canning, *The Unity of Love for God and Neighbour in St. Augustine* (Leuven: Augustinian Historical Institute, 1993); on the specific theme of this essay see pp. 301ff. I have used the text of P. Agaësse, *Sources Chrétiennes*, vol. 75 (Paris: Editions du Cerf, 1961). The translation used here for the sermons on both John's Gospel and 1 John is the version by J. W. Rettig, *The Fathers of the Church*, vols. 78, 79, 88, 90, 92 (Washington, D.C.: Catholic University of America Press, 1995).

themes found in the homily. The second half of the essay is devoted to sections of later homilies, in which Augustine looks directly at God as love. In the first sections of the essay, where I am simply expounding Augustine's commentary, I have prefaced each section with the biblical text on which Augustine is commenting.

II. THE CHURCH AS WITNESS TO THE INCARNATE WORD: TRACTATE 1.1-2

That which was from the beginning, which we have heard and which we have seen with our eyes and our hands have handled: the Word of life. And the life itself was manifested. And we have seen and are witnesses.

1 JOHN 1:1-2[4]

The first tractate as a whole comments on 1 John 1:1–2:11 and links a theology of the incarnation to an understanding of the role and function of the church in witnessing to that event. The sermon begins with the statement that Christ is the manifestation of God. This is a key theme of the whole series, and it is immediately interpreted as meaning that the Word that previously has been manifest only to the angels is now manifest to people:

"And the life itself was manifested" . . . and in what way was it manifested? For "it was from the beginning," but it was not manifested to men; it was, however, manifested to the angels, seeing [it] and feeding upon [it] as their bread. But what does Scripture say? "Man ate the bread of angels." Therefore, life itself was manifested in the flesh . . . in order that the reality that can be seen by the heart alone might be seen also by the eyes, in order that it might heal hearts.[5]

Augustine here introduces a key theme of his Christology by saying that the Word, which should naturally be manifest to the heart, is for us manifest now in the flesh, to the eyes. This statement hints at the importance in Augustine's thought of Christ as the one who can lead us through

4. This is Rettig's translation of Augustine's quotation, not a modern translation of the original Greek.

5. *Ep. Io. tr.* 1.1.

and in the material and temporal world to "see" God.[6] This is a theme to which he will return more than once later. This introductory passage also demonstrates that Christ is usually portrayed by Augustine, not abstractly or generally as the manifestation of "God," but concretely as the manifestation of Christ as "life itself," as the "one through whom all things were made" — that is, the Word.[7] This reading of the importance of "life itself" is borne out strongly by a parallel passage in the second of Augustine's tractates on John's Gospel, a passage that again parallels the Word's role in creation with the incarnate Son's revelation of God:

> "He was in the world, and the world was made through him." Do not imagine that he was in the world in such a way as the earth is in the world . . . [as] the stars, trees, cattle and men. . . . But how was he? As the master builder who governs what he has made. . . . God constructs while infused *(infusus)* in the world. He constructs while situated everywhere . . . by his own presence he governs what he has made. . . . "The world was made through him and the world knew him not." Did the skies not know their Creator? . . . "he came unto his own" — because all those things were made through him — "and his own received him not." Who are they? Human beings whom he made.[8]

Returning to the first homily on 1 John, in the paragraphs that follow his initial description of Christ's manifestation, Augustine continues his commentary on 1 John 1:1-2 and emphasizes both the physical, material side to the Word's appearance and the nature of Christian reaction to that appearance. Augustine takes the example of the martyrs and, in §2 of the homily,

---

6. The theme of Christ as mediator is set out in great depth in G. Rémy, *Le Christ Médiateur*, 2 vols. (Lille, 1978). Some of the key themes of Rémy's account are now available in an updated form as "La théologie de la médiation selon saint Augustin," *Revue Thomiste* 91 (1991): 580-623. See also the introduction of G. Madec, *La Patrie et La Voie: Le Christ dans la vie et la pensée de Saint Augustin* (Paris: Desclée, 1989).

7. Thus, although it is true that Augustine increasingly comes to think of humanity as being made in the image of the Trinity as a whole, and not just in the image of the Image (the Word), and although formally Augustine does occasionally indicate that any divine person *could* have become incarnate (so as not to introduce necessity into his theology of incarnation), his Christology is fundamentally defined by the fact that the Word became incarnate and by the congruence between the Word's "mission" and "procession" (although this terminology is from a later era). *Trin.* IV is a classic example.

8. *Io. ev. tr.* 2.10-12.

plays on the wording of his text of 1 John to make the equation between witnesses and martyrs.[9] The martyrs *and* witnesses — that is, the members of the contemporary church — are both living testimony to the Word's appearance; those in the church bearing witness to Christ are parallel to the martyrs bearing witness by dying for their beliefs.[10] In context, Augustine's point seems to be — and this interpretation will, I hope, be borne out by the development of the sermon — that the act of witnessing is a material, physical, "fleshy" act that testifies to the material, "fleshy" manifestation of Christ.[11]

Augustine ends this section (§2) with the complex and interesting statement that "the martyrs are God's witnesses. God wanted to have men as witnesses in order that men also may have God as a witness." This statement parallels one in §8 of the second tractate on John's Gospel: there Augustine explains that evil came into the world not because God departed but because people were deceived into willing against God. Our "witness" to God involves speaking of the truth present to us, learning to witness to that truth. However, in our fallen state we need some means of restoring and preserving our knowledge of and attention to that truth. God has not ever turned from us, in the sense of ceasing to be present to us; rather, our

9. Augustine's text reads: "the life was made manifest, and we saw it, and are witnesses *(et uidimus et testes sumus)*." The Vulgate reads: ". . . we saw it, and testify . . . *(. . . et uidimus et testamur . . .)*." This is a small point, but it does make more easy Augustine's statement *Vidimus, et testes sumus: uidimus, et martyres sumus* ("We saw and are witnesses: we saw and are martyrs"). *Sources Chrétiennes*, vol. 75 (Paris: Editions de Cerf, 1981), p. 114.

10. Augustine is here continuing the fourth- and fifth-century trend to find candidates to take over the role of the martyrs in the structures of Christian rhetoric and theology. It is of particular interest here that (a) Augustine does not opt for the frequent substitution of ascetic for martyr in Christian discourse, and (b) Augustine locates a theology of witness in general terms within Christology, as described in this essay.

11. It is important to note that here we see something of the polemical tradition within which Augustine's Christology developed. Augustine's thought is here shaped by the Latin anti-Nicene tradition of "Homoian" theology. Such theologians argued particularly that the visibility of the Son demonstrated his inferiority to the Father. Pro-Nicene theologians, such as Augustine, argued instead that his visibility functioned only to reveal the Word's consubstantiality and common invisibility with the Father. For "Homoian" theology see R. P. C. Hanson, *The Search for the Christian Doctrine of God* (Edinburgh: T. & T. Clark, 1988), ch. 18. Hanson tends to present Greek and Latin Homoians as virtually identical; against this tendency, and with specific reference to the Homoians engaged by Augustine, see M. R. Barnes, "The Arians of Book V and the Genre of *De Trinitate*," *Journal of Theological Studies* 44 (1993): 185-95; Barnes, "Exegesis and Polemic in Augustine's *De Trinitate*, Bk. I," *Augustinian Studies* 30, no. 1 (1999): 43-59.

primal act of will has "wounded our hearts," the organ by which he was previously "seen," with the result that we can no longer "see" God unaided.

In such a situation it is *as if* God has turned from humanity, *as if* we have been deserted. However, Christ has come in the flesh, in a way that we can now see, to enable us to offer testimony to that which has always been present. When we testify to Christ as the presence of the Word (through receiving the grace to do so[12]), we begin to grow again in awareness of the presence of God in the creation. Thus, Augustine understands the ongoing act of Christian witness, the confession of belief, as an act that reveals and in part effects the reeducation of the human being's love and attention: being given the grace to have right faith leads, eventually, to rightly formed love. One important way in which this theme may be seen in Augustine's thought is in his placing of the integration of the "inner" and the "outer" person at the center of his vision of Christian existence: attention to God's presence and rightly formed faith, hope, and action shape attention to God's presence, which in turn shapes a person's life at all levels.[13]

---

12. Augustine's account of the role of grace of course developed considerably during his career. Though against the attempt of P. Burns, *The Development of Augustine's Doctrine of Operative Grace* (Paris: Etudes Augustiniennes, 1980), to provide a clearly delineated history of the phases of his thought on this issue, see now I. Katayanagi, "The Last Congruous Vocation," in *Collectanea Augustiniana: Mélanges T. J. Van Bavel,* ed. B. Bruning et al. (Leuven: Leuven University Press, 1990) [= *Augustiniana* 40-41 (1990-91)], vol. 2, pp. 645-57. The text under consideration here appeared a few years before Augustine's mature account of the ways in which God draws the soul through delight, a theme that makes one of its earliest and most articulate appearances in *Io. ev. tr.* 26. For a brief introduction to some of the philosophical issues involved here see J. M. Rist, *Augustine: Ancient Thought Baptised* (Cambridge: Cambridge University Press, 1994), ch. 5.

13. The "inner" and "outer" parallel should not be read as a simple body/soul parallel: for the best and clearest recent account see D. Turner, *The Darkness of God: Negativity in Christian Mysticism* (Cambridge: Cambridge University Press, 1995), pp. 89-92. One of the most fundamental texts on the theme of integration is *trin.* XII-XIV. On these books see esp. R. Williams, "*Sapientia* and the Trinity: Reflections on the *De trinitate,*" in B. Bruning et al., eds., *Collectanea Augustiniana,* vol. 1, pp. 317-32; L. Ayres, "The Discipline of Self-knowledge in Augustine's *De trinitate* Book X," in *The Passionate Intellect: Essays on the Transformation of Classical Traditions Presented to Professor Ian Kidd,* ed. L. Ayres, Rutgers University Studies in the Classical Humanities, vol. VII (New Brunswick, N.J.: Transaction, 1995), pp. 261-96; and most radically J. Milbank, "Divine Triads: Augustine and the Indo-European Soul," *Modern Theology* 14 (1997): 451-74. Milbank especially argues (as all of these papers do to some extent) that Augustine sees the "integration" of the person occurring when it is truly integrated in its human and cosmic situation, governed from without by God. See also Rist, *Augustine,* ch. 4.

When Augustine says that, if we are witnesses to God, God will be *our* witness, he is in part making an eschatological statement. Using legal terminology — his rhetorical training provided him with a great deal of legal terminology and metaphor — Augustine is saying that, at the final judgment, God will "speak" for us. Our witness (itself something that is possible through the gift of grace) is mirrored by God's faithful return of our witness through the gift of eternal life (which, as we shall see, is simply life in Christ who is at one with the Father and the Spirit). However, this imagery is also closely related to the theme of grace-given faith as effecting the reorientation of the human person. We might also note here that, in §6 of the fourth homily on 1 John, Augustine uses the picture of a pocket stretched by what is put in it to describe the soul being "stretched" by God. The longing and the training that we learn through Christian lives are described as stretching our capacity to receive God when the longing is ended. The stretching is a training, and appropriate hope is formed through learning to love properly.

By drawing the close parallel between our witness and God's answering witness, Augustine emphasizes that, because Christ's life was the real manifestation of "life itself" in the flesh, we may be assured that our inability to see God's presence can slowly be overcome through imitation of Christ. Christ creates the possibility of a new accord between outer action and inner disposition that allows the human person to achieve full integrity and unity. In this light we can understand Augustine's frequent insistence that the true testimony of Christian faith may be relied on as something that *will* be taken up and fulfilled by God: through Christ, God enables a real and dependable continuity between our growing hope and the reality that awaits.[14]

So far we have seen that Augustine's theology of witnessing is closely related to his account of Christ as the manifestation of life itself, of the

14. This point is the essence of Augustine's annoyance at Cicero's skepticism about the relationship between present hope and the actual reality of God; see *trin.* XIV.19.25-26. For similar reasons Augustine strongly holds out against any justification of lying. In *trin.* VIII and XV he uses the Stoic theme of the inner word that is conceived in the mind and the outer word spoken on its basis as a metaphor for Christ's relationship to the Father. In both places Augustine contrasts the absolute accord between Son and Father with our own ability for deception and self-deception. Overcoming this lack of accord in us is at the heart of recovering the sense of God's presence to which Augustine so often returns: hence his horror at lying.

Word. His account of how the act of witness begins a process of reintegrating the human being, so enabling it to grow in awareness of God's presence, is interwoven with his account of how Christ creates the possibility of an accord between inner disposition and outer action. However, to see in more detail how Augustine's Christology is interwoven with his account of the salvation and restoration of humanity we must move on to the next section of the sermon, which concentrates on the accord between Christ's two natures and between God's presence and the "body" of Christ.

III. FAITH AND THE DRAMA OF CHRIST: TRACTATE 1.2.2-3

> *And we have seen and we are witnesses, and we declare to you the eternal life, which was with the Father, and has been manifested in us. The things which we have seen and heard, we declare to you.*

1 JOHN 1:2-3

Just as, in the first paragraphs of this sermon, Augustine's exegesis linked Christ's physical manifestation of the Word to the physical witness of the martyrs to God, so, in the next few paragraphs, Augustine uses the two natures of Christ's person to set out how Christ leads and educates his "body," the church. Augustine begins here using the picture of Christ as the bridegroom and champion in Psalm 19 and Isaiah 61, who pitches his tent in the sun that all may see him:

> But how could he who made the sun be seen in the sun except that "he has pitched his tent in the sun and he, as a bridegroom coming out of his bridal chamber, has rejoiced as a giant to run the course . . ." the true Creator . . . in order that he might be seen by carnal eyes that see the sun, he pitched his tent in the sun, that is, he showed his flesh in the manifestation of this natural daytime light.[15]

Augustine's allusion to Psalm 19 in particular emphasizes that Christ manifests at a particular point what should already be clear: as the bride-

---

15. *Ep. Io. tr.* 1.2.2.

groom or champion, Christ takes a place in the created order so that those who now see only according to the material part of that order may understand him. He does not take his place as *part of* that order — he is not himself created — but in order that we might see what is manifest in that order. Augustine immediately places the doctrine of the two natures at the core of his exposition of this theme. He continues, immediately after the passage quoted above:

> And the bridal chamber of that Bridegroom was the womb of a Virgin, for two have been conjoined in that virginal womb. . . . For it has been written, "And they will be two in one flesh" [Gen. 2:24]. . . . One person seems to speak, and he has both made himself the Bridegroom and the bride, because not two, but one flesh — for "the word was made flesh and dwelt among us." To that flesh the Church is joined, and there comes to be the whole Christ, Head and Body.[16]

The bridegroom coming forth from his chamber in order to be married is symbolic for Augustine of the Word taking flesh, the two natures becoming one. The significance of this equation (which has many other parallels in Augustine's work) is hinted at strongly through the last sentence of this quotation: the union of the two natures in Christ enables *both* the manifestation of the God who is continually in his creation *and* the assumption of redeemed humanity into the body of Christ.

To understand this last point we need to see that the "whole" Christ is manifest to us when the head is joined to the body, when the incarnate Word's revelation of God is understood as also involving Christ's assumption of the church as his body. If the first theme concentrates on the didactic and educative role of the incarnation, the second focuses on the salvific and effective role of the incarnation. We need also to note that the latter is the *context* for the former: the incarnation is able to function as educative because we may receive the grace to participate in the body of Christ and through so doing respond to and learn from that education. Augustine's exegesis in these passages is theologically very dense, but it should now be apparent that, like so much of the best exegesis of the early church, his presentation of the incarnation is inseparable from his presentation of how we participate in the incarnation as part of the body of Christ.

16. *Ep. Io. tr.* 1.2.2.

Elsewhere I have noted the importance of understanding the "dramatic" structure of Augustine's Christology.[17] By this I mean that Augustine conceives of the incarnation as part of a salvific drama that begins with the preparation for the incarnation in the history of Israel and finds its center in the incarnation itself. The next stage is that in which all Christians find themselves, the stage between the ascension and the judgment. At this stage in the drama Christ's physical body is absent, but he is present as the Word; Christ's physical body has ascended where the bodies of the saved will also be after the judgment. At this point in the drama, through increasing union with and in Christ, we may grow in knowledge and love of God and move toward the final unity of the body of Christ. The final stage of the drama is the judgment when we shall see God. This last stage is also deeply Christological in that the vision of God at the judgment involves the sight of Christ as human and as divine, as consubstantial with the Father: the vision of God, which is the sight of the Trinitarian union, comes through being drawn into the body of Christ.[18] That this drama governs the character of Christian existence is apparent from many texts in Augustine's work, for instance this passage on the eucharist from the twenty-sixth tractate on John's Gospel:

> thus he would have this meat and drink to be understood as meaning the fellowship of his own body and members, which is called the holy Church in his predestined, and called, and justified, and glorified saints and believers. Of these the first is already effected, namely, predestination; the second and third, that is the vocation and justification, have taken place, are taking place; but the fourth, namely, the glorifying, is at present in hope, but a thing future in realisation.[19]

17. See my "The Christological Context of *De trinitate* XIII: Towards Relocating Books VIII-XV," *Augustinian Studies* 29 (1998): 111-39. The only work on Augustine's Christology that sets out this dramatic perspective at length is E. Franz, "Totus Christus. Studien über Christus und die Kirche bei Augustin" (diss. Friedrich-Wilhelms-Universität, Bonn, 1956). On the theme of the body of Christ and the whole Christ see also T. J. van Bavel, *Recherches sur la Christologie de Saint Augustin*, Paradosis 10 (Fribourg, 1954), pp. 74ff.; I. Bochet, *Saint Augustin et le Désir de Dieu* (Paris: Etudes Augustiniennes, 1982), pp. 382-96; and M. Reveillaud, "Le Christ-Homme, tête de l'Eglise. Etude d'ecclesiologie selon les Enarrationes in Psalmos d'Augustin," *Recherches Augustiniennes* 5 (1968): 67-94.

18. On this theme see the early *div. qu.* 69; *trin.* I.13.30; and particularly clearly the later text (probably post–A.D. 420) *Io. ev. tr.* 110.4-5.

19. *Io. ev. tr.* 26.15.

Before returning to the homily under consideration it will be helpful here also to note one aspect of Augustine's eighty-second tractate on John's Gospel, a short sermon on the relationship between the Father's love for his Son and Christ's love for humanity. There, in a fairly dense argument, Augustine considers John 15:9: "As the Father has loved me, so have I loved you; abide in my love." For Augustine this statement needs to be understood as not referring simply to Christ's eternal relationship to the Father — telling us simply that the Father loves the Son, the second person of the Trinity. Rather, we should take this to be a statement about Christ's humanity, that which is united to divinity in the "person" of Christ. The text thus may be read as telling us, first, that the human nature is united to the divine in Christ not through the worth or merit of that human nature, but through grace. Second, just as the humanity of Christ has been joined to the Word by grace, we may be united to Christ through grace, not through our own effort. Third (in ways that are not discussed in any detail at all in this brief text), just as the Father has shown grace through the union of God and humanity in the person of Christ, so Christ himself functions as mediator between God and humanity, in some sense uniting us by grace to his own person. Our witnessing to Christ occurs *within* the body of Christ. Christ's person is not just a model for our being saved through grace; rather, it is the means by which and the place in which we are saved.[20]

Thus, the personal union of natures in Christ *enables* the new creation of redeemed humanity in the body of Christ. This theological picture of the union of natures importantly demonstrates that Augustine does not conceive of the incarnation as something *through* which we "see" God: rather, the incarnation is that which makes the mystery *(sacramentum)* present, and our participation in and learning of that mystery take the

---

20. On the way in which Christ's unity enables our progress back toward God see also *serm.* 263, 2-3: "just as he ascended, you see, and still didn't depart from us, so we too are now there with him . . . if he has attached us to himself as his members in such a way that even with us joined on he is his very same self . . . we too are going to ascend, not by our own virtue, but by our and his oneness"; and *trin.* IV.18.24: "we now practice faith in the things that were done in time for our sake, and by it we are cleansed, in order that when we have come to sight, as the truth follows the faith, so may eternity follow mortality . . . in order that it may come to pass . . . the truth itself, co-eternal with the Father, took a beginning from the earth, when the Son of God so came that he might become the Son of Man, and that he might take to himself our faith, and lead us to his own truth . . . our faith has now followed him, in some measure, to that place to which he has ascended."

form of a complex interweaving of our Christian practice and our contemplation.[21] This "complex interweaving" is a progress toward a redeemed created and transformed bodily existence.[22] The earlier picture I offered of a new accord between our bodily existence and the presence of God is here deepened and given further theological coherence through the link Augustine draws between the two-natured person of Christ and the nature of our incorporation into a redeemed humanity.

The previous paragraphs have been intended to provide some context for Augustine's assertion in the first tractate on 1 John of the unity of natures in Christ and our unity with him in the "body of Christ." In the next paragraphs of that homily Augustine returns to the meaning of witness, adding also to his picture of the incarnation and the church. At the core of this second mention of the witness theme is the figure of the apostle Thomas:

> We, therefore, have heard, but we have not seen. . . . And yet how does he add, "that you may also have fellowship with us"? They have seen, we have not seen, and nonetheless we are fellows, for we hold a certain faith. For a certain one, even in seeing, did not believe and wanted to touch and so believe. . . . And at a suitable occasion he offered himself to be touched by the hands of men, he who always offers himself to be seen by the eyes of angels. And that disciple touched him and exclaimed, "My Lord and my God." Because he touched the Man, he confessed the God. And the Lord — now sitting in heaven, comforting us who cannot with the hand physically touch him, but can come into contact [with him] by faith — said to him, "Because you have seen you have believed; blessed are they who do not see and believe."[23]

The physical touch led to the confession of what lies beyond: "Because he touched the Man, he confessed God" *(quia tetigit hominem, confessus est Deus)*. It is important that we notice how closely this presentation follows Augustine's earlier presentation of Christ's role: Thomas does not confess Christ himself but sees the significance of the Word's pedagogical appear-

---

21. Augustine's development of this theme in the slightly later context of the Pelagian dispute is clearly presented in R. Dodaro, "*Sacramentum Christi:* Augustine on the Christology of Pelagius," *Studia Patristica* 27 (1993): 274-305.

22. This theme is particularly well developed in Williams, "*Sapientia* and the Trinity."

23. *Ep. Io. tr.* 1.2.3.

ance in the flesh, and *God* is immediately confessed as present in Christ, as having acted in Christ. As Augustine says in §1 of tractate 79 on John: "he perceived and touched the living flesh, which he had seen in the act of dying, and he believed in the God enfolded in that flesh."[24]

In the course of offering this interpretation of Thomas's actions Augustine also passes comment on present-day Christians: "Christ, now sitting in heaven, comforting us who cannot with the hand physically touch him, but can come into contact [with him] by faith. . . ." Post-Thomas Christians stand in the light of Thomas: just as he touched and confessed, so too we may "touch" *in faith* and confess. In the case of Thomas, Christ's human nature acts as a revealer of God's action: God is not *seen* by Thomas but *confessed* by him. In our case we also cannot see Christ, but we may have the same faith as Thomas through believing without seeing.

However, in this passage Augustine is actually discussing the relationship between having faith and witnessing in order to illustrate how it is that we may have "fellowship" with Father and Son although we cannot see. To understand Augustine's account we need to place his account of witnessing against the background of the Christological themes that I have introduced in this section of the essay. Most importantly, Augustine clearly conceives of Christian existence as a participation in the "fellowship" of Father and Son, and yet he does so in a way that is conditioned by his account of the Christological drama. This is most clearly apparent in his statement that we may have that "fellowship" with him now "in faith": we have that fellowship in a way that may, through grace, lead to its fulfillment after the judgment (hence it is a *real* fellowship), but we have it at a stage of the drama where the final unity with and in Christ is not yet achieved (hence it is in faith, *not* in sight). Faith in this case is not faith in something that is not yet there; faith is a complex concept in Augustine's thought, but one key aspect of its usage is to describe belief in things that are present but not seen. In this light it may perhaps now be apparent that there is a parallel between faith's function to lead us (eventually) to a sight of Father and Son in union and the function of Christ in revealing visibly the invisible Trinity.[25]

---

24. Note that Augustine interprets John's text as indicating that Thomas did actually touch. John 20:25 is actually a little more ambiguous.

25. For an account of the distinctions between faith, hope, and love and for hints of what counts as a good foundation for faith see Augustine's *Enchiridion*, 2.7–2.8.

This section of the essay has taken up the importance of Christ's manifestation of the Word (explored in the previous section), and here we have seen something of how Augustine conceives of the church as a community of witnesses. This ecclesiology of witness is directly dependent on a Christology that sees the two-natured person of the incarnate Word as enabling the restoration of a created practice in accord with God's sustaining presence in his creation. In the next section I want to follow the way in which this account is immediately taken up and developed.

IV. FAITH, LOVE, AND HUMILITY: TRACTATE 1, 4-9

And this is the declaration which we have heard from him, and we declare to you, that God is light and in him there is not any darkness. But if we say that we have fellowship with him, and we walk in darkness, we lie and do not practice the truth. But if we walk in the light, as he also is in the light, we have fellowship with one another, and the blood of Jesus Christ, his Son, will cleanse us of every offense. . . . But if we confess our offenses, he is faithful and just to forgive us our offenses and to cleanse us of all iniquity. . . . but if anyone does sin we have an advocate before the Father, Jesus Christ the Just.

1 JOHN 1:5–2:1[26]

In this section I will begin to move toward specific discussion of God as love; but before we can approach that theme directly, we need to see something of Augustine's account of the role of love in Christian existence. At the beginning of §4 Augustine discusses 1 John 1:5: "This is the declaration which we have heard from him, and we declare to you, that God is light and in him there is not any darkness." For Augustine the second half of the verse gives us the very confession or teaching essential for true faith in answer to the question we might ask after having read the first half of the verse. The argumentation that draws out this reading is again very dense, but it is vital for the whole enterprise of these homilies.

The opposition of light and dark at the core of the "answer" given by

---

26. Augustine is here concerned with the whole of this text, but for the sake of space I have quoted only those verses on which the passages with which I am concerned comment.

1 John 1:5 is to be understood as an exhortation to a new way of life. This style of interpreting biblical metaphor follows a key principle outlined previously in his *On Christian Teaching (De doctrina christiana)*: whatever in the biblical text is unclear should be taken to refer to the building up of virtue or the expunging of vice. "So anyone who thinks he has understood the divine scriptures or any part of them, but cannot by his understanding build up this double love of God and neighbour, has not yet succeeded in understanding them."[27] Augustine thus tries to interpret 1 John 1:5 by describing how we should grow in awareness that "God is light and in him there is no darkness at all": such growth in awareness pertains directly to our love of God and neighbor.

We come to understand this statement in three stages: first comes the realization that God's light far surpasses what we know; second, a desire grows as sinful people to see that light and to be enlightened by it; and third, we realize that such "seeing" will come only when we learn to live in such a way that we do not sin. Thus, mirroring the Thomas episode, true confession of God, that is, true faith in the reality of God, leads to the expression of appropriate love, not to introspective despair about the possibility of "seeing" God.[28] Confession of God here involves confession of his existence symbiotically with confession of our sinfulness. In this process we do not *first* discover God's nature and *then* form our desire for him; rather, we are given the grace to confess, and that confession (of our sinfulness and of belief in God and God's intervention in history) begins to shape our desire for God. The third stage, the realization that seeing God comes only through learning to live correctly, is developed in the next section of the homily.

§5 of the homily concentrates on the difficulty of following this road to being "en-lightened" by God. We are able to *talk* of drawing near to God all too easily without noticing the *purpose* of the revelation that God is light. As we saw earlier, the purpose or goal of this revelation as described

---

27. *Doc.* I.36.40. I have used the new translation with text in R. P. H. Green, ed. and trans., *Augustine: De doctrina christiana*, Oxford Early Christian Texts (Oxford: Clarendon Press, 1996).

28. My argument is not that Augustine is unaware of the possibility of self-deception, or of the possibility of unquestioning fideism; rather, I am pointing toward a way of reading Augustine that does not accuse him of a modernist interiority and that takes full account of the classical rhetorical origins of his notion of faith, in which the building up of appropriate faith is all-important.

in 1 John 1:3 is fellowship *(societas)* with the Father and Son. Augustine re-inforces the imperative nature of the metaphorical light and dark image used by John by commenting on 1 John 1:6, "If we say we have fellowship with him while we walk in darkness, we lie and do not live according to the truth," which makes clear that we cannot simply *talk* of light but must also *"walk"* in it. Once we realize that this is the case, we might find ourselves in despair at the seemingly absolute separation of light and darkness (§5.2). However, we should not stop at this point, because the attempt to walk in the light is immediately preempted, followed, and facilitated by Christ's re-moval of our sins (§5.3): "Therefore, let a man do what he can; let him confess what he is, so that he may be healed by him who always is what he is. For he always was and is; we were not and are."

"Light" and "Truth" are equivalent here for Augustine. 1 John 1:8, "If we say that we have no sin, we deceive ourselves, and the truth is not in us," indicates that we cannot come near to God's "light" without entering a process of confession. In the first two part-sections of §6 Augustine bal-ances confession, humility, and love within the process of Christian life. In §6.1, then, our confession is essential to beginning a life of formed love: "Before all, therefore, confession, then loving" *(ante omnia ergo confessio, deinde dilectio)*. In §6.2 love and humility are described as essential to cor-rect confession and to the attempt to move beyond sin: "humility strength-ens love, love extinguishes offenses. Humility is conducive to confession by which we confess that we are sinners." Thus John calls us to love as the best way to avoid being overcome by the strains of post-baptismal life.

This dynamic of humility, love, and confession is again linked to Christology and to the invocation of God in §7 of the homily. Augustine again uses semi-legal imagery to emphasize the nature of invocation of God in two ways. First, to attempt persuasion before the final court while having lived badly will be to no good end; only true invocation of our only advocate will prepare us. Second, and taking up the centrality of Christ's removal of sin in §5, Augustine connects the possibility of constant confes-sion, which is necessary for us, with reliance on the constancy of our advo-cate. In this second sense he says,

> Make the effort not to sin, but if from the weakness of life sin stealthily creeps upon you, immediately look to it . . . immediately condemn it. And when you have condemned it, you will come before the judge, free of anxiety. There you have an advocate; fear not that you may lose the

case due to your confession . . . you are entrusting yourself to the Word . . . shout out "we have an advocate before the Father."

We come to understand true reliance on God through reflection on the true advocate: once again, attention to the incarnate visible Christ, learning to treat him as our advocate and point of appeal, will lead us to receiving the advocacy of the Triune God revealed in Christ. Augustine also emphasizes that we come to see the full nature of Christian humility by reflection on Christ's universal advocacy: in §8, John himself is taken to be careful to say that *we*, not *you*, have an advocate. Augustine characterizes the church as, in one key sense, a community of equals: although the bishops pray for the people, the people must also pray for the bishops, and all must pray to Christ as the one who will intercede. Taking account of Augustine's earlier emphasis on the link between confession of God and learning how to live — connecting awareness of God with awareness of the right relation between God and creation — humility is the virtue of beings taught by Christ to be aware of the constancy of their creator.

In §9 of the homily, commenting on 1 John 2:3, Augustine explores further how Christians come to knowledge of God. Once again the key is love: "and in this we know him, if we keep his commandments." Augustine then resolves "his commandments" into the one command of love and makes the statement that for us ultimate love is this: "even to love enemies, and to love them to this end, that they may be brothers." To love our enemies is to love them in order that they become our brothers; to love someone is to love them that they may be at one with us, that they also may love.[29] We love them that they may love, and hence also that they may equally desire humility before God. To be "at one" is always in this sermon to be at one under Christ, as we saw in discussion of Christ's advocacy. Augustine's interpretation of loving one's enemies is thus given a Christological foundation through interpretation of Christ's attitude to the thieves crucified with him: Christ prays for their absolute forgiveness, which is complete fellowship with him.

I want to leave this particular homily here, and it will be helpful for the rest of the essay if I summarize the argument so far in four points. First,

---

29. I have found Greg Jones's *Embodying Forgiveness: A Theological Analysis* (Grand Rapids: Eerdmans, 1995) particularly good in following through this theme in a modern context.

Christ manifests the one through whom all things were created. Second, at the stage of the incarnational "drama" between resurrection and judgment (the stage in which all Christians find themselves) Thomas is a model for Christian life: just as he touches Christ and confesses God's action, so we, too, with the help of grace may repeat that confession as a response to true teaching about the Word's appearance in the flesh. Third, through a dynamic of love and confession we may come to see how our witness reveals God's constant faithful and prior witness for us: our act of faith is responded to by God and is found to have been the result of God's presence. Through the mystery of the two-natured one person of the incarnation, we may be incorporated into the fellowship of Father and Son, which, as we shall see in the next section, is itself the communion of Father, Son, and Spirit. Fourth, such an incorporation takes the form of a struggle to see the presence of this movement in our lives, the struggle to be in accord with God's forming of a community in which we love that love may be in all. Already this argument raises a question that will be the subject of the remaining sections of this essay: what is the relationship between our love for God, enabled by grace, and God's nature as love?

V. GOD'S TRINITARIAN LOVE

I want now to turn to some of the passages later in the series of tractates on 1 John where Augustine directly comments on the theme of God as love, beginning with Sermon 7, which comments on 1 John 4:4-12. In §1 of homily 7 God is said to have indicated to the church that love *(caritas)* is the fountain, the pillar, which directs us through our desert. Indeed the whole of the gospel can be explained as the command of love; and love, says Augustine, is the reason for the incarnation.

In §2 denial of love, a failure to practice love, is also a denial of the incarnation, for one must judge the presence of the Spirit by acts rather than by words (Augustine here takes up a key theme of homily 6). Augustine goes on to say that we learn the nature of love by watching him who embodies love most fully. John 15:13, "Greater love has no man than this, that a man lay down his life for his friends," is to be understood as pointing to the example of Christ. Christ has shown us the supreme act of love and has done so as part of his taking flesh. The two themes of love as the test of faith and Christ as the focus for the formation of faith are joined: "How could the Son of God lay down his life for us unless he put on flesh whereby he could die? Whoever, then, violates love, whatever he may say with his tongue, by his life denies that Christ has come in the flesh." Later in the same sermon, in §7, Augustine links this display of love by Christ with the Father's display of love in sending his Son: both display the love of God. God does not hand over Christ as Judas hands him over; God hands over *himself* in love (for Father and Son are one in will and action), while Judas betrays his master. Thus we understand Christ's laying down his life as an expression of the common willing of Father and Son in love, an expression of the love of the Trinity toward us. (§7 is discussed again below.)[30]

Turning back to §4, we find Augustine commenting on that most famous passage of the letter, 1 John 4:6-9:

> We are of God. Whoever knows God listens to us, and he who is not of God does not listen to us. By this we know the spirit of truth and the spirit of error. Beloved, let us love one another; for love is of God, and he who loves is born of God and knows God. He who does not love does not know God; for God is love *(quia Deus dilectio est)*. In this the love of God was manifest among us, that God sent his only Son into the world, so that we might live through him.

In this text Augustine is happy to take the step from which so many theologians have shied and say that not only is God love, but hence love is God.[31] He moves to this statement in a number of stages. First, Scripture says we are "of God" because of the presence of love in us; second, Augustine adds that to act against love is to act against God; third, because the Spirit dwells in those who love, true love is thus the presence of God.

This third stage of the argument partly depends on some principles of Trinitarian theology. In §6 we find Augustine arguing,

> How then . . . "love is of God," and now "love is God"? The Son is God of God; the Holy Spirit is God of God. And these three are one God not three gods. For God is Father and Son and Holy Spirit. . . . If the Son is

---

30. A similar interpretation of John 15:13 is to be found in the eighty-fourth tractate on John's Gospel.

31. Unimpeded, it is important to note, by the significance of the article in the original Greek, which prevents the linguistic if not the theological move in that language.

God and the Holy Spirit is God and he in whom the Holy Spirit dwells loves, therefore love is God, but God because [it is] of God. For you have both in the epistle, both "love is of God" and "love is God."[32]

This is a dense argument, and it depends on the exegetical principle that, because of the "principal status" *(principium)* of the Father, things said both to *be* God and to be *of* God are best understood to refer either to the Son or to the Spirit (because of that *principium,* the Father is not "of" any of the other persons of the Trinity as are Son and Spirit).[33] Following this principle, Romans 5:5 ("God's love has been poured into our hearts through the Holy Spirit which has been given to us") indicates for Augustine that the presence of love within us is most properly the presence of the Spirit. Thus, to show love is to accept the gift of the Spirit, which is to accept the Spirit itself: "even an evil man can have all these mysteries [the sacraments]. But he cannot have love and be evil. This then is the peculiar gift. . . . For drinking of this the Spirit of God encourages you; for drinking of himself the Spirit of God encourages you." It is this theology of the Spirit's presence that completes the vision of the redeemed, loving community, loving through God's presence, which I began to outline in the first sections of the essay.

The gift of the Spirit is continually offered, and in §7 — in the passage mentioned only a few paragraphs ago — Augustine relates this theme of God as love to the overall thrust of the homilies by using 1 John 4:9 ("In this the love of God was made manifest among us, that God sent his only Son into the world, so that we might live through him") to emphasize once again that the gift is offered prior to our acceptance. The prevenience of the gift is demonstrated through the act of incarnation. This picture is reinforced in §9, where Augustine emphasizes the intimate relationship between the form and purpose of God's love. God has loved us in order that we might love and has offered himself as sacrifice: the way in which he offers himself thus mirrors the offering of love within the Trinity itself. Turning to *trin.* XV.26.47 we should note first the importance Augustine places

---

32. Most commentators agree that the parallel with John 1 is important to Augustine's making the equation between "of God" and being God.

33. See also *trin.* XV.19.37, where it is made clear that to call the Spirit "love" is also to speak of the Trinity as a whole as love. From *trin.* XV it is also clear that the Father is *principium* in the Trinity, a principle we find in Augustine's earliest extended discussion of the Trinity, *ep.* 11.

on the Father giving the Son "to have life in himself," taking this to imply that the Son is not temporally "after" the Father, and that the Father's self-gift to the Son does not imply a subordinationist Trinity. Second, in the same section, one might note that the Father's gift to the Son includes the power to bestow the Spirit, who is also the communion of both: the Father's act of generation and spiration involves an act of sharing himself absolutely as loving, continually self-offering communion. The Father is *principium* in the Trinity but is the originator of a truly self-giving reciprocal communion, not of a hierarchy of powers. Thus, returning to homily 7 of the 1 John series, if we are to love, love involves this form: "he offered himself. 'Most beloved, if God has so loved us, we also ought to love one another.'"

Two aspects of this vision of love that have been hinted at now need to be drawn out again. First, Augustine does not here offer a theology in which God offers his Son as propitiation, an exchange simply analogous to one subject's offering of an object.[34] Augustine rather combines an understanding of the Son's self-offering with a conception of the Father's self-gift through the use of their unity and separation in the Trinity. Although we use the language of a Father sending his Son, we understand the form of the transaction only when we see that although the Son comes to make an appropriate sacrifice he actually offers himself as victim. The Son, both God and human, offers himself as sacrifice, showing the extent of God's love for us. In addition, the absolute accord between the will of the Father and the will of the Son means that the whole "sending" is an act expressive of the exchange of love of the Trinity.

The second aspect that needs drawing out concerns Augustine's conception of the Spirit as the gift of love. The Spirit, as the gift of God that *is* God, continues to be a central part of his theology of God's self-offering on the cross. God's redemptive dispensation involves *both* the life, death, resurrection, and ascension of Christ *and* the sending of the Spirit. The incarnation reveals God's prior love for us, and the Spirit leads us to share in that love through forming the church into a community that participates in the love of the Trinity through incorporation into the body of Christ. Augustine's understanding of the work of the Spirit seems to involve two

34. Despite their different understandings of God's unchangeability, this theology is in some ways parallel to Hans Urs von Balthasar's theology of the cross, especially as seen in *Mysterium Paschale: The Mystery of Easter*, trans. A. Nicholls (Edinburgh: T. & T. Clark, 1990).

aspects. On the one hand, the Spirit is a "unifying" force, drawing us all into a form of loving that participates in the always prior loving exchange of God.[35] On the other hand, the Spirit permits a diversity through calling us to participate in this love by showing love to others that they may be our "brothers."[36] Only in the love of neighbor can we "see" the priority of God's love revealed in Christ.

This section of the essay has attempted to draw out Augustine's discussion of God as love and love as God. Because of the presence of the Spirit with us when we love, love is God. This picture is reliant on a theology of the Christian community as the community taken up by the gift of incarnation and Spirit into the life of the Trinity, and that in turn is understood here as expressive of the potential of creation: Christian practice is understood as a realization and discernment of God's presence to creation through attendance on the practices inaugurated within the body of Christ. Because of Augustine's theology of the person of Christ these practices draw us to participate in the incarnation that manifested God to us. In the next section of this essay I want to turn again to the relationship between "seeing" God and the practice of love.

VI. "SEEING" THE TRINITY

The "seeing" of God in the practice of Christian charity is the subject of the next few sections of tractate 7. In §10 Augustine searches for a way to reconcile 1 John 4:12, "No man has ever seen God," with Matthew 5:8, "Blessed are the pure in heart for they shall see God."[37] We should avoid trying to imagine God with the "desire of the eyes" *(concupiscentia oculorum)* because we would in that way be unable to avoid imagining God according to size and limit; rather, we need to see him according to the "eyes of the heart." This leads Augustine to state that we see God in love and in the actions of love:

> [This] is what you should imagine if you wish to see God: "God is love."
> What sort of face does love have? What sort of form does it have? . . . No

---

35. See *trin.* XV.17.31; XV.19.37.
36. See *trin.* XV.19.34.
37. The brief presentation of this theme here is mirrored at many other places in his work.

one can say. Nonetheless it does have feet, for they lead to the Church. It does have hands, for they are stretched out to the poor man. . . . It does have ears, about which the Lord says, "he who has ears to hear, let him hear." They are not members separated by places, but by means of the understanding he who has love sees the whole at one time. Dwell and you will be a dwelling, abide and you will be an abode.

Toward the end of §10 Augustine insists that love is something present to all people: the acceptance of love is not dependent on our taking something external to us; it is there with us prior to our acceptance. Nevertheless the preservation of love, which is the subject of §11, involves the formation of loving habits, a process of discernment and correction. The dove that descends on Christ at his baptism is a peculiarly appropriate form for the Spirit: the dove is both loving and yet defends its children; the dove expresses love and anger with love. The dove that descends rests above the head of Christ, symbolizing that Christ receives baptism in order that he may give it (just as he receives love and all that he is from the Father so that he may show love); we receive baptism from Christ and must refer all that we do back to him. His baptism is thus an expression of the Trinitarian life into which we are drawn.[38]

This passage can be helpfully supplemented with one from homily 9 in the series where Augustine directly examines the question of theological "analogy." In §3, commenting on 1 John 4:17 ("because as he is so are we in this world"), Augustine asks how far we may draw "likenesses" between our lives and our love and God.[39] The answer follows the general thrust of what one finds in considerations of "analogy" in the series (and Augustine himself points back to §9 of homily 4), but here Augustine adds to the picture his conception of our being made in the image and likeness of God. The argument can perhaps be set out in three stages. First, the "as" in the

38. I have attempted to set out and hint at the possible theological dynamic of this text without appropriating the particulars of its clear polemical context. Augustine is opposing the Donatists as schismatics on the grounds that they are claiming the right to have power over the sacraments that is properly Christ's (this parallels other treatments of Simon Magus in Augustine's corpus).

39. My use of "likeness" here is deliberate. Augustine never uses either of his two most direct technical terms for analogy *(analogia* or *proportio)* for the relationship between any part of creation and God. That *proportion* is simply and literally incomprehensible. Rather, he prefers less technical terms such as *similitudo* ("likeness"). For more discussion of this important issue see my "'Remember that you are Catholic.'"

phrase "we are *as* he is" is to be understood as indicating not (any degree of) equality but resemblance. There is a certain appropriate place in creation for us, a certain "measure" appropriate to us, and only by understanding this can we see how we resemble the Creator and how we do not. Second, this resemblance must be understood in the light of the theology of love given in these sermons; we may be like him in this world by following his example of love and by attempting to love our enemies. The increase in our love makes us resemble God more closely, more appropriately. Third, we never become equal to God because he is the one whose love is always prior; we love *because* he loved us.

This passage takes up and follows again the structure of homily 7, where we learn to love through our learning to attend to the love shown in Christ. Perhaps we can identify three key facets of Augustine's view of theological "analogy" here. First, our drawing of "likenesses" between the creation and God is dependent always on God's prior act toward us in the incarnation. Second, our drawing of "likenesses" is integrally related to our participation in the redemptive life of Christian love (because that love is simply God present in us), learning to see how the material acts as revelation of the divine, the created as revelation of the uncreated. Third, such life involves not the *supposition* of a theology of creation, but a continual *movement into* a theology of creation; only as we learn to see God as love under the impetus of the incarnation and the sending of the Spirit do we come to see the purpose of the creation and the truly appropriate relations between Creator and created. Theological "analogy" is thus a process integrally related to Christian life.

VII. CALLING GOD LOVE

Augustine's talk of learning to see God in love — and his more controversial willingness to say that love *is* God — must be understood in the context of his insistence that true love is the presence of the Spirit. It needs also to be said that, for Augustine, we are not called simply to see in our human love an image of the Trinity, as some readings of his Trinitarian theology suggest. Rather, we are called to see, through the process of faith and longing, how God is present to us and how the redemptive dispensation of God takes us up into the Trinitarian life and love. The process of theological "analogy" for Augustine depends on our coming to see beyond

our picture of a material or simply distant God and learning to see —
through increasing participation in it — how our lives may be both like
and unlike the exchange of love that is God. It is because of this perception
that Augustine is so insistent that we must undergo the discipline of
formed Christian love in community if we are to see how God may be
called love.

I have not devoted any space in this essay to examining whether or not
Augustine's theology of love is "platonic" or where it fits into a dynamic
between "eros" and "agape." On the one hand, these categories are simply
no longer adequate for the task, and scholars of Augustine gave up thinking that they were some time ago.[40] On the other hand, and without reference to these categories, I have been able to provide an introduction to the
theological themes that run through and provide the background for Augustine's account, focusing continually on questions of incarnation and
Trinitarian theology. It is through attention to these most fundamental of
theological themes that we will best come to see how Augustine talks of
God as love — and how he appropriates the many philosophical sources
available to him. Both Stoic and Neoplatonic sources are important in providing the background to his statements that all virtues are identical and
that they find their only full instantiation in the very being of God; but the
particular articulation and combination of these ideas that we find in Augustine's thought will be greatly misunderstood without close attention to
the doctrinal matrix within which he situates them. Calling God love is for
Augustine an activity that makes sense only within the slow process of
coming to realize that the one who *is* love has revealed himself and that he
has inaugurated a practice of formed love and confession through which
we may share in the Triune life of love itself.

My intention here has been to provide an introduction to one key resource, and indeed just one key text, for thinking about God as love. Having provided that introduction, I want finally to go further and suggest
that the theological structure of Augustine's account may provide one of
the most important and most basic models for modern theological writing
in this area. On the one hand, Augustine locates his exposition of this

---

40. Indeed, the substantive issues that Anders Nygren attempted to raise in his discussion of Augustine in these categories were answered as long ago as J. Burnaby's now classic
Amor Dei: A Study of the Religion of St. Augustine (Norwich: Canterbury Press, 1991 [origi-
nally 1938]).

theological theme within Trinitarian theology, showing how what it means for God to be love is learnt only by attention to the structures of love within the Triune life of God. On the other hand, he approaches the question of how we come to know (and live within) those structures through reflection on the function of the incarnation in shaping and leading human lives. I suggest that these two moves are fundamental to any Christian theology of God as love. There are many theological and ontological questions we may wish to take up with Augustine's work; but in thinking through what it means to call God love, we can do far worse than think through the moves Augustine has already made.

CHAPTER 5

How Do We Define the Nature of God's Love?

TREVOR HART

The question that forms our title can be read in two ways. It can be taken on the one hand as an inquiry after an appropriate theological method: how do we go about the task of defining the nature of God's love? Or, on the other hand, we could read it as a request to know the results of such definition. What, in fact, do we *say* about the nature of God's love? Much will be said in answer to this second question in the other essays in this book. But, while I have chosen to focus on the methodological problems of definition, it will be clear, particularly in the latter parts of this essay, that the two questions cannot really be separated and that the implications for theological content of different strategies of approach are considerable. I want first to raise in a very general way some of the problems of definition involved in speaking of God's love, and then I will turn to consider some different approaches to the task.

I. THE PROBLEM OF DEFINITION IN HORIZONTAL AND VERTICAL PERSPECTIVE

Love, the words of the song remind us, is a many-splendored thing. This, of course, is offered to us by the songwriter as a virtue. But for the Christian theologian the multifaceted and diverse nature of human experiences of love has its distinct drawbacks. "God is love," 1 John 4:8 and 16 tell us.

But what seems at first sight, perhaps, to offer a refreshingly straightforward intellectual handhold on the otherwise sheer, slippery, and apparently inaccessible rock face of the divine nature proves upon closer inspection to do nothing of the sort. The very familiarity with love in the human context that draws us to it also serves to convince us of its potential risks and dangers as a point from which to begin the climb of a description of the one in whom we live and move and have our being.

There are, after all, so many different human loves to choose from: the love of lover for his or her beloved; the love of husband for wife and wife for husband; the love of parent for child; the love of child for parent; the love of brother for sister and sister for brother; the love of grandparent for grandchild; the love between close friends; the love we have for our pets, for nature, for art, for good food and drink — and the list might easily be extended. In none of these cases are we speaking of precisely the same thing, even if we prune the list of some of the more evidently metaphorical and strained uses of the verb. And in any one instance, the love of which we speak is a highly complex and elusive quantity. So simply to repeat the biblical assertion that "God is love" is certainly not to answer any significant theological questions. It is, in fact, where the hard work of theology begins rather than ends. Given the complexity and diversity of that which the word "love" evokes, which, if any, we must ask, of the strands presenting themselves to us for consideration are relevant or appropriate to the interpretation of this statement? And on what grounds are we actually able to make a valid selection? That, it seems, is the first problem we face.

But it is far from being either the only or indeed the major problem. Alongside it we must set the more general problem of knowing what precisely is entailed in speaking of God at all and of the meaning of any resultant statements. This is a problem that any religious or philosophical tradition that entertains belief in a genuinely transcendent God must necessarily face. Theology is a craft in which the chief tools are words and the ideas to which they are related. But these words and ideas are inevitably finite; they are drawn from the available pool of human language and experience and handled by human thinkers and word-smiths who can make no claim to have transcended their own finitude and sinfulness in the process, any more than can their readers in receiving the results. How, then, is it that these creaturely linguistic and conceptual tools, fashioned in order to bring to expression finite realities, are applied to the infinite Creator of all things? That they *are* so applied is not in doubt. Theology has no other language, no other conceptuality, no other experience to draw upon in its task than those of this world. What remains to be answered is the question of how or on what basis this dual application of terms across the boundary between finite and infinite, created and uncreated, proceeds; and, crucially, what are its implications for the respective meanings of the terms that theology deploys in this linguistic joining of heaven and earth.

Karl Barth delineates the precise contours of the question for us:

> Does there exist a simple parity of content and meaning when we apply the same word to the creature on the one hand and to . . . God on the other? We are aware, or we think we are aware, of what being, spirit, sovereignty, creation, redemption, righteousness, wisdom, goodness, etc. mean when we use these terms to describe creatures. We are also aware, or think we are aware, what we are saying when in the sphere of the creature we say eye, ear, mouth, arm or hand, or love, wrath, mercy, patience and such-like. Does all this mean the same thing when we also say it about God?[1]

Barth goes on to remind us what Christian theologians have always known; namely, that if we assume a univocal use of terms as applied to creatures and to God, we effectively deny God's transcendence, or else we deify the creature, subsuming both God and the creaturely under common categories of description. If, on the other hand, we suppose that human terms assume a wholly new and different meaning when they are predicated of God, then our theology rapidly collapses into nonsense, and we effectively rob ourselves of any consequent knowledge of God at all, since, being finite, we are not in any position to know what these different meanings might be.

Returning, then, to our particular piece of theological construction, we must now face the fact that an intelligent account of the claim that God is love must cope not only with the inherent slipperiness of the word "love" itself in general discourse, but also with the complications introduced by tacking these other words "God is" in front of it. There is, as it were, a vertical as well as a horizontal dimension to the problem of definition with which we are concerned. To develop our rock-climbing image, we are not faced simply with a choice of numerous possible alternative routes across the rock face, some of which may prove fruitless or even lead

---

1. Karl Barth, *Church Dogmatics* II/1 (Edinburgh: T. & T. Clark, 1957), p. 224.

us into danger, but also with the apparent risk that even the *best* of those routes may lead us ultimately only to the edge of a semantic crevasse that cannot be bridged, leaving us facing a gap of unknown proportions between our words and any meanings they might or might not have as applied to God. The problem of defining the love of God (or any other aspect of his being and activity) lies chiefly here, in discerning how, if at all, this gap may be closed, and our words terminate on the reality of God himself, rather than falling short or bouncing back, leaving us forever trapped in one form or another of agnosticism. I say "if at all" advisedly, because, to anticipate briefly, it seems to me that the terms in which our question is phrased are presumptuous. Perhaps we should be asking, "*Do* we define the nature of God's love?" while preparing ourselves for the possibility of a negative answer. There is, I think, a sense in which such an answer must be allowed.

It may be at this point, however, that someone will finally wish to unmask the rather obvious weakness in the metaphor I have used. Surely, it might be objected, attempts to liken the theological task to a rock climb — scaling unknown heights, choosing routes, and facing insurmountable obstacles — are poorly conceived. It suggests that our task is one of climbing up to God, rather than grappling seriously with the claim implicit within most Christian theology in some form or another that God has come down to us and made himself known. This is a vital methodological point, and one with which we shall certainly have to reckon. And it probably does highlight the main weakness of my chosen image. But appeals to revelation and neat and tidy distinctions between approaches to theology "from above" and "from below" can be introduced too quickly and in ways that finally fail to recognize the problems I have outlined rather than resolving them.

To begin with, immediate resort to the category of revelation does not resolve the "vertical" problem of the ontological and noetic gap between transcendent and immanent, created and uncreated, God and the world. This gap, it might be claimed, while it is unbridgeable from our side, is not unbridgeable from God's, and he has in fact bridged it, making himself known on our side of the gap: supremely in flesh-and-blood terms in the incarnation, but with a vital associated cognitive and hermeneutical matrix that we find in its raw form in the biblical writings. God has spoken. And on the basis of this speech we too now may speak of him, repeating after him, as it were, the words in which he speaks of himself.

But the claim that the Word of God has assumed *flesh,* far from resolving the linguistic, epistemological, and ontological problem of the relationship between God and the world, simply serves to raise it in a particularly acute form, as the history of Christology bears adequate witness. On the one hand, the fact of God's self-accommodation to human forms — in a human life, in human text, in human proclamation — robs us of the possibility of remaining silent. It demands an obedient response from us. Having heard God's word, we must now speak and make sense of what we say in order that others might hear and understand. Yet, on the other hand, it is precisely *because* this self-revealing takes *human* form (as it must if we are to hear and receive it) that the problem of a semantic *unio hypostatica* presents itself to us. For, whatever the relationship between the uncreated and the created may be supposed to be, God cannot be accommodated completely within human language any more than within human flesh. And inasmuch as revelation takes place in human terms, therefore, it will always be a veiling as much as a revealing, as Barth recognizes.[2] There will always be an extent to which even those forms which God assumes and drafts into his service fall short of bringing the infinite to expression within the terms of the finite. It cannot be done, any more than we can give an adequate rendering of a Mahler symphony on the triangle or render the smell of fish and chips into verbal form. In both cases, something inherently inadequate about the tools at our disposal renders even our best efforts little more than a pale reflection of the original, and such that we could never infer the original from mere familiarity with the copy. Likewise, the fact that God becomes human and employs human modes of knowing in communicating with us raises, rather than resolves, the question of how those human realities may be supposed to refer beyond themselves and beyond their ordinary human context in their specifically theological application.

A theology that affirms an incarnational revelation insists that God immerses himself in the messiness and contingency of history and the flesh in making himself known to humans. In doing so he does not lift us up out of our creatureliness, elevating us to some deified state in which we are able to contemplate divine realities directly, from a "God's eye" perspective. This means, of course, that we cannot ignore or circumvent the

---

2. See, e.g., Barth, *Church Dogmatics* I/1 (Edinburgh: T. & T. Clark, 1975), pp. 320f.; II/1 (Edinburgh: T. & T. Clark, 1957), pp. 234f.

familiar and ordinary associations that words and realities taken up into the service of divine revelation have for us. We begin, and remain, within the sphere of the human in theology. Insofar as we know God, we do so because he comes to be with us in this same sphere, and not because he lifts us out of it.

To this extent, a theology of the love of God cannot short-circuit or set aside the contribution that human experiences and understandings of love have to offer; rather, it must take them fully into account. We may in due course wish to speak of God's love or Jesus' love as informing and transforming our thinking about human love — as, for example, when H. R. Mackintosh reminds us that in the Sermon on the Mount, Jesus presents God's love as a pattern for, rather than a reflection of, human love.[3] It is not that he loves like us, but that we are urged to love like him. But the hermeneutical realities of the situation are more complicated than beginning with God and moving to the human. First we have to obtain an understanding of the divine love; and such an understanding will already be fashioned from the messy stuff of human experience and ideas. That is what is entailed in the affirmation of incarnation. As George Newlands suggests, the Christian will certainly want to argue that the great gap between God's love and ours has been bridged in the person of Jesus, where the divine life is in some sense earthed in a human life. "Through the humanity of God revealed in the humanity of Jesus Christ," he writes, "we may come to understand the true nature of the human. But even Barth recognised on occasion that there must be something in our experience of the human which enables us to recognise a perfection of humanness in Jesus."[4] We cannot, therefore, afford to overlook the obvious fact that that which comes "from above," unless it remains above, must at some point become incarnate in the humdrum reality of what exists here below, and as a consequence that reality must form some sort of resource for theological reflection and development.

But in coming down, in assuming the flesh, God does not, of course, leave it as he finds it. And this is a point of at least equal significance for our approach to theological language. For if in coming he does not lift us

3. H. R. Mackintosh, *The Christian Apprehension of God* (London: S.C.M., 1929), p. 186.

4. George Newlands, *Theology of the Love of God* (Cambridge: Cambridge University Press, 1981), p. 132.

out of our *creatureliness,* God does, Christians claim, lift us out of our *sinfulness.* The process of incarnation does not entail change for God alone, leaving the familiar forms of the "flesh" unaffected. That which is assumed is, as the Greek fathers suggested, in some sense healed or redeemed in the process, being taken up and reconciled from its sinful condition to a state in which it reflects more appropriately the being of the one who now indwells it. And this, we may suppose, is no less true of human language and conceptuality than it is of human flesh. Its assumption by the divine Word entails refashioning and recasting, a semantic shift that overcomes the incapacities resulting from its fallenness, even if those resulting from its creatureliness inevitably remain.

To say, then, that theology must begin and remain within the sphere of the flesh must not be supposed to mean that in making sense of the forms that revelation takes we can rest content with any simple trawl of our own experience and understanding in order to identify the common meanings and significances that ordinarily attach to those forms. As in Christology we cannot simply construct a portrait of the human Jesus rooted in our own perceptions of empirical humanity but must always reckon with those things which differentiate his humanity from ours, precisely because it is in these very elements that his revelatory and salvific significance resides, so too in this matter of theological definition, while our starting point must inevitably be with our own creaturely and sinful perceptions and experiences of love, fatherhood, righteousness, and the rest, we must expect and allow the limits of these perceptions to be ruptured and their content transformed as they refer us beyond the ordinary and familiar to the humanity of God, and beyond still, to God's own life and being.

In short, if we are to make sense of the claim that God is love, then, precisely *because* this claim reposes on a revelation of God in the flesh, we must come to terms with and seek to explore the implications of the recognition that we are dealing with "love, . . . but not as we know it"! There are both similarity and difference. God's love both is and yet is not like ours. The task of theological definition, whether we base it upon an appeal to revelation or not, is, therefore, somehow to feel our way toward a grasp of the shape and dimensions of the difference. And this task will involve us in a human intellectual activity the results of which, whatever the quality of the raw materials, will and can only ever be provisional and imperfect. It does not follow from this, however, that all results must be equally (in)adequate.

Thus we arrive at the suggestion that the theologian is at some point forced to admit some version of the doctrine of analogy in both its linguistic/conceptual and ontological aspects. We must suppose, that is to say, that words such as "love," drawn as they are from our creaturely language, are applied to God neither univocally nor equivocally but in a way that involves both likeness and unlikeness to their everyday use. And, unless we consider theology to be a matter of words and the relationships between words alone, behind this supposition will lie another — namely, that the relationship between God and creaturely reality is such that it is somehow possible for human words to refer to him in such an analogous manner. To say that such analogies between the divine and the human exist, however, is not necessarily to suppose that human beings are in any position to know of them or to discern their nature and contours. Assumptions concerning this epistemic circumstance, and theological strategies constructed on the basis of them, may differ quite substantially.

I want next to consider two contrasting approaches to the question of what is involved in speaking of God's love and see where they might lead us.

II. THE METAPHOR OF GOD AS LOVER

Sallie McFague roots her so-called metaphorical theology expressly in the soil of human experience. Hence her particular reason for speaking of God's love (or, more specifically, of God as lover) is not tied specifically to biblical themes or to any of the ways in which these have been developed in Christian theology over the centuries. It is rather because she is convinced that here she has identified a metaphor offering an imaginative construal of the God-world relation that resonates with contemporary experiences of relatedness to God. Theology, she insists, must be credible: that is to say, it must ring true for those whose assumptions and values are those of modern society.[5]

But, for McFague, the theologian's task is not that of definition — so in the strict sense we do not define the nature of God's love, or anything else to do with God. Rather, the theologian is a philosopher-poet whose task is to try out new metaphors and models drawn from general experience in order to bring to expression aspects of the God-world relation as *it*

---

5. Sallie McFague, *Models of God* (Philadelphia: Fortress, 1987), p. 32.

is experienced by men and women today. Metaphors are imaginative leaps across distance, daring attempts to think differently and to express the quality of our experience of being related to God by borrowing human images and ideas. In this sense metaphorical theology is heuristic, experimenting and testing out new ways of thinking and speaking. It is by definition open to all possibilities. No metaphor can be excluded from consideration, although all must be tested, and there is always the risk "that the leap across the abyss will be unsuccessful."[6] The criteria of selectivity are not those of resort to the traditional authorities, although McFague insists that some level of identifiable continuity with the past is important. But, since "how language, any language, applies to God we do not know, what religious and theological language is at most is metaphorical forays attempting to express experiences of relating to God,"[7] and it is the proven persuasiveness and appropriateness of a particular metaphor (which seems in practice to amount to its popularity and ready assimilation in the contemporary context) that eventually secure it a place as a legitimate expression of Christian faith for our time.

Although McFague eschews the normative role of tradition and makes experience her primary datum in theology, nonetheless, at the heart of the relatedness to God of which she speaks, the themes of salvation and of the "transforming love of God" figure large. While the particular ways in which she construes these differ considerably from the mainstream of Christian theology, it is difficult to suppose that the basic categories themselves have not ultimately been borrowed, eclectically (and perhaps unconsciously), from that same tradition. What we must seek today, therefore, McFague suggests, are metaphors and models that speak to our generation of caring, mutuality, nurturing, support, empathy, service, and self-sacrifice at the level of ultimate reality. The metaphors she especially favors are those of Mother, Lover, and Friend, to the second of which we now turn.

While the Christian tradition has from its earliest days wished to speak of love in God, McFague notes, it has been equally reluctant to engage the particular metaphor of God as lover. Yet such love, she notes, is "the most intimate and important kind of human love."[8] Surely, then,

---

6. McFague, *Models of God*, p. 35.
7. McFague, *Models of God*, p. 39.
8. McFague, *Models of God*, p. 126.

it cannot be irrelevant to an attempt to apply the language of love to God? While it is sometimes supposed to be the erotic associations of the idea that have rendered it inappropriate for Christian theological description, Eros as such, McFague notes, has its essence not in sex but in finding value in someone else and in being found valuable by that someone. To speak of such love between God and the world, she argues, while it may not have been tolerable to the classical Greek philosophy that so shaped and influenced Christian theology in its most formative years, holds enormous potential for those who live in an ecological-nuclear era. In such an era, she suggests, we need to be told not that we are valueless in ourselves, that God has no need of us and showers his love upon us out of sheer grace, but that life is valuable and wondrous in itself, that God loves it because it is loveable, and that our reciprocal love is something that "fills a need in God the lover," rather than something that he can take or leave. "We need to feel that value," she writes, "in the marrow of our bones if we are to have the will to work with the divine lover toward including all the beloved in the circle of valuing love, . . . if we are to have any hope of attaining an ecologically balanced, nuclear free world."[9]

While there are elements in McFague's protest against the abstract theism of the tradition that resonate fairly evidently with voices from across the theological spectrum, it is clear that her use of the lover metaphor takes her a very long way from the mainstream and its discussion of the love of God. Cutting herself loose from the moorings of Scripture and tradition, and appealing to experience and credibility as her guides, in effect she allows human experiences and construals of love to determine what she will say about God — or rather, about human experience of God. For McFague, in a manner directly reminiscent of Schleiermacher, makes no profession to be able to say anything about God as such. The metaphors that theology fashions and develops are imaginative leaps across a yawning crevasse beyond which the mystery of God lies. Such metaphors, we should recall, are adverbial; they express ways of relating to or experiencing God. Of the nature of God they can and do say nothing whatever. They offer "likely accounts," and the criteria of likelihood, like the selection of the metaphors themselves, lie in the hands of human beings and what they will find persuasive and credible.

9. McFague, *Models of God*, p. 133.

C. S. Lewis writes that "The human loves can be glorious images of Divine love. No less than that: but also no more."[10] The danger that McFague's theology falls foul of, perhaps, is that of reversing the logic of 1 John 4:8. Throwing up conceptions of love drawn directly from human experience, and lacking any objective standard of comparison by which to adjudge their worth, she effectively deifies them. At the end of the day such an approach seems likely to tell us little about God (even in poetic fashion) and rather more about the texture and color of the human situation from within which it issues.

III. BARTH AND THE SELF-DEFINITION OF GOD IN REVELATION

To come to Barth after McFague, while in historical terms anachronistic, is in many other ways an entirely appropriate and informative procedure. The theology that Barth set himself against in the early decades of the twentieth century was similar in some fundamental methodological respects to that which McFague espouses. Barth's contention was that every attempt to found human talk about God by pointing to the possibility and actuality of anthropological phenomena (whether latent rational truths, a sense of absolute dependence, an experience of the numinous, or whatever) simply invites the Feuerbachian reduction of theological statements to anthropological ones and ultimately traps theology within the confines of the possibilities and impossibilities of the human. For Barth, the utter transcendence of God taken together with human sinfulness renders every and any attempt at an intellectual storming of the gates of heaven utterly futile. "God," he writes, "does not belong to the world. Therefore he does not belong to the series of objects for which we have categories and words by means of which we draw the attention of others to them, and bring them into relation with them. Of God it is impossible to speak, because He is neither a natural nor a spiritual object."[11] At least, if it is *not* impossible to speak of God, if speech of him, if theology is in fact a possibility for human beings, then for Barth it is so only because God himself spans the gap that creation posits and human sin exacerbates. "What if," he asks, "God be

---

10. C. S. Lewis, *The Four Loves* (London: Geoffrey Bles, 1960), p. 18.
11. Barth, *Church Dogmatics* I/2 (Edinburgh: T. & T. Clark, 1956), p. 750.

so much God that without ceasing to be God he can also be, and is willing to be, not God as well. What if he were to come down from his unsearchable height and become something different?"[12] This, of course, is precisely what the Christian tradition insists that God has done, in a radical self-objectification, giving himself to be known in cognitive, verbal, and fleshly historical created forms. The possibility of human speech about God rests, for Barth, entirely upon this contingent fact. Theology, therefore, is not a matter of heuristics in the sense of some enterprising human exploration of the divine regions, but rather of obedient response to a given revelation.

For all his emphasis on revelation, however, Barth is anything but naive in his treatment of the problem of theological definition. The self-objectification of God involves God precisely in becoming "not God," which means that the media of revelation — verbal, conceptual, fleshly — in their very mediation raise the problem of their own relatedness to God. In the event of revelation in which they are, as it were, united with God's Word by the Spirit and given a transparency that in and of themselves they lack, they do not, nonetheless, become other than they always were. There is no transubstantiation, no docetic co-mingling of the divine and the creaturely that presents the divine to us immediately. Thus, Barth writes, "what we see, hear, feel, touch, and inwardly and outwardly perceive is always something different, a counterpart, a second thing,"[13] and never God himself and as such. Thus Barth realized that, even in the light of God's gracious condescension in revelation, the problem of theological language must be addressed and must finally be resolved by some version of the doctrine of analogy. Only thus, only if, notwithstanding the absolute transcendence of God over against the creature, there is some created analogy between God's existence and our language can the truth of God's self-revealing in human form be safeguarded without compromising his transcendence. In short, when human beings, on the basis of God's self-revelation, speak of him as loving, it is either because he is loving in the precise way that we are (which is precluded by a due recognition of his transcendence), or else it is because the love of which we speak has nothing whatever in common with human love (in which case it is a meaningless statement and tantamount to an untruth), or else it is because there is

12. Karl Barth, *Göttingen Dogmatics*, vol. 1 (Edinburgh: T. & T. Clark, 1992), p. 136.
13. Barth, *Göttingen Dogmatics*, vol. 1, p. 136.

that in God to which human love is in some respects analogous, given that there are other respects in which it is not. Thus, by his self-revealing economy God has granted to human language the power to refer appropriately to himself, albeit in an analogous, and thereby an indirect and veiled, manner.

There is, of course, a vital difference between Barth's handling of the doctrine of analogy and its classical development in the theology of Aquinas. For Thomas, the doctrine of analogy is not simply an account of what is going on in theological discourse; it is also a means of acquiring knowledge of God and of his relatedness to the world outside of the context created by revelation.[14] It is, in other words, a tool deployed in the construction of a natural theological metaphysic. In the metaphysical principle first aired by Proclus that "Everything which by its existence bestows a character on others, itself primitively possesses that character, which it communicates to the recipient,"[15] Aquinas identifies a basis for theological speech about God. Since creatures relate to God in the same way that effects relate to their cause, he writes, "we can be led from them so far as to know of God whether He exists, and to know of Him *what must necessarily belong to Him* as the first cause of all things, exceeding all things caused by Him."[16] Thus the analogical method yields substantive knowledge of God's character. By analogical predication we name perfections that belong to God properly, even though, drawing our language from creatures, the mode of signification is imperfect and falls short of naming them adequately. This differentiation between the *perfectio significata* and the *modus significandi* is crucial, since it allows Thomas to avoid appearing to subsume Creator and creatures under a common category of being.[17] Hence God and creatures manifest goodness, for example, in ways appropriate to their quite distinct modes of existence.

From Barth's perspective, however, the problem that remains is that analogy in its Thomist version lays claim just as surely as McFague's metaphorical theology to a basis for human talk about God that is independent

14. George Newlands would seem to me to be incorrect in his denial that this is so. See his *God in Christian Perspective* (Edinburgh: T. & T. Clark, 1994), p. 46.

15. Proclus, *The Elements of Theology* 18, trans. E. R. Dodds (Oxford: Clarendon, 1953), p. 21.

16. Aquinas, *Summa Theologica*, 1.12.12. My italics.

17. See Battista Mondin, *The Principle of Analogy in Protestant and Catholic Theology* (The Hague: M. Nijhoff, 1963), 170.

of God's self-revealing act in Jesus Christ.[18] Hence it lies within the grasp of human reason to discover which perfections must necessarily belong to God and which cannot. But God, Barth insists, is not and could never be at our disposal in this way. That there must be some analogy between God and the creature is clear, but that human beings are in any position to trace the precise nature and contours of this analogy is not; and Barth rejects the claim to have identified a basis for doing so via empirical observation and logical inference, as if the relationship between Creator and creature could be reversed and controlled to human theological advantage. In any case, he avers, since creation is *ex nihilo,* and God is not simply the first link in a chain of cause and effect, all we should find by such a method, were it in fact to be successful, would be the nothingness out of which we were first called into being.

While, therefore, Barth embraces a doctrine of analogy as a necessity, it is for him only a *factual* necessity, established by the contingency of God's creative and revelatory action, and not an *absolute* necessity determined by some metaphysical principle to which God and humans are alike subject.[19] Consequently human beings, Barth argues, are in no position to extrapolate from their own creaturely natures some account of the divine nature. The analogy between God and humans, if such there be, can be known only by that which drives us to speak of it in the first place — namely, God's revelatory and redemptive act in Jesus Christ, in the course of which we find human language and conceptuality taken up and legitimated as a means of referring appropriately to God.

In other words, if we are to speak of love in God, then it can only be because this is how God has first spoken to us of himself, and we must be careful to allow our use of the term to be driven and guided from first to last by the particularities of that prior use. The verbal formula of 1 John

18. See, e.g., the discussion of analogy in *Church Dogmatics* II/1, p. 232: "The moderate doctrine of analogy in natural theology, as it has been and is represented in particular in the Catholic Church, stands in the closest material and historical connexion with the Liberalism which, under appeal to God's omnipotence, affirms all analogies . . . [and] shows a basic readiness in almost every connexion to discover new analogies in the world."

19. "All kinds of things might be analogous to God, if God had not made and did not make a very definite and delimited use of His omnipotence in His revelation; that is to say, if the analogy of the creation and creaturely word effected by His revelation did not mean a selection, determined and carried out by Himself, from among the infinitely many possibilities and definitely referred away from others." Barth, *Church Dogmatics* II/1, p. 232.

4:8, Barth notes, might at first sight encourage us to think in terms of an equation of God with some abstract universal idea, a Form of love in which he and others participate to differing degrees. But, he reminds us, the exegetical context makes it quite clear that we are intended to think not abstractly but concretely at this point.[20] "This," the apostle makes clear, "is how God showed his love among us; he sent his one and only Son into the world that we might live through him. This is love . . . that he loved us and sent his Son as an atoning sacrifice for our sins" (1 John 4:9-10, NIV); "This is how we know what love is: Jesus Christ laid down his life for us" (3:16, NIV). We must begin our reflection on God's love, therefore, not with some general concept of love, or with one of any number of different possible human experiences and exemplifications of love. Whatever role these may have to play in our subsequent thinking and theological development, they cannot be the dogmatic point of departure.

"It is not," Barth writes, "that we recognise and acknowledge the infinity, justice, wisdom" (and we might add love) "of God because we already know from other sources what all this means and we apply it to God in an eminent sense, thus fashioning for ourselves an image of God after the pattern of our image of the world, i.e., in the last analysis after our own image."[21] Rather, we must begin and continue for a considerable while with the testimony to God's love that is contained in the form of his revealing act itself. Of course, this cannot mean any pure and simple reiteration or a refusal to do more than receive and preserve in its original form the revelation that he bestows. We are called upon to interpret, to make sense, to present what we have learned in new and persuasive and compelling ways, to relate it to existing knowledge and experience in such a way that others may be able to hear and receive it. Thus "The humility of our knowledge of God does not consist in the laziness of the servant who took his pound and buried it (Mt 25.18), but in the fact that, invited and authorised by revelation to do so, we give God the honour which belongs to Him, to the very best . . . of the ability which He Himself gives us."[22] But, in using and developing and translating the words in which he teaches us to speak of himself, we must ever seek to allow him to be the interpreter of these words, rather than cutting our-

20. Barth, *Church Dogmatics* II/1, p. 275.
21. Barth, *Church Dogmatics* II/1, p. 333.
22. Barth, *Church Dogmatics* II/1, p. 336.

selves loose from the normative forms of his revelatory engagement with the flesh.

We need do little more here than list a couple of the things that Barth believes Christians are thereby compelled to say of God's love in order to see how his contrasting approach leads him to a very different picture from that arrived at by McFague.[23]

First, God loves us as the one who loves in freedom. He loves us, that is to say, not out of any lack or need in his own being, but because he wills our existence as an other over against himself and sharing in fellowship with himself. To be sure, God is love in his innermost being, but not an unrequited love that demands the creation of an object and a reciprocal response in order to find fulfillment. As Father, Son, and Spirit he is eternally fulfilled in his love, and his love for us issues out of an overflow rather than a deficit of love. If, therefore, we may speak of a need love in God in relation to his creatures, it can only be with the proviso attached that this need, the desire for the creature's love, which also furnishes the capacity for pain and a sense of loss, is something contingent upon God's willing to enter into such a relation in the first place, to place himself under certain relational constraints, to be limited in his freedom by the existence of a genuinely free other.[24]

Second, God's love for his creature takes a very particular form. This love for the other craves response but is itself unconditioned by any capacity for response, or any inherent virtue or value, in that other. Indeed, it is love for those who not only are not loveable but who actively hate and reject and despise the lover. It is love that burns in anger at the existence and effects of sin and evil, yet never ceases to love those who are gripped by and the agents of sin, and it manifests itself supremely in the form of forgiveness.[25] It is, in other words, unlike any other love that we know, uniquely Holy Love.[26]

---

23. See §28 of *Church Dogmatics*, II/1.

24. See, e.g., Barth, *Church Dogmatics* II/1, pp. 273-75.

25. "The love of God always throws a bridge over a crevasse. It is always the light shining out of darkness. In His revelation it seeks and creates fellowship where there is no fellowship and no capacity for it, where the situation concerns a being which is quite different from God, a creature and therefore alien, a sinful creature and therefore hostile. It is this alien and hostile other that God loves. . . . That . . . is the miracle of the almighty love of God." Barth, *Church Dogmatics* II/1, p. 278.

26. See Barth, *Church Dogmatics* II/1, pp. 353f.

A careful focus on the form of God's self-revealing act helps us, therefore, to delimit the horizontal spread of different human options signified by our ordinary uses of the term "love." We whittle down the field, attending to the particularities and peculiarities of this specific application of the term, until we are left with a pool of usable language and conceptuality that we may trust to refer us appropriately to their divine object only because he blesses our use of them. But what exactly do we mean by saying this? And where does it leave us? Specifically, what are we now to say of the vertical relation of these delimited human terms and ideas to the being of God? These may well be the most appropriate ways of thinking and speaking that we have, being the ones that God himself grants us and encourages us to develop and reflect upon, but may we say that in them we have the means to define God's love, or any other feature of his being and activity?

The truth is, surely, that the problem of theological language remains, and we have not solved it simply by narrowing the field of language available for our use and allowing our use of it to be controlled by the particularities of God's self-objectification in human and created forms. We are still faced with the vital question: just how does this human reality relate and refer to the divine reality lying beyond it? When we say that God's love is "love . . . but not as we know it," we are saying much more than that the form which God's love takes on the human plane when it is incarnate differs significantly from any other human love that we are familiar with. We are also admitting that even *this* love is but a fleshly representation, a God-given analogy, of the divine reality itself. Barth writes: "God is what man in himself never is, what man himself can only understand as he looks to Him, admitting that of himself he does not know what he means when he says it."[27] And again, "We may and must venture to bring the concept of love (the peculiar and final meaning of which we admit we do not know . . .) into the service of . . . the declaration of the act and therefore of the being of God."[28]

Thus, while in obedience we are called to speak of God in *this* language and not another language of our own choosing or devising, the fact remains that of ourselves we do not know what we are saying when we say that God is love, so far as its reference to God himself is concerned. We do

27. Barth, *Church Dogmatics* II/1, p. 284.
28. Barth, *Church Dogmatics* II/1, p. 276.

not, in other words, know the nature of the dissimilarity between what our human words signify in ordinary discourse and what they signify in theological discourse. Precisely because, in revealing himself, God takes human form, all revelation is at the same moment a veiling. It is never revealedness under the form of the human. The givenness of the humanity of Christ, and of the language and conceptuality that form its creaturely matrix for interpretation, do not in and of themselves, therefore, provide us with that which we seek — namely, a definition of God's love. Even in the light of revelation we cannot, as it were, climb up the vapor trails left by the divine descent and find our way to heaven. The tangible forms of that revealing are but the opaque media of an event in which, in and through those forms, God opens himself and his truth to our knowing and our participation. But this event is not at our disposal. We "know" how these human media refer beyond themselves as we are drawn into a relationship with the object to which they refer us, as we know him in faith, as the knowledge of God is granted us new every morning. Such knowledge cannot be pinned down, held on to, packaged, and handed on to others. We can only point to the human media faithfully in order to direct others to the reality of which we speak.

This situation is not unique to theology, of course. Something similar may be found wherever the semantic range of our language is extended metaphorically to refer to hitherto unknown and unspoken aspects of reality in order to grant us epistemic access. In the process of accommodating language to the world, we are forced to borrow from our existing stock of words and images and to misuse them in order to draw parallels between the known and the only newly discovered. But precisely what the relation between the two is, what the analogy between them is, and what, therefore, the familiar term *means* in its new metaphorical application can be discerned only by those who are willing to submit themselves to the knowing relation. It is through our contact with the real that the meaning of our statements about it can finally be grasped. In the case of God, of course, since he is supremely subject and not object, we are not able to engage in such heuristic enterprise of our own accord. He must give himself to be known. But in other respects it would seem that the problem of theological language is simply a particularly clear instance of the problem of human language and its mode of reference to the real in general. What does it mean, we might legitimately ask, to *define* anything? And can we do it? If creaturely reality is less mysterious than divine reality, nonetheless it may be altogether more mysterious than has sometimes been supposed. In this case, of course, we are forced to the uncomfortable but perhaps inevitable conclusion that the doctrine of analogy tells us, not about some peculiar linguistic circumstances, but about the conditions of human speech in general.

IV. CONCLUSION

To our original question, "How do we define the nature of God's love?" it would seem that we are driven finally in one way or another to respond that we don't, at least in any strict sense. For McFague, theology is not about defining God but about fashioning metaphors that express our experience of relatedness to God, and none of these can be supposed in any way to penetrate the ether and speak of God as God is in Godself. They are "likely accounts," pictures that may help us to think of our relation to the ultimate, but that lay claim to no specific knowledge of God as such. Even Aquinas, with his application of the analogy of intrinsic attribution, differentiating carefully between the perfection signified and the mode of signification, leaves us having to admit that, while we may specify which perfections God, as the cause of the world, must necessarily possess, we cannot specify precisely how he possesses them, and therefore we cannot define precisely what the words we use to describe them mean in their specifically theological application. And then there is Barth, for whom we do not define God, but God defines himself for us, assuming our words and conceptuality just as surely as he assumes our flesh in order to reveal himself, and yet doing so in such a way that it never lies within our grasp to cash out the metaphors in literal terms, any more than we can capture the eternal Son simply by analyzing the humanness of the historical Jesus. In both cases, the truth is known only as the event of revelation happens, and we are drawn into a relationship with God himself through a transparency that the created media of that relationship do not possess in and of themselves.

The difference between Barth's account and those of McFague and Aquinas, however, is that, at the end of the day, we can trust that there is an appropriate analogy between our language and God himself at these points, because the basic metaphors are of his making and choosing rather than ours. We can trust, too, that as we deploy them to speak of him, he will be faithful and will speak of himself in and through our speaking, thereby opening out their ultimate reference and meaning for us so that we "know," through something resembling intuition, how these words refer. Perhaps the fact that we cannot capture that meaning and pin it down in neat logical formulae bothers us. But is this anything more than our eschatological impatience, which always seems to want certainty and clarity now, rather than resting content in the assumption that what we are granted now is sufficient, and being happy to wait for that time when we shall know fully, even as we are fully known?

CHAPTER 6

Is Love the Essence of God?

ALAN J. TORRANCE

To ask whether love is the essence of God commits one to giving particular consideration to the questions of language that are integral to this issue. Is love to be predicated univocally, equivocally, metaphorically, or analogically of the being of God and of human beings? Are we speaking about the same thing when we speak of divine love and human love, or is the meaning of the word different when affirmed of God on the one hand and humanity on the other? If the meaning of the word *agape* is quite different when used of God on the one hand and the contingent order on the other, then why use the same word? This leads in turn to the further question as to how we can be sure that, as human beings, we really know what we mean if and when we speak of God in this way.

Furthermore, can we mean what we say when we speak of divine love, given that we are not just finite but alienated in our conceptualities and cognitive orientation[1] such that we require to be "reschematized in our minds"?[2] In sum, what exactly are we saying and what precisely is going on when, with John, we affirm that "God is love"?

1. The argument of Colossians 1:21 is that we are *"echthroi te dianoia"* (lit. "enemies in our minds"). Calvin uses the phrase *"alienati mente,"* which is simply the Vulgate translation of the Greek.
2. Cf. Romans 12:2, where Paul argues that we are not to be "schematized" *(suschematizesthe)* by the secular world (Vulgate: "saeculum") but rather transformed *(metamorphousthe)* by the renewal of our minds.

Clearly, if we are successful in addressing these issues we will *already* have addressed the wider question whether and in what sense we might describe love as denoting the *essentia* or *ousia* of God.

It is important to emphasize right from the start that there is and can be no dichotomy between first-order theological statements about the being and nature of God and second-order statements relating to the functioning of our language in describing God. The functioning of our language will be seen to be irreducibly bound up with the being-in-act of God. To attempt to separate these two is one of the most serious confusions to be found in recent theological debates! With this proviso we shall now turn briefly to the relevant debates concerning language.[3]

The essential challenge to all theological description and all attempts to describe God is what Frederick Ferré refers to as a "perplexity" created by apparently contradictory axioms. This "perplexity" is generated, he writes, by "the *prima facie* conflict between repeated Biblical warnings that God is wholly incommensurable with his creation and . . . fairly explicit statements on the Deity's purposes, emotions, and characteristic modes of behaviour." The Christian theologian finds herself committed, therefore, to axioms that appear to contradict each other: "On the one hand, God, to be the God of the Bible or of the philosophers, must be so utterly different from all finite created beings that no statement with God as referent can mean what it would mean if it had any other referent," while, on the other hand, "genuine knowledge of God — of some kind — must be insisted upon if God has somehow been revealed to men."[4]

In short, when we say that God loves and that Mother Teresa loves, are we affirming the same thing or quality in both contexts? If we are, then are we not in danger of anthropomorphic projection and of failing to take seriously the transcendence of God? If we are affirming something completely and utterly different (when referring to God on the one hand and Mother Teresa on the other), then is theology not driven into sheer equivocation in all reference to God? If there is no continuity of meaning, then when we refer to God we must simultaneously acknowledge that all the

---

3. The following section constitutes a condensed form of the argument in chapter three of my book *Persons in Communion: Trinitarian Description and Human Participation* (Edinburgh: T. & T. Clark, 1996).

4. Frederick Ferré, "Analogy in Theology," in *The Encyclopedia of Philosophy*, vol. 1, ed. Paul Edwards (New York: Macmillan, 1967), p. 94.

terms we are using of God mean something that bears no continuity or relation to our experience and apperceptions as finite creaturely beings. This of course would reduce theology to an "Alice in Wonderland" scenario. Like Humpty Dumpty, theology would be utilizing terms such as "love" in the knowledge that their meaning is entirely different and discontinuous when used of God.

The traditional way out of this dilemma between assuming the univocal use of the term "love," which suggests that God loves and we love in exactly the same way, and an equivocal use of the term, which assumes that there is no continuity or similarity of meaning whatsoever between the two contexts, is offered by the theory of analogy. When terms are used of God they are used neither univocally nor equivocally, but analogically. But what does this mean?

In Western thought the most influential analysis of analogy has been Cajetan's classification of St. Thomas's theory. It is in terms of this classification that Gerald Phelan, for example, distinguishes three kinds of analogical predication:

1. The common character or *ratio* belongs really and truly to each and all of the participants in the same way, but in unequal degrees of intensity or under conditions of existence that are not identical. Men and dogs are equally animals, but they are not equal animals; the common character that makes them both animals really and truly belongs to each, but it does not exist in dogs and human beings under the same conditions of existence. This is what is usually referred to as the *analogy of inequality* or the *analogy of generic predication*.
2. The common character or *ratio* belongs properly to only one of the participants but is attributed by the mind to the others. Health, for instance, belongs properly speaking only to an organism, but, because of the relation in some order of causality that other things like food, medicine, and exercise bear to the health of the organism, these too are called healthy. This is usually referred to as the *analogy of attribution*.

Neither of these forms of analogy has traditionally been deemed to offer theology a sufficiently satisfactory way through the dilemma. Hence, Phelan argues, the solution to the problem is to be found in a third alternative:

3. The common characteristic or *ratio* belongs really and truly to each and all in proportion to their respective being *(esse)*. This is the *analogy of proper proportionality*.

It is in the light of this threefold classification that the heart of Aquinas's theory of analogy, as traditionally understood, is expounded. In the Thomist doctrine of analogy, Phelan claims, "the basic proposition . . . in its strict and proper meaning, is that *whatever perfection is analogically common to two or more beings is intrinsically (formally) possessed by each*, not, however, by any two in the same way or mode, but by each *in proportion to its being*."[5]

Love is possessed by human beings, by angels, and by God, but not in the same way. The way in which human beings love is proportionate to the being that humans have; the way in which angels love is proportionate to the being that angels have; and, likewise, the way in which God loves is proportionate to the being that God has. This is not to say that there is a direct equivalence between these proportions but rather that there is "a strict proportion of proportions in which the terms of one proportion are not proportionate to the terms of the other proportion, but the whole proportion between the terms on one side of the relation is proportionate to the whole proportion between the terms on the other side of the relation."[6]

Therefore if we say that "God loves," we are saying that God loves in a way appropriate to God and that this corresponds proportionately to the relation between human beings and their loving, where human beings love in a way appropriate to human beings. In this way, it is believed, we can assert analogically that "God loves" without ascribing to God human loving, and consequently we are not therefore speaking anthropomorphically of God. In this way we respect the divine transcendence and the categorical difference between God and humankind. We acknowledge, that is, the divine incommensurability with the created order.

But this solution clearly will not do. The analogy of proper proportionality is actually making two claims — first, that the predication holds analogously for creatures and the Creator, and second, that there is an analogy between the proportionality that exists between the analogates

---

5. Gerald B. Phelan, *Saint Thomas and Analogy* (Milwaukee: The Aquinas Lecture, 1941), p. 22, italics mine.

6. Phelan, *Saint Thomas and Analogy*, p. 23.

and the properties predicated of them. But this second statement is simply another and different statement of the same form as the first. In no sense does adding this second statement concerning an analogical proportionality of relations solve the problem as to how love can be predicated of God in a manner that suggests both that we know what we are affirming of God and that we are not engaging in anthropomorphic projection.

The weaknesses of this Cajetanian classification (a classification widely adopted, not least, by Reformed thinkers) do not, however, allow any easy dismissal of Thomas Aquinas's own thinking. Although Cajetan's interpretation of Aquinas was adopted almost universally for centuries, Suarez stood against this stream and opposed this interpretation. Rather than grounding theological description on an *analogy of proportionality* between God and creatures, Francisco de Suarez asserts that Aquinas teaches an *analogy of intrinsic attribution,* that is, "an analogy where the denominating form exists intrinsically in both (or all) the terms, in one absolutely and in the other or others relatively, through intrinsic relation to the former."[7] In other words, certain perfections (*agape,* for example) can be predicated of the created order due to the intrinsic relation of the created order to God. This means that there is an analogical and intrinsic continuity between the two contexts, which can mean that human language (appropriate to the created context) may be used of the Creator.

It is not our concern to engage here with the history of the interpretation of Aquinas. What is of real relevance to our discussion, however, are Aquinas's insights into theological description as these are elucidated by Battista Mondin (following Suarez).

On this alternative interpretation, the primary type of analogy as it is used in theological statements is for Aquinas the analogy of one to another according to priority and posteriority *(Analogia unius ad alterum per prius et posterius).* In these terms Aquinas advocates a form of analogy, of theological description, which claims direct (analogical) similarity between perfections attributed to God and the same perfections attributed to humanity — a direct similarity of the predicate, that is, rather than a similarity of proportions.

7. Battista Mondin, *The Principle of Analogy in Protestant and Catholic Theology* (The Hague: M. Nijhoff, 1963), p. 40. It may be noted that Mondin's work follows the lead given first of all by Etienne Gilson and continued by George P. Klubertanz in his book *St. Thomas Aquinas on Analogy* (Chicago: University of Chicago Press, 1960).

The weakness of the analogy of proportionality is that it fails to take due cognizance of either of the essential ingredients in Aquinas's interpretation. As Mondin comments, it "does not indicate either the causal nexus between God and creatures or God's priority over His creatures."[8] By focusing on an analogy between the proportions rather than the respective perfections themselves, it fails to address the fact that one is deliberately using the *same* word and concept when one asserts that as God loves us so must we love one another — and that just as love constitutes the being of God,[9] so must love constitute our being as participants in the new creation.

I. A NEW CLASSIFICATION OF AQUINAS'S MODES OF ANALOGY[10]

As a result of his analysis of the text of Aquinas and his critique of the problems inherent in the traditional exposition of analogy, both as interpretations of Aquinas and as offering a solution to the problem of human talk about God, Mondin offers a new and concise classification of types of analogy. The distinctions he draws are between the following four types of attribution:

1a. The *analogy of intrinsic attribution;* this is "formally" based on a relation of efficient causality between the analogates.

This, he argues, is the fundamentally theological form of analogy underlying the very possibility of God-talk.

1b. The *analogy of proper proportionality;* for example, the flight of an angel is to an angel as the flight of a bird is to a bird.

8. Mondin, *The Principle of Analogy in Protestant and Catholic Theology,* p. 50.
9. Catherine Mowry LaCugna is one recent writer who stresses the ontological significance of the love of God for the being of God. She interprets John Zizioulas's position as suggesting that "love causes God to be who God is" (*God for Us* [San Francisco: Harper, 1991], p. 261). Although we are not aware of Zizioulas using the term "cause" in precisely this way — the term is used not of love, nor of communion but of the person of the Father — his position does suggest that love constitutes the being of God.
10. Mondin, *The Principle of Analogy in Protestant and Catholic Theology,* pp. 51-53.

This is also an analogy of intrinsic denomination, but it is based, not on the divine agency and the relation of creation to Creator as effect to cause, but on a similarity of relations.

There is then another category not relevant to the theological task.

2a. The *analogy of extrinsic attribution;* for example, Peter is healthy and food is healthy.

(At certain points in the *Church Dogmatics,* Karl Barth's discussion comes too close to identifying with this kind of option — one that is ultimately incompatible with his central theological emphases.)

2b. The *analogy of improper proportionality* or the *analogy of metaphorical proportionality;* for example, Achilles is a lion and that beast is a lion.

In the light of Mondin's analysis, the impressive virtues of Aquinas's exposition of analogy (liberated from the confusions of Cajetan's) become clear.

1. The analogical attribution of a perfection to God must always be *unius ad alterum* (of one to another). It must never be *duorum ad tertium* (of two to a third) — that is, where we subsume God and creatures under some higher concept or category such as, for example, a Platonic form. In the same way, Aquinas shows that it must never be "of many to one" — as if we have an ideal of love under which we subsume God, Jesus, Paul, Gandhi, and Mother Teresa. If love is to be affirmed properly of God and humanity, it must be on account of a direct relationship between God and humanity — it must be *unius ad alterum,* from one to the other.

2. Analogical description must invariably be *per prius et posterius* (according to priority and posteriority) — recognizing the primacy or priority of God over the created order. The perfection is primarily affirmed of God and only secondarily and in a derivative sense of the creature. It applies to God first and to the human being second.

In sum, analogy reposes on an ontological relation between God and the creaturely domain and must recognize the order implicit in this relation. Consequently, God must never be subsumed together with his creatures under any more ultimate form or category. The analogy of "one to another" and "according to priority and posteriority" denotes two essential requirements of God-talk if it is to be true, meaningful, comprehensible by the human mind, and reverent (obviating, that is, all forms of anthropomorphism).

But this immediately raises the question as to the ontological presuppositions that underlie the possibility of the analogy of intrinsic attribution conceived in this way. Here we must turn to a further useful aspect of Mondin's analysis of Aquinas's theory of analogy — namely, the extent to which it exposes the underlying worldview or cosmology operative in (and integral to) the Thomist conception of analogy. As Mondin explains, intrinsic attribution requires

> a real similarity between analogates and that this similarity is based on a relation of efficient causality. . . . For instance, we may know that an omelette has been prepared by the Chinese Chiang, but this fact gives us no assurance that the omelette is Chinese. We may have this assurance only if we can appeal to the principle of the likeness between cause and effect. Only if the Scholastic principle *omne agens agit simile sibi* (every agent acts in a way similar to itself) is valid are we justified in believing that there is something Chinese about the food. The possibility of analogy of intrinsic attribution rests, then, on the validity of the principle of likeness between cause and effect.[11]

The primary complaint against Cajetan's interpretation is that this key principle undergirding Aquinas's entire theory of analogy was lost.[12] Mondin's analysis shows that the roots of the Thomistic doctrine of analogy are to be found in a cosmological principle — a principle of universal

---

11. Mondin, *The Principle of Analogy in Protestant and Catholic Theology*, p. 67.

12. "Cajetan and Cajetanists (like Phelan) do not recognise intrinsic attribution. This forces them to turn analogies of natures into analogies of relations. For instance, if wisdom is predicated of God and man, according to the Cajetanists, wisdom is not predicated of both of them because in their natures there is some similarity with respect to wisdom, but because the relations Wisdom-God and wisdom-man are similar. But is this what we intend to say when we attribute wisdom to both God and man?" (Mondin, *The Principle of Analogy in Protestant and Catholic Theology*, p. 69). "Intrinsic attribution explicitly signifies the similarity between the primary and secondary analogate. The secondary analogate is an imperfect imitation of the primary with respect to the property caused by the primary in the secondary analogate. Intrinsic attribution implicitly expresses also that the relation of the analogous property to the secondary analogate is an imperfect imitation of the relation of the same property to the primary analogate" (p. 70).

(as this includes the divine realm) similarity between agents and that which they cause to exist or produce, that is, create.

This interpretation clearly echoes some of the findings of Hampus Lyttkens's earlier and substantial volume *The Analogy between God and the World*, in which he writes, "Our conclusion will accordingly be that, on the grounds of the natural equipment of man bearing some likeness to God and of the likeness of creation to God, St. Thomas holds that man has a natural way to a knowledge of God which, although deficient, is nevertheless true."[13]

On this interpretation of the ontology underlying analogy, two serious and closely related problems arise for the Thomist position — of which Mondin neither offers any discussion nor even seems to be aware. First, if the principle *"omne agens agit simile sibi"* is applied to God and God's relation to the created order, then God is apparently being subsumed under a kind of generic category, namely, the class of "agents" to whom it applies universally that their actions bear some likeness to themselves. The real strength of Aquinas's advocacy of the analogy of intrinsic attribution was precisely his insistence that analogy must be *unius ad alterum* (of one to another) and not *duorum ad tertium* (of two to a third) and that God must not be subsumed under some general category with respect to which he is obliged to portray certain general features. *Deus non est in genere* (God does not belong to a class). The question emerges whether there is not to be found here a thinly veiled form of the analogy "of two to a third" or "of many to one" of precisely the kind that Aquinas rejected. Second, this argument works on the basis of the supposition that there is some kind of empirical necessity here that is so all-pervasive that it includes God. This is not an argument from probability but from necessity. Given that the argument is of the form "All agents are such that . . ." rather than "It would seem probable that all agents may be of such a kind that . . . ," a directly perceived universal necessity is relied on to undergird the very possibility of God-talk.

In sum, the ontological presupposition undergirding the Thomist theory of theological description involves projecting onto God a conception of agency formed in the context of — and deriving from — finite, human experience and doing so in a manner that risks subsuming God under a common category with respect to whose members certain rules apply uni-

---

13. Hampus Lyttkens, *The Analogy between God and the World: An Investigation of Its Background and Interpretation of Its Use by Thomas of Aquino* (Uppsala: Almqvist & Wiksells, 1953), pp. 480-81.

versally. Both of these moves or presuppositions clearly require extensive justification — both theological and philosophical. It is difficult to see how David Hume's criticisms of the cosmological and teleological arguments for the existence of God may be avoided as rendering an insurmountable critique of this kind of move.[14]

This brings us to one of the most important questions in theology. Is there an alternative ontological ground consistent with Aquinas's impressive insights into the imperatives of theological description in which terms function *unius ad alterum* and *per prius et posterius?*

As I pointed out at the beginning of this essay, in the West it is often assumed that Aquinas offered the first thoroughgoing theological exposition of analogy. But the concept of *analogein* is central to Athanasius's theology.[15] In debate with Arianism, Athanasius distinguished between the anthropomorphic projection of our opinions *(epinoiai)* onto the divine — what he termed *muthologein* (mythologizing) — and *theologein* or *analogein*. In *theologein* (God-talk proper), our terms are extended to project *(ana-logein)* beyond their ordinary context of use in such a way that they refer to the reality of God. No longer mere *epinoiai* (arbitrary human opinions or ideas projected mythologically onto the transcendent), these terms become *dianoiai* — concepts that project through *(dia)* to the reality and being of God. The condition of this is *meta-noia*, as Paul interpreted it — that is, the transformation of our thinking and concepts *(noiai)* and thus our terminology. The implication is that there is a semantic shifting of our concepts in parallel with the "reschematization" of our minds (Rom. 12:2) so that they might truly and appropriately refer to the divine. In sum, *theologein* — that is, valid or truthful *(alethos)* reference to God — requires a reconciliation of our *noiai* to the extent that we are, in Paul's

---

14. The point at issue here is expressed with clarity by Karl Barth in volume 3, part 3 of his *Church Dogmatics*. He writes: "If the term *causa* is to be applied legitimately, it must be clearly understood that it is not a master-concept to which both God and the creature are subject, nor is it a common denominator to which they may both be reduced. *Causa* is not a genus, of which the divine and creaturely *causa* can then be described as species. When we speak about the being of God and that of the creature, we are not dealing with two species of the one genus being" (*Church Dogmatics* III/3 [Edinburgh: T. & T. Clark, 1960], p. 102).

15. For the following I am indebted to A. I. C. Heron's "Homoousios with the Father," in *The Incarnation*, ed. T. F. Torrance (Edinburgh: Handsel, 1981), and T. F. Torrance's discussions of Athanasius in *Theology in Reconstruction* (London: S.C.M., 1965) and *Theology in Reconciliation* (London: Geoffrey Chapman, 1965).

words, *echthroi te dianoia,* alienated or hostile in our conceptualities. This reconciling takes place so that we might have that mind which is in Christ Jesus and thereby participate in the new, transformed semantics (or "language games") of the Body of Christ — where our *logoi* participate in the *Logos,* who is God concretely present within the created order.

In this way, an "Athanasian" account safeguards precisely what Aquinas would later affirm through his insistence on the *per prius et posterius* and *unius ad alterum* principles — namely, the transcendence, priority, and initiative of God and the ontological relationship between the divine being and the contingent human order. Our terms refer to God in and through their being grounded in the Logos, just as the incarnate Logos constitutes the community of the church in and through which the "sense" and thus the "reference" of terms[16] is redefined and refined such that, through the reconciling work of the Spirit and the dynamic presence of God with us in Christ, our language is enabled to refer to the eternal and transcendent God. This is what Calvin refers to in his doctrine of the divine *balbutire*[17] and the work of the Spirit in the church. It is also that to which Eberhard Jüngel refers in his concept of the divine commandeering of language in and through revelation.[18]

So what is the ontological principle that underlies Athanasius's theory of analogy? Here we see the difference between the static categories of Western medieval Scholasticism and the dynamic categories of the Greek fathers. For Athanasius, the God-given control on *theologein* is quite simply the *Logos theou.* Where our God-talk is true to, and reoriented by, the one who is *(ephapax)* Immanuel, then our language refers to God in truth *(alethos)* — it is true to the Truth of God come to humanity in all its alienation and confusion. Consequently, the ontological ground of *analogein* and *theologein* is not some universal, ontological likeness *(homoi-ousia!)* between cause and effect — so absolute and universal that it includes God!

---

16. This distinction is borrowed from Frege who interprets the sense *(Sinn)* as the mode of designation of the reference *(Bedeutung).* Cf. "On Sense and Reference," in *Translations from the Philosophical Writings of Gottlob Frege,* ed. P. Geach and M. Black (Oxford: Blackwell, 1952).

17. God "prattles" with us like a mother to a child, accommodating his revelation to our level of understanding.

18. Cf. Eberhard Jüngel, *The Doctrine of the Trinity: God's Being Is in Becoming,* Eng. trans. (of *Gottes Sein ist im Werden,* 2nd edition) by Horton Harris (Edinburgh: Scottish Academic Press, 1976).

— but the oneness of being of the Son and the Spirit with God the Father. The *homoousion* becomes, in other words, the sine qua non of the analogical functioning of our terms, where, by the Creator Spirit, our minds and our conceptualities are reconciled and united with Christ as the One in whom we have the fullness of the Being of God with us. And as our *echthrai noiai* (alienated minds) are transformed and reconciled, by the Spirit, within the communion of the Body of Christ, so we are brought to participate in the Son's unique knowledge of the Father, to have that mind which was in Christ Jesus. "I have revealed you to those whom you gave me out of the world. . . . I gave them the words *(rhemata)* you gave me and they accepted them" (John 17:6, 8).[19]

One of Calvin's greatest contributions was his recovery, over and against the Scholastic rationalism that preceded him, of the Pauline insight into the need for the reconciliation of our alienated minds if there is to be true reference to God.[20] For Calvin, in contrast with Aquinas, the created order points to the Creator not because of any necessary traces of divine agency but because God freely inscribes in it *certae notae Gloriae Dei* (specific marks of the glory of God). These *would* furnish our *notitia Dei* (awareness, or idea, of God) and *would* validly serve the referential function of our conceptualities *si integer Adam stetisset* (if Adam had remained uncorrupted). But since humanity does not remain whole, and since our minds and paradigms are alienated accordingly, the attempt to read nature in the light of the divinely implanted *semen religionis* (the seed of religion) drives us into idolatry and does not direct us to the one God and Father of our Lord Jesus Christ.

The issues and debates outlined above become particularly relevant when we ask what is happening when we affirm, with John, that God is

19. This "acceptance" should be construed in terms of the Johannine metaphors, which suggest that having the eyes to see and the ears to hear requires our being "reborn from above," that is, created anew by the Spirit in our thinking and paradigms — in other words, in our whole orientation.

20. As Alvin Plantinga argues in his book *Warrant and Proper Function* (Oxford: Oxford University Press, 1993), truth claims require an appropriate "cognitive environment" if they are to have warrant (p. 82). What he terms the "design plan" concerns not simply ourselves as individuals but also our social contexts. The implications of ecclesiology that this suggests for theological epistemology and, indeed, analogy are clear. Just as there is no private language, there is no private knowledge of and reference to God. All such knowledge takes place within the reconciled community that is the Body of Christ.

agape (ho theos agape estin) and when we also come to ask whether and how we might affirm simultaneously that to love *(agapân)* does not simply refer to God but may and must also be able to describe human relationships.

So the questions to which we now turn are these:

1. whether we might affirm that *agape* applies properly both to God and to human beings;
2. how we can understand continuity of meaning and reference between the two contexts; and
3. how the ontological basis of any such continuity is to be conceived.

The "Scholastic" Approach — Following Mondin's Reclassification of Aquinas

On the "Scholastic" approach, the ontological similarity between the world, the created order, and the Creator (the agent or cause of its existence) constitutes the ground by which terms that are furnished within the created order may refer to God. Consequently, if the word *agape* can be used meaningfully of God, it must be on the ground of some discernible and intrinsic likeness of the created order, as it is and in its totality, to the *agape* that denotes the being of the Creator. There is, and must be, an analogical, ontological continuity between the being of God and the created order, as a whole, since this is the very ground of theological semantics.

But does not the gospel suggest that that specific love we have and find in Christ, by the Spirit, is, in a fundamental sense, new to the created order, that it is intrinsic to a new humanity, a new creation, and that the presence of this *agape* is integrally related to the concrete, historical presence of God? Does it not denote the free presence of the Spirit of Christ, who turns our natural understanding, desires, and orientations on their heads and creates them anew in a reconciling event? The New Testament witness would seem to suggest that the *agape* we meet in Christ is, as self-giving, almost subversive — a counter-natural form of love that takes place *precisely* at that point when nature would prescribe hate or disgust or abhorrence or fear.[21] It is *agape* for people when our natural, created desires would encourage *eros.* It is an *agape* for our enemy at the cost of family and

---

21. Perfect love drives out all (natural) fear.

friends — in the face of our natural *storge* and *philia*. Moreover, far from being a static, "encaused" state that is necessarily replicated in nature by its First Cause, it denotes the gift of self-giving realized in us by our being brought into communion with the Self-giving of God in Christ.

This would suggest that, theologically interpreted, *agape* is very much more than a mere improving, heightening, perfecting, or repairing of that which is causally conditioned in the created order by virtue of its createdness. In sum, the creation of the new humanity constitutes a rupture of the natural order whereby new wine is poured into a new vessel.

Here we can see the impropriety of making the principle *"omne agens agit simile sibi"* the ground of theological reference. A form of foundationalism displaces, and thus denies, the place of Christ as our "sole foundation." It pours into old wineskins what is appropriate only to the newness of Christ.

The theological ontology that we are suggesting here reposes not on a foundational principle *("omne agens . . .")*, as this includes and subsumes God, but rather on an acknowledgment of the form *Hic agens agit simile sibi* (This agent acts in a manner similar to himself) as this refers to God's being and agency in Christ. When this acknowledgment remains the control of our understanding, *Hic agens . . .* becomes the affirmation of the glory and integrity of God and the divine *agape* in the face of Christ — *Hic agens,* the One through whom, and for whom, all things were created.

The Idealist or Platonist Approach

Idealist approaches tend to sidestep the analogy debate by interpreting all ethical concepts as denoting an eternal form or idea that is divine and real. I shall argue that they cannot accommodate the concept of *agape* for the same reason.

For the idealist, to the extent that we are real we participate (naturally) in the forms and thus exemplify them — albeit in varying degrees. The relevant predication is treated as univocal, albeit with a degree of proportionality. Abraham, Jesus, Paul, Gandhi, Mother Teresa — and, indeed, all of us, to the extent that we participate in the good — exemplify ultimate reality. And, as Plato established in the *Meno,* this is necessarily able to be discovered and analyzed by enlightened reason. For the Platonist, *gnothi seauton* — rational, analytical self-knowledge — must offer access to *agape* to the extent that *agape* is right, true, divine, and our duty. On this count, Jesus might be a particularly impressive exemplification of *agape*, but, as Kierkegaard has shown so effectively in his *Philosophical Fragments,* he does not and cannot, on this view, teach us anything new — he can have no "decisive significance." Like a good Platonic midwife he can at most be an incidental means of the "discovery" of that which is immanent within us. The truth is that which we always knew (albeit dimly perhaps), to which we never ceased to have access, and which is known by ceasing to "escape our notice."[22]

The essential appeal of the Platonic approach lies in the fact that it explains how we can recognize *agape* to be good. It appears to solve the Meno paradox at the ethical level. How do we recognize actions described in terms of *agape* to be good and right? We do so in precisely the same way that we recognize Jesus to be good and his teaching to be morally commendable — because the knowledge of ethical propriety and goodness is already innate and thus immanent within us. Jesus advocates, preaches, and exemplifies the ethics of *agape* but in no sense introduces us to anything new, since, if he were to do so, we simply would not have the capacity to recognize that to which we were introduced. He has not, therefore, given us the eyes to see anything we could not see already if we were to look hard enough. At best, he facilitates a sharpening up of our perceptions and thus functions as a kind of ethical therapist or "in depth" psychotherapist — facilitating the discovery of what lies deep within our souls.

As Kierkegaard showed, the implications of this view are unambiguously clear. If Jesus (or, indeed, Gandhi) is to be deemed an effective teacher, in this sense, helping simply to give birth to what is already within us *(maieuesthai),* then he must fade from view as we are brought to "remember" or "recover" the relevant clarity of insight. His significance is transitory and must never be more than that. It is the learner's relation to the ideals that is of ultimate importance and not the teacher. Indeed, any focusing on the teacher per se can only serve to distract from, and hence to undermine, our relation to the ethical truths that are our real concern and our real focus. It is the truths (the ideas and ideals) that are divine and emphatically not the "occasion" or the means of their recall.

A related appeal of this approach is that the universal immanence

22. Martin Heidegger points out that the Greek word for truth *(a-letheia)* originally meant the "un-concealed" or "dis-covered," lit. "that which does not escape us." (Cf. *Being and Time,* trans. John Macquarrie and Edward Robinson [London: S.C.M., 1962], 57n.1.)

within us of the capacity to appreciate *agape* constitutes a point of connection *(Anknüpfungspunkt)* between the gospel and the world. Consequently, we can confidently preach the idealist gospel of love to the world, knowing that the world must immediately recognize it to be right, proper, and good and the essence of what reality, as a whole, is all about.

The combination of these apologetic and epistemic concerns has brought about a situation whereby an incipient idealism has become the unacknowledged system underlying the contemporary advocacy of love by "liberal" theologians and church leaders operating with immanentist, "spiritual" suppositions. The concept of an innate *imago Dei* (assumed to justify a spiritual *"gnothi seauton"* or analytical self-knowledge) is too easily utilized in support of this. This points to a further element in the appeal of this approach. It seems to cater to human "spiritual" needs or desires — in particular, the desire for self-transcendence.

William George de Burgh's classic work *Towards a Religious Philosophy* constitutes an impressive example of precisely the kind of approach I am criticizing. De Burgh discusses how true statements can be made by finite human beings about the God who is infinitely transcendent. The only possibility is if we can find some "concept, generated in direct religious experience, which is applicable both to God and to man univocally, and not analogically . . . with identity of meaning." The answer, he suggests, is to be found in the concept of love, where "God's love for man and man's love for God differ not in kind but in degree."[23] Here we can have an identity of meaning and relation. But this, he continues, "holds not between God's love for man and that of man for other finites, but only between God's love for man and man's love for God and Him alone." In this experience "man is literally more than finite." What becomes clear is that what is being advocated is not *agape* but the classical form of heavenly *eros* — the desire of God for his human counterpart and an identical, univocal (and individualistic) desire on the part of the human subject for God.

That this kind of approach appeals beyond the bounds of Christian theology is reflected in a book written by Allan Bloom shortly before his death in 1993 entitled *Love and Friendship*.[24] In it, the author of that devas-

---

23. William George de Burgh, *Towards a Religious Philosophy* (London: Madonald & Evans, 1937), pp. 125-26.

24. Allan Bloom, *Love and Friendship* (New York: Simon and Schuster, 1993). (See especially the introduction, "The Fall of Eros," and Part 3, "The Ladder of Love," pp. 429ff.).

tating critique of the egoism, hedonism, and narcissism of contemporary North American culture, *The Closing of the American Mind*,[25] proffers an analysis of classical literature — Shakespeare, Jane Austen, and others — in an attempt to establish that what is required in the modern world is the recovery of an emphasis on that highest human emotion or desire, namely, love. But, again, the love of which he speaks is not *agape* but *eros*, and Bloom calls us back to Plato's *Symposium*, the desire for goodness, truth, beauty, and morality — that is, to the "divine" ideals.

It is imperative for the Christian theologian to recognize, before making common cause with this kind of response to the ethical confusion and agnosticism of our age, the inherent incompatibility of idealism with that irreducibly historical (not timeless) and relational (not "possessional") personal commitment (not desire) that is denoted by the concept of *agape*. Ethical obligation here concerns "persons" and not "divine ideals" as the immediate objects of value.

In sum, *agape* is not a response to intrinsic values or ideals; it is not something whose value we can argue for or establish by introspection, since it is not a natural desire with its own object. It is not a form of natural attraction of any higher kind — the love of like for like. Nor is it a natural sentiment, a form of sympathy to be conceived in Humean terms. It simply does not denote any natural facet inherent within — that is, replicated within or naturally infused within human nature. The love revealed in Jesus Christ is not a love *for the sake of* any "thing." In radical contradistinction to the thrust of idealism, it is a love that creates value by giving value to what it loves. It does not desire to receive, or to fulfill itself; it simply gives — and its human object may be worthless and degraded. Far from being an object of Socratic understanding, it is the love which "passes all understanding," which does not belong to our natural understanding or worldview, and which remains foolishness to the Greek mind.

But in addition, as the one who loves in this sense does not love for the sake of any "thing," so on the other hand what God wishes to impart is not any "thing" but his own Self. In the incarnation, the cross, and the resurrection, the One who is Immanuel gives *himself*. The focal event of a theology of *agape* is thus the Self-giving of the crucified God. As A. E. Taylor, Jürgen Moltmann, Donald Mackinnon, and many others have empha-

---

25. Allan Bloom, *The Closing of the American Mind* (New York: Simon and Schuster, 1987).

sized, the sacrifice of Christ on the cross is of a radically different kind from the death of Socrates as we have it in the *Phaedo*. And to reduce it to the expression or exemplification of any universal form or ideal, far from simply exhibiting a failure to understand the divine *agape*, is to advocate a *metabasis eis allo genos* of the gospel — its transformation into something of a radically different and foreign kind.

To the extent that the life of Christ denotes the irreducibly historical Self-giving of God in the deliverance of a lost humanity, it constitutes the essential ground of our affirming *agape* of God. This means that to affirm that God is *agape* is to affirm that God *is* what God is toward us in Christ; to affirm the divine *agape* without the incarnation is meaningless.[26]

It should be clear also, therefore, that *agape* does not refer to some supererogatory ethical "extra" attributed either to the humanity of Christ or to the divinity of God. It constitutes an ontological category in the same way that, as John Zizioulas argues, *koinonia* does.[27] The argument of John is that it denotes the being, the *ousia*, the *essentia* of God — the being, that is, of the God whose *ousia* is to be ontologically identified with its *ekstasis* in Christ, "God with us."

II. AFFIRMING *AGAPE* OF THE HUMAN[28]

The arguments I have offered above reflect the contrast drawn by Anders Nygren (as also by Emil Brunner[29] and, more famously, by C. S. Lewis in

---

26. The one who utters "I will be who I will be" identifies himself as *agape* in the crucified Christ — where God's historically enacted *hesed* (steadfast love) toward Israel finds its fulfillment in the once-and-for-all event of the new covenant for all people.

27. Cf. John Zizioulas, *Being as Communion: Studies in Personhood and the Church* (New York: St. Vladimir's Press, 1985), and also his earlier essay, "On Human Capacity and Incapacity: A Theological Exploration of Personhood," *Scottish Journal of Theology* 28 (1975): 401-48.

28. I am especially indebted here (as elsewhere) to my father, Professor James B. Torrance, and to an unpublished essay he wrote entitled "Love and Justice in God and Man."

29. Cf. Emil Brunner, *The Divine Imperative*, trans. Olive Wyon (London: Lutterworth, 1937), pp. 343ff.; *The Christian Doctrine of God*, vol. 1, trans. Olive Wyon (London: Lutterworth, 1949), pp. 185ff.; *Justice and the Social Order*, trans. Mary Hottinger (London: Lutterworth, 1945), p. 115; *Man in Revolt*, trans. Olive Wyon (London: Lutterworth, 1939), pp. 219, 283. Cf. also John McIntyre's discussion of Nygren's distinction in *On the Love of God* (London: Collins, 1962), pp. 28ff.; and Reinhold Niebuhr, *An Interpretation of Christian Ethics* (London: S.C.M., 1936), p. 221.

The Four Loves[30]) between *agape* and *eros;* we shall now turn to Nygren's arguments and consider them in further detail.[31]

Eros is love for something because it is worthy of love. Its aim is the fulfillment of function in the acquisition of value. It is love "motivated" by the value of its object.

But the love of which the New Testament speaks, *agape,* is that new kind of love revealed in Jesus Christ which gives value to what it loves, even where its object may be degraded and worthless. Articulating the very grammar of the gospel as the Self-giving of God in Christ and in the Spirit for sinners, it refers to that "new way of fellowship with God," which constitutes, in Nietzsche's phrase, "the reversal of the values of antiquity."

Four points are made:[32]

1. *Agape* is spontaneous and "uncaused." God's love for humanity is not grounded in human worthiness or value.
2. Therefore, *agape* is indifferent to human merit. Jesus came to save sinners. He does not love their sin; he loves them in spite of their sin. Moreover, in loving the righteous he does not love them because of their righteousness.
3. *Agape* is creative. That which is in itself without value acquires value by the fact that it is the object of God's love. The value of the one whom God loves consists solely, therefore, in the fact that he or she is loved by God. Interpreting the fact of the divine *agape* in this way, we cannot affirm with Ritschl, therefore, the infinite value of the human soul as if this provides a reason for God's love. As creative and uncaused, the love of God is always in the nature of a gift.[33]

30. C. S. Lewis, *The Four Loves* (London: Geoffrey Bles, 1960).

31. Anders Nygren, *Agape and Eros,* 2 vols., trans. A. G. Herbert et al. (London: S.P.C.K., 1932).

32. Nygren, *Agape and Eros,* vol. 1, pp. 52ff.

33. An important implication of this point is that it is no longer necessary (or appropriate) for us to say that God loves the sinner but hates the sin. This all too common assertion is motivated by an attempt to affirm God's love while repudiating that God loves — with the assumed implication that he thus *endorses* — that which is sinful. The problem with this statement is that it falsely separates our sin and our alienation from our *being*. Our sins become extrinsic to our being. But this reflects a failure to appreciate the nature of sin. Sin is not ontologically insignificant or incidental. It denotes what we *are*, that is, our "being-in-act" and our whole orientation — our "minds." We are not essentially God's lovable friends and hostile only in our extrinsic acts. We are loved as enemies and *as sinners* — while we are yet sinners.

4. *Agape* opens the way for fellowship with God. There is no way from humanity to God; we cannot attain to God by ourselves. God alone can and does create and open up a way for humanity.

But there is a weakness in this account to the extent that it suggests that *agape* is thus found only in God, that it is essentially divine and not human, thereby reducing human loving to a form of *eros*, the acknowledgment and response to that which has intrinsic worth and value. Without disagreeing that there is a proper and, indeed, important place for *eros* conceived as the human pursuit of ethical and aesthetic values and ideals, the New Testament witness requires us to say more.

This is not to say, with de Burgh, that there is a simple univocity between divine and human love. The concept of *agape* may not be used univocally of both God and humanity. However, we would argue that it is not only the case that *agape* may be affirmed but also that it must be affirmed of the truly human properly and intrinsically — albeit analogically. This means, in Aquinas's language, that it is affirmed of God and humanity *unius ad alterum, per prius et posterius.* But what then constitutes the ontological ground of this claim — what is its warrant? It is certainly not any form of *gnothi seauton* (or navel-gazing under the supposed auspices of the *imago Dei*); it is rather the *homoousion* of the Son and the Son's presence with humanity in Christ, not merely as God but as man, as truly human. The witness of the New Testament makes it utterly inappropriate to affirm that the divine in Christ is the subject of *agape* but the human Jesus is capable only of a sublime form of *eros.*

In Christ we find *agape* requiring to be affirmed not simply of God but also of the one who is truly human, namely, the Second Adam. And it is from this ground and on this basis that, by the Spirit, *agape* may be conceived as constituting the being of women and men as they participate in the new humanity, in the Body of Christ.

In Christ, Creator and creature, nature and grace are one. And when we take the humanity of Jesus seriously, as also the New Testament witness, we do not find here simply a *channel* of the love of God, conceived in Apollinarian or docetic terms, but a loving that is truly *human.* The love Jesus bore for outcasts and sinners was not only the love of God incarnated in his person but also his own love as a human being. The uncaused, spontaneous *agape* he bore for sinners was a love he manifested not merely because he was God but also because he was truly human — freely and sinlessly man, the perfect embodiment of all God meant and means humanity to be. It is precisely here, therefore, in the true Adam that we see human nature for the very first time as God intends it to be — to have its being in participating in his *koinonia* and his *agape*.[34]

The weakness of the Lutheran approach toward divine and human love, as we find it in Nygren, parallels precisely the weakness that Calvin found in Osiander, who stressed the divine righteousness in Christ at the cost of Christ's human righteousness. Indeed, Calvin's arguments bring into focus a number of the issues that we have been addressing.

In Book 3 of the *Institutes of the Christian Religion*, we find Calvin referring to a "kind of monstrosity" that is Osiander's "essential righteousness" (*Institutes* 3.11.5). This, Calvin suggests, undermines the "free righteousness" of Christ, thereby clouding in darkness the grace of God, which is to be interpreted in terms of the humanity of Christ. The notion of an essential, divine righteousness effectively vitiates "that righteousness, which was procured for us by the obedience and sacrificial death of Christ" by maintaining instead that we are "substantially righteous in God by an infused essence as well as quality."

For Calvin, Osiander's problem constituted a form of Manichaean dualism, in that he failed to take seriously that in Christ we have not simply *divine* righteousness but a truly *human* righteousness. This confusion arose from a failure to perceive the "mode" of the dwelling of God in humanity, that is, that "the Father and the Spirit are *in Christ*; and as in him the fullness of the Godhead dwells, so in him we possess God entire" (3.11.5, my italics). The problem with this kind of approach is that it threatens to "lead us away from the priesthood of Christ, and his office of Mediator, to his eternal divinity" (3.11.7). He was made our righteousness not simply in respect of his *divine* nature but also in respect of his *human* nature. And just "as Christ cannot be divided into parts, so the two things,

---

34. It is important to note here that the Father's *agape* for the true Adam does not, as *agape*, bestow value on the valueless any more than the eternal *agape* within the Trinity creatively bestows value on its divine objects that they would otherwise not have. Nevertheless, it is appropriate and, indeed, necessary to speak of *agape* in both contexts and to see the intra-Trinitarian *agape* as constituting the grounds of the creative overflowing of that same *agape* — resulting in a creative valuing, claiming for relationship, elevating into relationship, and sustaining in relationship of that which does not, in and of itself, warrant any such bestowal of value or, indeed, participation in the Triune life.

justification and sanctification, which we perceived to be united together in him, are inseparable" (3.11.6).

Calvin concludes: "If it is asked, in what way are we justified? Paul answers, by the obedience of Christ. Did he obey in any other way than by assuming the form of a servant? We infer, therefore, that righteousness was manifested to us in his flesh" (3.11.9).

The parallelism speaks for itself. Just as there can be no dichotomy between divine righteousness and human righteousness, between justification and sanctification, similarly there can be no dichotomy between the divine and human *agape* in Christ. Similarly, God's grace cannot be reduced to the infusion of any ideal or essential righteousness or morality into humanity. As the righteousness of God is inseparable from the righteousness of the human Jesus, so the *agape* of God is inseparable from the human *agape* of Christ. In him, therefore, *agape* can be affirmed to be intrinsic to what God is in truth, as also to what the true Adam is in truth. In this way Jesus Christ becomes the very means of our being brought to understand the *agape* that constitutes the being of the transcendent God.[35]

The possibility, therefore, of speaking of the love of God within the human context and of recognizing a real continuity between the two is not grounded (a) in any essential likeness between Agent and effect, or (b) in any idealistically conceived essential love that is necessarily universal, or (c) in an "immanentist" infusion of the divine love into the human. None of these constitutes an appropriate ontological framework for interpreting the dynamics at the heart of the Christian faith. They no more hold forth a free *agape* than Osiander's infused righteousness held forth the "free (human) righteousness" that Calvin saw to be integral to the grace of God.

Rather, the ground of our speaking of the love of God, as it constitutes human *agape* in the new creation, remains the incarnation alone — the fact that in Christ we have God come *as God* in pure *agape*, and God come *as human* to live a human life of *agape*.

Just as Athanasius affirmed the *homoousion* as constituting the fullest and final ground of, and control upon, our theological semantics, so we see the particular significance of this when we seek to understand the con-

35. This is not to deny, however, that our understanding of God's love remains, in Calvin's words, *quodammodo praesens* (in a certain manner present) and *quodammodo absens* (in a certain manner absent). As Paul argues (1 Cor. 13) our understanding of the love of God is through a mirror darkly; there remains an eschatological and thus analogical tension in our understanding.

tinuity between that divine *agape* which denotes the form of God's being toward us, as this "takes place" in an "event" (lit. *e-venire*) of *agape,* and the event itself, namely, the truly human *agape* of God as the human Jesus. Here the dynamic that controls, structures, and warrants God-talk is seen to be one and the same with the specific dynamic that we affirm when we affirm the love of God. To utilize the distinction made by Gottlob Frege, the human "sense" is, and can be, the mode of the designation of the divine "reference" precisely because the Reference actively designates (or, to use Jüngel's term, "commandeers"[36]) the human "sense." That is, we are enabled to refer to the divine *agape* to the extent that our conceptualities are not conformed to this world but "reschematized" (Rom. 12:2) by the one who took the "form" of a servant in *agape.* Here it is supremely the case that, as Luther argued, "*omnia vocabula in Christo novam signifi-cationem accipere in eadem re significata* [in Christ all our terminology receives new meaning in and through the reality signified]."[37]

It must be emphasized that the provision of "ears to hear" new dimensions of meaning is not a private event, and the language game with which this understanding is bound up is not a private language. The semantics of *analogein* and *theologein* are integral to the reconciled life of the Body of Christ, and our being true in *agape (aletheuontes en agape)* within it. This *koinonia* or fellowship stems from the creative *agape* of God, which creatively bestows on the language of the Body of Christ fuller dimensions of meaning than could otherwise be contemplated. Our participation in the Body of Christ is *koinonia* (and *not* the Platonic *methexis* [participation]), and it takes place by the Spirit in Christ — the sole priest and mediator of our confession of the love of God. To the extent that we are given by grace that mind which was in Christ Jesus (the author and inaugurator of the new humanity, which constitutes a new creation) we are brought to glimpse forms of life, love, and communion that will ultimately be realized only in the *eschaton.*

We started out this essay by looking at the question of language and whether it is possible for human creatures meaningfully to affirm love of God. Our question concerned whether we might say that *agape* is the essence (or *ousia*) of God. We end by seeing the folly of the order of this essay's argument! It is when we comprehend the length and breadth and

---

36. Jüngel, *The Doctrine of the Trinity,* p. 12.
37. Martin Luther, *Luther's Works,* Weimar Edition, 39/2, 94, 17-18.

depth of the divine *agape*, as we find it in the Being-of-God-as-Christ, that we perceive what Eberhard Jüngel refers to as God's "coming to speech." In an event that confirms the utter folly of God-talk from any other ground, we find that in an *agape* that is the faithful, unconditional, and historical giving of himself for humanity in its inability to speak and love, in its *echthros* (alienated) orientation and conceptuality, we are given the speech, the *rhemata*, that we would not otherwise have. God's *agape* thus bestows value on our *echthrai noiai*, our alienated concepts and language games, which of themselves have no intrinsic capacity to function theologically. In this manner, by way of an otherwise unanticipatable and inconceivable event, God elects humanity to participate (semantically and noetically) in the *koinonia* constitutive of his Triune being.

In conclusion, therefore, what is our response to the question with which we began: is love the essence of God? The fact that love is of the very being *ousia (essentia)* of God constitutes the ground of the possibility of our referring to God at all. Without the Self-giving of God that is divine *agape* for a lost and confused humanity there can ultimately be no *analogein* or *theologein*. There can be no genuine semantic participation in or access to the divine *ousia*. To affirm that the Logos was made flesh is to affirm that the being of God is *agape*. To affirm this is to affirm, by the Spirit alone, the possibility, also by the Spirit alone, of *analogein* and of *theologein*.

The sentence with which Jesus concludes his high priestly prayer, as it is recounted in John's Gospel, sums up the relationship between analogy and knowledge of God and the connection between divine and human *agape*: "I have made you known to them, and will continue to make you known in order that the *agape* with which you love me may be in them and that I myself may be in them" (John 17:26).

CHAPTER 7

The Wrath of God as an Aspect of the Love of God

TONY LANE

I. THE NEGLECT OF THE WRATH OF GOD

Two experiences have influenced my thinking in this area. When I was about ten I was taught by a retired man who went by the title of professor. A decade or so later, while studying for my theology degree, I met him again. It transpired that he had studied theology in the heyday of liberalism, prior to the Barthian revolution, and had taught it at a university in Asia. At the stage when we met, in his closing years, he was questioning some of his beliefs. "Where is the God of love in the Old Testament?" he asked. A few minutes later he asked again, "How can you believe in a God of love with so much suffering in the world?" What he did not seem to notice was that the Old Testament and empirical reality cohered; it was his sentimental liberal concept of the love of God that was out of step. Or, as Goethe put it, the whole course of history shows that the God of providence and the severe Jehovah of the Hebrews are

---

The thinking behind this paper was originally stimulated by a reading of John Stott's *The Cross of Christ* (Leicester: Inter-Varsity Press, 1986). It is offered to him out of appreciation for the benefit that I have received from reading that and others of his works.

one and the same.[1] The dilemma faced by the professor is typical of that faced by so many in the West today. The sentimental view of the love of God proclaimed almost without respite by the Western churches may appear very attractive, but it is not in the last resort credible.

The second experience was more recent. At a church service the reading was from Romans chapter 12. "Love must be sincere," began verse 9. The next word came as a shock. "Hate." "Hate what is evil." For most Western Christians hate is the last word that would be associated with love. But a love that does not contain hatred of evil is not the love of which the Bible speaks. It is most fitting therefore that a volume on God's love should include an essay on the wrath of God. This is necessary, not because we need to balance God's wrath with his love, as rival attributes, but *because God's love itself implies his wrath. Without his wrath God is simply not loving in the sense that the Bible portrays his love.*

The modern silence regarding God's wrath is well described by R. P. C. Hanson:

> Most preachers and most composers of prayers today treat the biblical doctrine of the wrath of God very much as the Victorians treated sex. It is there, but it must never be alluded to because it is in an undefined way shameful. . . . God is love; therefore we must not associate him with wrath. God is love; therefore he is indefinitely tolerant. Presumably it is for such reasons that the Christian churches of the twentieth century have in practice turned their backs upon the biblical doctrine of the wrath of God.[2]

But it was not always thus. The most infamous sermon on the topic is probably Jonathan Edwards's "Sinners in the Hands of an Angry God," preached to great effect at Enfield in New England in 1741. In this sermon Edwards is unrestrained in the language that he uses to describe God's wrath:[3]

> The bow of God's wrath is bent, and the arrow made ready on the string, and justice bends the arrow at your heart, and strains the bow,

1. I have yet to trace this passage, but a similar thought appears in Goethe's *Maximen und Reflexionen* no. 1304: "Die Natur ist immer Jehovah. Was sie ist, was sie war, und was sie sein wird" (M. Hecker [ed.] [Weimar: Goethe-Gesellschaft, 1907], p. 273).

2. R. P. C. Hanson, *God: Creator, Saviour, Spirit* (London: S.C.M., 1960), p. 37.

3. Sermon 7 in *The Select Works of Jonathan Edwards*, vol. 2 (London: Banner of Truth, 1959), pp. 183-99, with the punctuation modernized in places.

and it is nothing but the mere pleasure of God, and that of an angry God, without any promise or obligation at all, that keeps the arrow one moment from being made drunk with your blood. . . . The God that holds you over the pit of hell, much as one holds a spider or some loathsome insect over the fire, abhors you and is dreadfully provoked. His wrath towards you burns like a fire; he looks upon you as worthy of nothing else, but to be cast into the fire; he is of purer eyes than to bear to have you in his sight; you are ten thousand times more abominable in his eyes, than the most hateful venomous serpent is in ours. You have offended him infinitely more than ever a stubborn rebel did his prince. And yet it is nothing but his hand that holds you from falling into the fire every moment.

O sinner! consider the fearful danger you are in. It is a great furnace of wrath, a wide and bottomless pit full of the fire of wrath, that you are held over in the hand of that God, whose wrath is provoked and incensed as much against you, as against many of the damned in hell. You hang by a slender thread, with the flames of divine wrath flashing about it, and ready every moment to singe it and burn it asunder. . . . Consider this, you that are here present, that yet remain in an unregenerate state. That God will execute the fierceness of his anger implies that he will inflict wrath without any pity. When God beholds the ineffable extremity of your case, and sees your torment to be so vastly disproportioned to your strength, and sees how your poor soul is crushed and sinks down, as it were, into an infinite gloom; he will have no compassion upon you, he will not forbear the executions of his wrath, or in the least lighten his hand; there shall be no moderation or mercy, nor will God then at all stay his rough wind; he will have no regard to your welfare, nor be at all careful lest you should suffer too much in any other sense, than only that you shall *not suffer beyond what strict justice requires.* Nothing shall be withheld because it is so hard for you to bear. Ezek. viii.18. "Therefore will I also deal in fury; mine eye shall not spare, neither will I have pity; and though they cry in mine ears with a loud voice, yet will I not hear them."

God will have no other use to put you to, but to suffer misery; you shall be continued in being to no other end; for you will be a vessel of wrath fitted to destruction; and there will be no other use of this vessel, but to be filled full of wrath. . . . [God] will not only hate you, but he will have you in the utmost contempt; no place shall be thought fit for you, but under his feet to be trodden down as the mire of the streets. . . . And seeing this is his design and what he has determined, even to show how terrible the unrestrained wrath, the fury and fierceness of Jehovah is, he will do it to effect. There will be something accomplished and brought to pass that will be dreadful with a witness. When the great and angry God hath risen up and executed his awful vengeance on the poor sinner, and the wretch is actually suffering the infinite weight and power of his indignation, then will God call upon the whole universe to behold that awful majesty and mighty power that is to be seen in it.

Is this how the wrath of God should be preached? Leaving aside the fact that such a sermon would not be appropriate in our current context, is the picture of God presented true to the Bible? Is the manner of presenting the wrath of God in keeping with the emphasis of the New Testament? This question will be answered in due course.

Today one would have to travel far to hear a sermon remotely like Edwards's. The problem with today's theology and preaching is not that the wrath of God is exaggerated but rather that it is muted or even suppressed. There are four different ways in which this happens. These will be considered in turn, with the greatest emphasis on the third.

The first way is simple denial of the wrath of God. Given the wealth of material in the Bible about God's wrath, this approach is relatively rare, but not unknown, in Christian theology.[4] But while explicit denial may be rare, implicit denial by virtue of simply ignoring the topic is very common.[5] Also, open denial is more likely to be found at a popular level. At the church to which I belong there was recently a preparation meeting for a children's holiday club. The biblical material chosen for the week, wisely or otherwise, was the early chapters of the Book of Joshua. At one point it was suggested that the treatment of this material should include some element of the idea of judgment. This suggestion was vigorously rejected by a minority, for whom true Christianity did not include any such negative ideas. Such a reaction at the popular level would be far from uncommon today. As often happens, the unsophisticated layperson expresses bluntly what

4. G. H. C. MacGregor, "The Concept of the Wrath of God in the New Testament," *New Testament Studies* 7 (1960-61): 101-2.

5. H. G. L. Peels, *The Vengeance of God* (Leiden: Brill, 1995), pp. 271-74, notes the way in which Old Testament theologies have all but ignored the related theme of God's vengeance.

some more sophisticated theologians really think but are not prepared to state openly.

Interestingly, the idea that wrath is unworthy of God is nothing new. Lactantius in 313 or 314 wrote one of the very few Christian books devoted to this theme, his *De ira dei*. He begins by recording the opposition of Greek philosophers (Stoics and Epicureans) to the idea:

> Many persons hold this opinion, which some philosophers also have maintained, that God is not subject to anger; since the divine nature is either altogether beneficent, and that it is inconsistent with His surpassing and excellent power to do injury to any one; or, at any rate, He takes no notice of us at all, so that no advantage comes to us from His goodness, and no evil from His ill-will.[6]

The second way, more sophisticated than philosophical denial, is the theological approach of Marcion, the Christian thinker who took the principle of Christological concentration with full seriousness, *really* believing that God is revealed only in Jesus Christ. Marcion differentiated between the wrathful God of justice revealed in the Old Testament and the merciful God of love revealed in those parts of the New Testament that remained after he had, as Tertullian put it, exercised textual criticism with the knife rather than the pen.[7] Tertullian describes the Marcionite gospel in words that might well apply to much contemporary preaching: "a better god has been discovered, one who is neither offended nor angry nor inflicts punishment, who has no fire warming up in hell, and no outer darkness wherein there is shuddering and gnashing of teeth: he is merely kind. Of course he forbids you to sin — but only in writing."[8] Tertullian is biting in his critique. Marcion views God as a being of simple goodness, to the exclusion of other attributes (like his wrath), which are transferred to the Creator God. Marcion has removed from God "all functions involving severity or criticism." But when Marcion's God delivers humanity, he rescues us from a rival God, the Creator God of the Old Testament. This rivalry must, says Tertullian, in-

6. Lactantius, *A Treatise on the Anger of God* 1, in *The Ante-Nicene Fathers* (reprint; Grand Rapids: Eerdmans, 1969-73), vol. 7, p. 259.

7. Tertullian, *The Prescription against Heretics* 38.

8. Tertullian, *Against Marcion* 1.27, in *Tertullian Adversus Marcionem*, ed. E. Evans, vol. 1 (Oxford: Clarendon, 1972), p. 77.

volve ancillary passions, such as anger, hatred, and displeasure. Further-more, Marcion's God issues commands. But "to what purpose does he lay down commands if he will not require performance, or prohibit transgressions if he is not to exact penalties, if he is incapable of judge-ment, a stranger to all emotions of severity and reproof?" Commands without a penalty are ineffective, for "in real life an act forbidden with-out sanctions is tacitly permitted." Again, Marcion's God is not really of-fended by sin. For "if he does take offence, he ought to be displeased; and if displeased, he ought to punish. For punishment is the outcome of dis-pleasure, as displeasure is the due reward of offence, and offence . . . is at-tendant upon wishes set at naught. But as he does not punish, it is plain that he is not offended." Again, a God, says Tertullian, "can only be com-pletely good if he is the enemy of the bad, so as to put his love of good into action by hatred of the bad, and discharge his wardship of the good by the overthrowing of the bad."[9]

While crypto-Marcionism is a powerful influence at the popular level, modern biblical studies are too responsible to subscribe to such a crude approach. Few would dissent from the judgment of MacGregor that "it is clear that Scripture definitely regards 'wrath' as an attribute of God; we must reject the Marcionite view that the contrast between the God of the O.T. and the God of the N.T. is that between a wrathful, avenging deity and a loving Father who is incapable of anger."[10]

There is a third and more subtle way in which the wrath of God is un-dermined. C. H. Dodd, in a brief but highly influential section of his Moffatt Romans commentary, offers a reinterpretation of the concept.[11] Talk of God's anger is too anthropomorphic. "Paul never uses the verb, 'to be angry,' with God as subject." While the original meaning of "the wrath

---

9. Tertullian, *Against Marcion* 1:25-26, on pp. 69-75. ("Displeasure" in this passage translates the Latin word *ira*, which is more appropriately translated "wrath" or "anger.") R. P. C. Hanson makes a similar point, describing the popular concept of God as an impo-tent God who is "too gentlemanly to involve anybody in wrath, and too tolerant to punish anybody" and who therefore "seems to be no more effective than the United Nations" (*God*, p. 39).

10. MacGregor, "The Concept of the Wrath of God," p. 103. R. V. G. Tasker, *The Biblical Doctrine of the Wrath of God* (London: Tyndale Press, 1951), p. 26; G. Stählin, "ὀργή," in *Theological Dictionary of the New Testament* (hereafter *TDNT*), vol. 5 (Grand Rapids: Eerd-mans, 1967), p. 422, makes the same point.

11. C. H. Dodd, *The Epistle of Paul to the Romans,* 2nd ed. (London and Glasgow: Col-lins, 1959), pp. 47-50.

of God" was the passion of anger, by the time of Paul it had come to refer to an impersonal process of cause and effect, the inevitable result of sin. Thus, "anger as an attitude of God to men disappears, and His love and mercy become all-embracing. This is, as I believe, the purport of the teaching of Jesus, with its emphasis on limitless forgiveness." Essentially Paul agrees, but he retains the concept of the wrath of God, "which does not appear in the teaching of Jesus, unless we press certain features of the parables in an illegitimate manner." In Paul the wrath of God describes not "the attitude of God to man" but "an inevitable process of cause and effect in a moral universe." "In the long run we cannot think with full consistency of God in terms of the highest human ideals of personality and yet attribute to Him the irrational passion of anger."

Dodd's approach has stimulated considerable debate, and it would be hard to find a recent serious English-language discussion of the wrath of God that does not refer to him. A. T. Hanson, in his substantial monograph on the subject, *The Wrath of the Lamb*,[12] follows broadly in Dodd's footsteps. Dodd and those who follow him are united in affirming that the wrath of God is to be understood purely as *effectus*, as the effects or consequences of sin, rather than *affectus*, as a prior emotion or feeling on God's part.[13] God is not to be thought of as angry and loving, either at the same time[14] or alternately.[15] We should not speak of "God's displeasure," because displeasure suggests a personal feeling in God.[16] "The wrath of God is wholly impersonal and does not describe an attitude of God but a condition of men."[17] But there is some ambiguity in these writers about the extent of God's involvement in this *effectus*. At times the impression is given, as in Dodd's brief account, that this is purely an inevitable byproduct of sin, not in any way willed by God. R. P. C. Hanson, by contrast, is willing to talk robustly of God punishing, while denying that God's wrath is an *affectus*.[18]

How should this approach be assessed? D. E. H. Whiteley wryly ob-

---

12. A. T. Hanson, *The Wrath of the Lamb* (London: SPCK, 1957).

13. A. T. Hanson, *The Wrath of the Lamb*, pp. 69, 110, 126, 186, 197, and *passim;* R. P. C. Hanson, *God*, pp. 45-46.

14. A. T. Hanson, *The Wrath of the Lamb*, p. 197; R. P. C. Hanson, *God*, p. 47.

15. J. S. Stewart, *A Man in Christ*, 2nd ed. (London: Hodder & Stoughton, 1972), p. 220.

16. A. T. Hanson, *The Wrath of the Lamb*, p. 104.

17. A. T. Hanson, *The Wrath of the Lamb*, p. 110.

18. R. P. C. Hanson, *God*, pp. 48-52.

serves that "the wrath of God is a matter about which theologians feel deeply, but little precision of thought and language has been attained." He rightly adds that there is more common ground than is sometimes acknowledged.[19] So it is appropriate to begin by recognizing the positive points in the Dodd approach.

First, it must be recognized that talk of God's wrath is anthropomorphic or, to be more precise, anthropopathic. While God is rightly described in human terms, we must recognize that these terms are true by analogy rather than univocally.[20] But of course, this is not true only of the wrath of God. Talk of God's love is also anthropopathic, and we must not fall into the error of equating the divine love with human love in all its imperfection and distortion. "The Enlightenment called such ideas [as God's wrath] 'the crude anthropopathisms of an uncultured age' . . . but they are no more anthropopathic than what the Bible says about the fatherly love of God; like this they belong inalienably to the biblical concept of the personal God."[21] To concede that talk of God's wrath is anthropopathic is not, of course, to deny that there is a reality to which it corresponds. What that reality is is precisely the point at dispute.

Second, the wrath of God should not be understood in a crudely literal fashion. The divine wrath is very different from human wrath. It should certainly not be understood as an irrational passion, to use Dodd's words. As John Stott puts it, God's wrath against sin

> does not mean . . . that he is likely to fly off the handle at the most trivial provocation, still less that he loses his temper for no apparent reason at all. For there is nothing capricious or arbitrary about the holy God. Nor is he ever irascible, malicious, spiteful or vindictive. His anger is neither mysterious nor irrational. It is never unpredictable but always predictable, because it is provoked by evil and by evil alone.[22]

Almost every writer on this topic emphasizes the dangers of understanding God's wrath in terms of human anger.

19. D. E. H. Whiteley, *The Theology of St. Paul* (Oxford: Basil Blackwell, 1964), pp. 61-62.

20. The issue of analogical language is discussed fully in some of the other chapters of this volume.

21. Stählin, "ὀργή," in *TDNT,* 5:425.

22. Stott, *The Cross of Christ,* p. 173.

Third, it can be conceded that there is in the New Testament a tendency to depersonalize the wrath of God. MacGregor softens and qualifies Dodd's position in such a way as to bring out the real case that Dodd has. "God's 'wrath' in the N.T., and particularly in Paul's letters is conceived of in terms less completely personal than is his love."[23] This fact casts doubt on the wisdom of Edwards's sermon. Edwards heightens the affective character of God's wrath by bringing together in concentrated form the strongest elements of the Old Testament teaching, while the New Testament writers seem to move in the opposite direction. The New Testament speaks of God's wrath almost entirely in terms of *effectus* rather than *affectus*.

Finally, it should be recognized that wrath is not fundamental to God in the same way that love is. Isaiah describes God as rising up in wrathful judgment "to do his work, his strange work, and perform his task, his alien task" (Isa. 28:21). Luther picked up this idea, distinguishing between God's wrath as his *opus alienum* (alien work) and his mercy as his *opus proprium* (proper work).[24] Karl Barth makes the same distinction between God's wrath and his grace[25] as does Emil Brunner between his wrath and his love.[26] There are two different points to be noted here. First, God *is* love, yet one could not say that God is wrath. In other words, love is a fundamental and eternal attribute of God, while wrath is no more than an outworking of God's character in response to sin. Before creation God was love, and this love was active within the Trinity; but God's wrath was no more than a potentiality. "Unlike holiness or righteousness, *wrath never forms one of the permanent attributes of the God of Israel.*"[27] Wrath is not an attribute of God in the way that his love or holiness is. His wrath is his response to something outside of himself. Second, it is also true that before creation God had no occasion to exercise his mercy. But this does not put wrath and mercy on the same footing. The Old Testament repeatedly af-

23. MacGregor, "The Concept of the Wrath of God," p. 103, cf. pp. 104-5.

24. E.g., A. E. McGrath, *Luther's Theology of the Cross* (Oxford: Blackwell, 1985), pp. 154-56.

25. K. Barth, *Church Dogmatics*, I/1 (Edinburgh: T. & T. Clark, 1936), pp. 204-5.

26. E. Brunner, *The Mediator* (Philadelphia: Westminster, 1947), pp. 445, 520-21; *Man in Revolt* (London & Redhill: Lutterworth, 1939), p. 163.

27. W. Eichrodt, *Theology of the Old Testament*, vol. 1 (London: S.C.M., 1961), p. 262 (his emphasis). Cf. Peels, *The Vengeance of God*, p. 289: "Wrath is not a permanent 'attribute' of God, but neither is it 'uncharacteristic' of God."

firms God's reluctance to exercise his wrath and his delight in showing mercy.[28]

There is much that is true in Dodd's thesis. God's wrath is an anthropomorphism not to be taken in a crudely literal fashion. It is not to be put on the same level as the love of God, and the New Testament does tend to speak of it in impersonal terms. But having gladly conceded these points we must point to the serious deficiency in the Dodd thesis: the reduction of the wrath of God to a process of cause and effect, to the inevitable consequences of sin in a moral universe.[29] Of course, God's wrath does indeed work in this world primarily in the way that Dodd describes. God's wrath normally operates through means. MacGregor rightly cites James Denney to the effect that "The divine punishment is the divine reaction against sin expressing itself through the whole constitution or system of things under which the sinner lives."[30] The problem lies not with what Dodd affirms but with what he denies.

There are various problems with the purely impersonal view of God's wrath. Anselm, because of his belief in divine impassibility, explained God's compassion as follows:

> But how are You consistently both merciful and impassible? For, if You are impassible You have no compassion. And if You do not have compassion, You do not have a heart sorrowful out of compassion for the wretched — the very thing which being merciful is. And if You are not merciful, from where do the wretched derive their great consolation? . . . You are merciful according to our experience but not merciful according to Your experience. For when You behold us in our pitiable condition, we feel the effect of Your mercy, but You do not feel any emotion. And so You are merciful because You save us miserable creatures and

---

28. E.g., Exod. 34:6-7; Num. 14:18; Neh. 9:17-18; Ps. 30:5; 86:15; 103:8; 145:8-9; Isa. 54:7-10; Ezek. 18:23, 32; 33:11; Hos. 11:8-9; Joel 2:13-14; Jon. 4:2; Mic. 7:18-20. Cf. Peels, *The Vengeance of God,* pp. 294-95, on the relation between God's love and his vengeance/wrath: "There is no balance between vengeance and love; the preponderance of God's faithful love is evident in the whole Old Testament. . . . God's heart is not in the vengeance, but he does so when there is no other option."

29. Dodd, *The Epistle of Paul to the Romans,* pp. 49-50; A. T. Hanson, *The Wrath of the Lamb,* passim; MacGregor, "The Concept of the Wrath of God," pp. 105-6; Stewart, *A Man in Christ,* pp. 219-20.

30. Denny, cited in MacGregor, "The Concept of the Wrath of God," p. 106.

spare us though we sin against You. And You are not merciful, because You experience no compassion for misery.[31]

In other words, God's compassion is an *effectus,* but not an *affectus.* Such a doctrine of divine impassibility has rightly been rejected by recent theologies that have stressed the suffering of God. How ironical that at the very same time the reverse process has taken place with regard to the wrath of God!

The seriousness of this issue can be seen by a simple example. A. T. Hanson expresses the Dodd view clearly by emphasizing that God's wrath is not an *affectus,* a feeling or emotion, and that God does not have a personal feeling like "displeasure."[32] (This is not on the basis that God cannot have any *affectus,* since his thesis is that God's wrath, *unlike* his love, is impersonal.) It follows, therefore, that God views the sexual molestation and murder of a little child without any feeling of displeasure. Is this really the New Testament picture of God's wrath, any more than Anselm's is the New Testament picture of God's compassion? It is not open to Dodd or Hanson to say that God feels displeasure toward the sin but not the sinner. They make no differentiation between those passages which speak of God's wrath against sinners and those which speak of his wrath against sin. To grant that God feels anger or displeasure against sin would be to undermine the whole basis of their exegetical case. If they wished to make the distinction between God's wrath against sin and his wrath against sinners they would have to rebuild their case from scratch.

Dodd's position is not immune from the charge of deism, as was preemptively noted by P. T. Forsyth.[33] A. T. Hanson rejects the charge as follows: "Wrath is part of the natural moral order, and it is no more deistic to conceive of God as allowing the process of the wrath to work impersonally, than it is to conceive of his allowing the process of the laws of nature to work impersonally."[34] This is an unfortunate choice of analogy. Of course God works both through "the laws of nature" and through "the natural

31. Anselm, *Proslogion* 8, in *St Anselm of Canterbury,* ed. J. Hopkins and H. Richardson, vol. 1 (London: S.C.M., 1974), pp. 97-98.

32. Cf. nn. 13 and 16, above.

33. P. T. Forsyth, *The Work of Christ* (London: Hodder & Stoughton, 1910), pp. 239-40.

34. A. T. Hanson, *The Wrath of the Lamb,* pp. 187-88.

moral order." But just as it is deistic to allow God no further role in creation than setting up impersonal laws of nature that work like clockwork, so it is deistic to conceive of God's wrath as no more personal than setting up a "natural moral order." Those, like R. P. C. Hanson, who are willing to speak of God actively punishing are immune from this particular criticism. But for others the aim in talking about impersonal wrath appears to be to dissociate God from wrath and punishment, to portray wrath as a mere by-product of sin, not actually willed by God. Such a position is not free of deistic implications.

Similarly, Dodd in particular is not exempt from the charge of neo-Marcionism. He argues that in the New Testament "anger as an attitude of God to men disappears, and His love and mercy become all-embracing. This is, as I believe, the purport of the teaching of Jesus with its emphasis on limitless forgiveness."[35] Wrath and punishment are the impersonal by-product of the moral order, and God is dissociated from them. This approach is avowedly contrary to the teaching of the Old Testament; it is based upon a particular interpretation of Paul and is supported by a truncated (as we shall argue) appeal to the teaching of Jesus. The similarities to Marcion are striking.

But what of the biblical evidence? Space permits no more than a brief review. First, let us look at the Old Testament. Baird refers to six different words used for the wrath of God a total of 406 times, while Morris extends the list to over twenty words used more than 580 times.[36] There is an "indissoluble link between the proclamation of God's wrath and the whole message of the OT."[37] "Wherever in the Old Testament one finds a reference to the love of God, his wrath is always in the background, either explicitly or implicitly, and we neglect this element to the impoverishment of the Hebrew concept of love."[38] This wrath is God's displeasure and his venting of it, the opposite of his good pleasure.[39] Because of his holiness, righteousness, and justice, God is by nature intolerant of sin and impu-

---

35. Dodd, *The Epistle of Paul to the Romans*, p. 50.

36. J. A. Baird, *The Justice of God in the Teaching of Jesus* (London: S.C.M., 1963), p. 46; L. Morris, *The Apostolic Preaching of the Cross*, 3rd ed. (London: Tyndale, 1965), pp. 149-50.

37. J. Fichtner, "ὀργή," in *TDNT*, 5:407. Peels likewise notes that "instead of being an element foreign to God's nature, vengeance is an essential component of the Old Testament revelation of God" (*The Vengeance of God*, p. 292; cf. p. 284).

38. Baird, *The Justice of God*, p. 46.

39. Eichrodt, *Theology of the Old Testament*, p. 259.

rity.[40] God's wrath against sin is portrayed in the Old Testament both as *affectus* and as *effectus*.[41] "If God enacts punishing judgment, he does not do that 'emotionlessly'. He is then very angry concerning sin, injustice and blasphemy. God's vengeance is not an impersonal, cold disciplinary action but it is a retribution in which the heat . . . of God's deep indignation is sometimes evident."[42] "While disaster is regarded as the inevitable result of man's sin, it is so in the view of the Old Testament, not by some inexorable law of an impersonal Nature, but because a holy God wills to pour out the vials of His wrath upon those who commit sin. Indeed, it is largely because wrath is so fully personal in the Old Testament that mercy becomes so fully personal, for mercy is the action of the same God who was angry, allowing His wrath to be turned away."[43] The anger of God signifies his emphatically personal character.[44]

What of the New Testament? Dodd claims that in the teaching of Jesus "anger as an attitude of God to men disappears, and His love and mercy become all-embracing." The wrath of God, he states, "does not appear in the teaching of Jesus, unless we press certain features of the parables in an illegitimate manner."[45] A rather different conclusion is reached by Baird. He finds in the New Testament "the entirety of the Old Testament view of judgment," including the wrath of God. In the New Testament teaching on judgment, and especially in the teaching of Jesus as found in the Synoptics, he finds the full Old Testament teaching with an emphasis on "God's condemnation and wrath." "The Synoptics record Jesus saying well over twice as much about the wrath of God as he ever did about his love."[46] Why such different conclusions? A major difference is that Baird works from the whole sweep of Jesus' teaching on judgment and wrath while Dodd ap-

---

40. Baird, *The Justice of God*, p. 49. Peels judicially comments: "The moral motivation for God's wrath is not immediately evident in a few of the older texts, but the central thought is certainly that this wrath is a reaction to the misdeeds of mankind" (*The Vengeance of God*, p. 289).

41. Whiteley, *The Theology of St. Paul*, p. 64; Fichtner, "ὀργή," in *TDNT*, 5:397, 407. A. T. Hanson argues, however, that in parts of the O.T. material, such as Chronicles, a view emerges of wrath as an impersonal and inevitable process (*The Wrath of the Lamb*, pp. 21-26).

42. Peels, *The Vengeance of God*, pp. 289-90.

43. Morris, *The Apostolic Preaching of the Cross*, p. 152.

44. Eichrodt, *Theology of the Old Testament*, p. 258.

45. Dodd, *The Epistle of Paul to the Romans*, p. 50.

46. Baird, *The Justice of God*, pp. 59-60, 72.

pears to look solely at the use of the *word* wrath, a procedure criticized by James Barr in his *The Semantics of Biblical Language.*[47] It is true that Jesus does not in the Synoptics[48] use the word "wrath" in relation to God except at Luke 21:23 ("There will be great distress in the land and wrath against this people"), where it is possible to deny that the wrath referred to is God's. But there are many passages where he clearly expresses the divine hostility to all that is evil, though without using the actual term "wrath."[49] Baird warns against a crudely anthropomorphic interpretation of God's wrath but rightly concludes that to grasp Jesus' meaning the concept must not be "depersonalized."[50]

What of the parables? In the parable of the unmerciful servant, the master in anger hands him over to the jailers to be tortured (Matt. 18:34). In the parable of the wedding feast, the master is angry at the excuses made by the invited guests (Luke 14:21). In the Matthaean version the guests killed the servants who brought the invitations, and the king is so enraged that he sends his army to destroy them (Matt. 22:7). Is it legitimate to deduce the wrath of God from these parables? Dodd, followed by A. T. Hanson, claims that we can no more conclude from this parable that God is angry than we can conclude from another parable that he is an unjust judge.[51] But the comparison is not fair, since the point of these parables seems to be that God does act like the angry lord, while he is explicitly contrasted with the unjust judge.[52]

What of Paul? The impersonal character of his talk about God's wrath should be acknowledged, but not exaggerated. In the first chapter of Romans Paul three times states of the depraved that God "gave them over" to various sins (vv. 24, 26, 28). "The thrice-repeated παρέδωκεν αὐτοὺς ὁ θεός is surely so emphatic as to suggest that a deliberate, positive

---

47. J. Barr, *The Semantics of Biblical Language* (Oxford: Oxford University Press, 1961). Geoffrey Grogan, in his chapter in this volume, notes that it is nowhere clearly stated in the Synoptic Gospels that God loves human beings, but that it would be rash to deduce from this that the authors did not believe in God's love for humanity.

48. John 3:36 refers to God's wrath, but it is far from certain that John is attributing these words to Jesus.

49. Morris, *The Apostolic Preaching of the Cross,* p. 181, lists many.

50. Baird, *The Justice of God,* pp. 71-72.

51. Dodd, *The Epistle of Paul to the Romans,* p. 50; A. T. Hanson, *The Wrath of the Lamb,* p. 121.

52. Tasker, *The Biblical Doctrine of the Wrath of God,* pp. 28-29; Baird, *The Justice of God,* pp. 63-71, maintains that the Synoptic parables clearly portray God's wrath.

act of God is meant."[53] Again, Romans 3:5 speaks of God bringing wrath upon us, which suggests an active role on God's part. Romans 12:19 refers to God's wrath in impersonal terms, but Paul proceeds to state that vengeance is God's and he will repay, quoting Deuteronomy 32:35, the text for Edwards's infamous sermon! In 1 Corinthians 10:22 he refers to God's jealousy, a passage of which A. T. Hanson disapproves, stating that here "Paul is not at his most profound with respect to the wrath."[54] Finally, if one looks at a passage like 2 Thessalonians 1:7-9, with its vivid portrayal of Christ coming in judgment at the Parousia, it is hard to talk of God's wrath in purely impersonal terms. In short, while much of Paul's talk about God's wrath is relatively impersonal, the evidence of his writings as a whole is that he did not wish to eliminate the concept of wrath as *affectus*. Stählin's conclusion is fair: "In most NT passages ὀργή is in fact the divine work, destiny or judgment of wrath" but "the idea of an actual attitude of God cannot be disputed in respect of many NT verses, any more than this is possible in respect of [love and mercy]." "As in the OT . . . so in the NT ὀργή is both God's displeasure at evil, His passionate resistance to every will which is set against Him, and also His judicial attack thereon."[55]

If this conclusion is at least plausible for the teaching of Paul, it is much clearer in Hebrews. The author (3:10-11; cf. 4:3) quotes from Psalm 95:10-11 the statement that God was displeased or angry (προσώχθισα) with Israel and swore against them in his anger (ὀργῇ). This is the one place in the New Testament where God is unequivocally the subject of a verb meaning "to be angry."[56] Later passages, such as 10:31 ("It is a dreadful thing to fall into the hands of the living God") and 12:29 ("Our God is a consuming fire"), reinforce the impression that for the author of Hebrews God's wrath was no impersonal process of cause and effect.

Finally, there are places where judgment of sin in this age is portrayed as the direct act of God (Acts 5:1-11; 12:23; 1 Cor. 11:30; Rev. 2:22-23). The case that God's wrath is *purely* an impersonal process of cause and effect, the inevitable consequence of sin in a moral universe, can be maintained only with considerable difficulty. It necessitates rejection of the clear

---

53. C. E. B. Cranfield, *A Critical and Exegetical Commentary on the Epistle to the Romans*, vol. 1 (Edinburgh: T. & T. Clark, 1975), p. 120.

54. A. T. Hanson, *The Wrath of the Lamb*, pp. 77-78.

55. Stählin, "ὀργή," in *TDNT*, 5:424-25. Paul is explicitly included in this judgment.

56. A. T. Hanson, *The Wrath of the Lamb*, pp. 132-33.

teaching of the Old Testament, dubious interpretation of some passages of the teaching of Jesus and Paul, and the rejection of other New Testament passages. This neo-Marcionite procedure (rejection of the Old Testament teaching and selective use of Jesus and Paul) yields no more than a silence about the affective side of God's wrath. No passage in either Testament is alleged that *denies* the personal and affective nature of God's wrath. The case rests simply on an argument from the (alleged and highly contestable) silence of Jesus and Paul.

The fourth way in which God's wrath is muted is that found in the majority of Western evangelical churches today. The wrath of God is not denied and is indeed given formal recognition. But in practice it is neglected. In preaching and teaching it is ignored, largely or totally. "Those who still believe in the wrath of God . . . say little about it. . . . The fact is that the subject of divine wrath has become taboo in modern society, and Christians by and large have accepted the taboo and conditioned themselves never to raise the matter."[57] This is a very serious matter, for, as Brunner comments, "a theology which uses the language of Christianity can be tested by its attitude towards the Biblical doctrine of the wrath of God, whether it means what the words of Scripture say. Where the idea of the wrath of God is ignored there also will there be no understanding of the central conception of the Gospel: the uniqueness of the revelation in the Mediator."[58] More simply, "only he who knows the greatness of wrath will be mastered by the greatness of mercy."[59]

As Hanson notes, "the contemporary rejection by Christians of the biblical doctrine of the wrath of God is a typical example of our allowing secular, non-Christian ideas to creep into our understanding of the Christian faith in such a way as to distort it."[60] But why does the idea of God's wrath arouse so much displeasure today? There are at least three ways in which it offends against the Enlightenment mind-set. First, if there is any room for God in a "world come of age" it is for a God whose purpose is to serve humanity. A genuinely theocentric concept of God is intolerable, because "modern man, through the influence of the thought of the Enlightenment, is so accustomed to think that God's function is to stand surety

---

57. J. I. Packer, *Knowing God* (London: Hodder & Stoughton, 1973), p. 164.

58. Brunner, *The Mediator*, p. 152. For a similar idea, cf. K. Barth, *Church Dogmatics*, II/1 (Edinburgh: T. & T. Clark, 1957), pp. 393-94.

59. Stählin, "ὀργή," in *TDNT*, 5:425.

60. R. P. C. Hanson, *God*, p. 38.

for human purposes."[61] Second, it follows from this that any "God" who wishes to be accepted today must be a tolerant God who respects human rights.[62] Finally, the sentimentality of the Enlightenment has given birth to a sentimental view of God and his love,[63] one that suits carol services at Christmas but does not cohere either with Scripture or with empirical reality. Such a proclamation of God gives birth to benevolent, skeptical apathy. By contrast, the response to proclamation of the wrath of God is more likely to be very different, either hostility or conviction of sin (John 16:8-11). Christians are, of course, not exempt from these pressures, and sentimental, anthropocentric views of God are to be found in almost every sector of the modern Western church. Why has the biblical doctrine of the wrath of God not been more effective in correcting these trends? One reason may be the fear that it is incompatible with God's love, a misconception that this essay will seek to dispel.

II. THE WRATH OF GOD AND ITS RELATION TO OTHER DOCTRINES

The conclusion thus far is that God's wrath is to be understood neither as purely impersonal nor in crudely anthropomorphic terms. So to what does "the wrath of God" refer? It is God's personal, vigorous opposition both to evil and to evil people. This is a steady, unrelenting antagonism that arises from God's very nature, his holiness. It is God's revulsion to evil and all that opposes him, his displeasure at it and the venting of that displeasure. It is his passionate resistance to every will that is set against him.[64]

These "definitions" raise an issue that is often ignored. What is the ob-

---

61. Brunner, *The Mediator*, pp. 467-68.

62. R. P. C. Hanson, *God*, pp. 37-38; Stott, *The Cross of Christ*, pp. 108-9. It must of course be acknowledged that belief in the wrath of God in the past has often gone hand in hand with cruel and inhumane human behavior, whether in war or in penal systems. But those wishing to blame the latter practice on the former belief would do well to consider the inhumane cruelties of atheistic regimes in the twentieth century.

63. Brunner, *The Mediator*, p. 464.

64. These "definitions" are drawn from Morris, *The Apostolic Preaching of the Cross*, p. 180; idem, *The Cross in the New Testament* (Exeter: Paternoster, 1967), p. 191; Stählin, "ὀργή," in *TDNT*, 5:425; Stott, *The Cross of Christ*, p. 173; W. Temple, *Christus Veritas* (London: Macmillan, 1924), p. 259.

ject of God's wrath? Is God angry with evil or with evil people? In the New Testament both are true. Often God's wrath is referred to without precisely specifying the object of that wrath (e.g., Matt. 3:7; Luke 3:7; Rom. 4:15; Rev. 14:19; 15:1, 7). In one place the object of God's wrath is evil (Rom. 1:18), although even here the perpetrators are mentioned. Where an object is mentioned it is usually evildoers (e.g., Luke 21:23; John 3:36; Rom. 2:5, 8; Eph. 5:6; Col. 3:6; 1 Thess. 2:16). Thus a comprehensive verdict would be to say that God's wrath is directed primarily against evildoers because of the evil that they do.

Where does this leave the modern cliché that "God hates the sin but loves the sinner"? Like most clichés it is a half-truth. There are two ways in which it could be taken. The first, which is undoubtedly the way that most people take it in the modern liberal West, is as a comment about the wrath of God. God's displeasure is against sin but not against the sinner. Apart from the fact that this reverses the emphasis of the New Testament, there are problems with it. As William Temple observes, "that is a shallow psychology which regards the sin as something merely separate from the sinner, which he can lay aside like a suit of clothes. My sin is the wrong direction of my will; and my will is just myself as far as I am active. If God hates the sin, what He hates is not an accretion attached to my real self; it is myself, as that self now exists."[65] It is incoherent to say that God is displeased with child molestation but feels no displeasure toward child molesters. In what sense, then, is the cliché true? It is to be understood not as limiting the objects of God's displeasure to sinful *actions* but as affirming God's grace. God loves sinners, not in the sense that he does not hate them along with their sin, but in the sense that he seeks their salvation in Christ. While his attitude to sinners as sinners is antagonism and wrath, his good will toward them actively seeks their conversion and forgiveness.[66]

But does the Bible ever talk of God actually hating people?[67] Mostly it speaks of God hating evil deeds (e.g., Deut. 12:31; Prov. 6:16-19; Isa. 61:8; Amos 6:8; Rev. 2:6), but there are seven passages that speak of his hatred for people. First, there is the repeated statement that God loved Jacob but

---

65. Temple, *Christus Veritas*, p. 258.

66. Temple, *Christus Veritas*, pp. 258-59.

67. This is related to the issue of God's enmity toward sinners. Cf. Brunner, *The Mediator*, pp. 515-22; Morris, *The Apostolic Preaching of the Cross*, pp. 220-25.

hated Esau (Mal. 1:2-3; Rom. 9:13). We should beware of reading too much into this given the question of the extent to which it is individuals or nations that are in mind, and the question of whether "hate" here is to be understood as in the injunction to hate one's own relatives and one's own life (Luke 14:26; cf. Matt. 10:37). Second, it is thrice stated that God hates evildoers (Psalm 5:5; 11:5; Prov. 6:16-19). Finally, God twice states that he hates Israel (Jer. 12:8; Hos. 9:15). Clearly these last affirmations do not preclude God's love for Israel, as is proclaimed especially by Hosea. Perhaps we would remain closest to the emphasis of the Bible if we spoke of God's hatred of sin and his wrath against sinners, though we cannot exclude talk of God's wrath against sin or his hatred of sinners. A new slogan might be "God hates the sin and is angry with the sinner."

Two of the leading theologians of the church have tackled the question of God's love and hate. Augustine, in discussing the atonement, warns against the idea that God did not begin to love us until Christ died for us. He wrestles with the tension between the fact that Christ's death flows from God's love for us (Rom. 5:8) and the fact that God hates evildoers (Ps. 5:5). He reaches the paradox that God both hated and loved us. He hated us for our sin and loved us for that which sin had not ruined and which is capable of being healed.[68] Thomas Aquinas also tackles Psalm 5:5. He maintains that "God loves sinners as being real things of nature," as created. But "in so far as they are sinners they are unreal and deficient" and as such God "holds them in hatred."[69] Again, wrestling with Malachi 1:2-3, Thomas notes that "God loves all men and all creatures as well, inasmuch as he wills some good to all." But at the same time, "in that he does not will to some the blessing of eternal life he is said to hold them in hate or to reprobate them."[70]

The wrath of God relates to a number of other themes, some of which can be mentioned briefly in passing. The first theme is the question of the moral order and the exercise of moral judgment. Jonathan Sacks laments the situation that prevails in our society, a situation that is not unrelated to the rejection of the wrath of God. In our society, he maintains, the word "judgmental" is used "to rule out in advance the offering of moral judge-

---

68. Augustine, *Homilies on the Gospel of John* 110.6, in *The Nicene and Post-Nicene Fathers, First Series* (hereafter NPNF)(reprint; Grand Rapids: Eerdmans, 1956), 7:411.

69. Thomas Aquinas, *Summa Theologiae*, 1a.20.2, *ad* 4, in vol. 5 (London: Eyre & Spottiswoode; New York: McGraw-Hill, 1964), p. 63.

70. *Summa Theologiae*, 1a.23.3, *ad* 1 (vol. 5, p. 117).

ment." He gives the recent example of a church leader who was lambasted for daring to criticize adultery. Adultery is acceptable; judgment is not. A worthy and biblical reticence in passing judgment on individuals has been confused with an unwillingness to make moral judgments, to distinguish between what is morally good and what is evil. "So morality becomes a matter of taste and choice, and *de gustibus non est disputandum:* there is no point in asking an expert which to prefer."[71] S. T. Davis argues that the wrath of God rescues us from just such a moral relativism by showing us that right and wrong are objectively real and pointing us to the moral significance of our deeds.[72]

The second theme is the fear of God. Together with the demise of the wrath of God there is the rejection of fear as a valid motive.[73] This is another of those dangerous half-truths. Augustine rightly observed that the person who fears hell fears burning, not sin.[74] The mainstream Christian tradition has always recognized that true obedience is motivated not by fear but by love. It is not a reluctant, fearful, slavish obedience that God seeks but a joyful, free response of love. But the mainstream Christian tradition has not been so naive as to imagine that this dispenses with the need for fear. Augustine, whose grasp of human psychology was profound, came to recognize that the free response of love is often preceded by the constraints of coercion. Children need initially to be disciplined at least in part by fear. But if the process of discipline is successful the values being conveyed are internalized. That which initially is done in order to avoid parental disapproval or punishment is done freely and willingly. The motivation of fear is not invalid (as is so often implied today) but insufficient. Jesus had no qualms about telling his disciples to "fear him who, after the killing of the body, has power to throw you into hell" (Luke 12:5).[75] Lac-

71. J. Sacks, *Faith in the Future* (London: Darton, Longman & Todd, 1995), pp. 37-39.

72. S. T. Davis, "Universalism, Hell, and the Fate of the Ignorant," *Modern Theology* 6 (1989-90): 184-85.

73. The rejection of the fear of God is another example of neo-Marcionism. Tertullian attacks the Marcionites for their boast that they did not fear their God (*Against Marcion* 1.27).

74. Augustine, *Letters* 145.4, in NPNF, 1:496. The index to Augustine in *Patrologiae Cursus Completus,* Series Latina, ed. J. P. Migne (Paris, 1844-64), 46:635-36, gives many similar passages, as well as passages that affirm the positive role of fear.

75. Baird, *The Justice of God,* pp. 61-62, tackles the difficulty that some have today in accepting this. Wayne Grudem's comment that "we should feel no fear of God's wrath as Christians" (*Systematic Theology* [Leicester: Inter-Varsity Press; Grand Rapids: Zondervan, 1994], p. 206) is not the whole truth.

tantius notes that there is no true religion or piety without some fear of God and that without the wrath of God there is no fear of God.[76] "The fear of the LORD is the beginning of wisdom" (Prov. 9:10), and while the term "fear" here embraces much more than the fear of God's anger, it does not exclude it.

A third theme is the doctrine of hell. It is very popular today to portray hell as locked on the inside only.[77] God's role in condemning people to hell is simply reluctantly and sorrowfully to consent to the choice that they have made. Again we have here a half-truth. The mainstream Christian tradition has always acknowledged that God's "No" to the unrepentant at the Last Judgment is in response to their "No" to him in this life. Again, the Bible testifies to God's reluctance in executing judgment (e.g., Ezek. 33:11; 2 Pet. 3:9). But there is another side to the picture that should not be suppressed. It is not enough to say that God's punishment is simply the sinner punishing himself.[78] God's role in judgment is not merely passive. The final judgment involves God's wrath as well as his sorrow (e.g., Rom. 2:5, 8; 1 Thess 1:10). While it remains true that those who are lost have excluded themselves from heaven, it is also true that God actively excludes those who at least at one level wish to be included (e.g., Matt. 22:11-13). Jesus emphasized not the difficulty of escaping from God's grace but the need to strive for it: "Make every effort to enter through the narrow door, because many, I tell you, will try to enter and will not be able to" (Luke 13:24). He stressed not the perpetuity of the opportunity to enter but the great danger of ignoring it until too late (e.g., Matt. 25:1-13; Luke 16:26).

The final theme is the cross. Belief in the wrath of God has, as its correlate, belief in the work of Christ in dealing with that wrath. A. T. Hanson explicitly rejects the idea that God's wrath is an *affectus* on the grounds that this leads to theories of propitiation.[79] Dodd's interpretation of the wrath of God is closely linked with his rejection of the concept of propitia-

76. Lactantius, *A Treatise on the Anger of God* 6, 8, 11.

77. An influential example is C. S. Lewis, *The Great Divorce* (1946; Glasgow: Collins, 1972). For a full discussion of these issues, cf. J. L. Kvanvig, *The Problem of Hell* (New York and Oxford: Oxford University Press, 1993).

78. As A. T. Hanson, *The Wrath of the Lamb*, p. 198; Stewart, *A Man in Christ*, p. 219.

79. A. T. Hanson, *The Wrath of the Lamb*, pp. 192-94. His brother speculates that contemporary reluctance to consider any doctrine of God's wrath "is caused by a reaction away from the distorted and unjustified doctrine that Christ appeased God's wrath" (R. P. C. Hanson, *God*, p. 47).

tion.[80] Those who recognize God's wrath as *affectus* have been more willing to say that Christ on the cross bore in our place the wrath that was our due.[81]

III. THE WRATH OF GOD AND THE LOVE OF GOD

The time has come to turn to our central concern, the relation between the wrath of God and the love of God. In the popular imagination they are simply opposed to one another. Yet, as has often been observed, "the opposite of love is not wrath but indifference."[82] It is the thesis of this essay that God's wrath should be seen as an aspect of his love, as a consequence of his love. As Barth puts it, if we truly love God, "we must love Him also in His anger, condemnation and punishments, or rather we must see, feel and appreciate His love to us even in His anger, condemnation and punishment."[83] In seeking to do this we will need to explore the ways in which God's wrath both expresses his love and can be contrasted with it — though it might be happier to contrast wrath with *mercy*, seeing both as expressions of God's love.

First we should note that there is no true love without wrath. The Old Testament teaching on the wrath of God has been summarized thus: "the wrath of YHWH is a personal quality, without which YHWH would cease to be fully righteous and His love would degenerate into sentimentality."[84] Anders Nygren likewise accuses the Marcionite view of love, which is separated from the idea of judgment, of sentimental-

---

80. E.g., C. H. Dodd, *The Bible and the Greeks* (London: Hodder & Stoughton, 1935), pp. 82-95. Among the very many responses, cf. Morris, *The Apostolic Preaching of the Cross*, pp. 144-213.

81. E.g., Barth, *Church Dogmatics*, II/1, pp. 396-99; idem, *Credo* (London: Hodder & Stoughton, 1936), pp. 46-47; Forsyth, *The Work of Christ*, p. 243; Stählin, "ὀργή," in *TDNT*, 5:445-46. A related issue is the revelation of the wrath of God in the event of the cross. Cf. Barth, *Church Dogmatics*, II/1, pp. 398-99; Cranfield, *A Critical and Exegetical Commentary on the Epistle to the Romans*, 1:109-11; Stählin, "ὀργή," in *TDNT*, 5:425, 431-32. I would hold that God's wrath is revealed *supremely*, but not *solely*, in the cross.

82. Whiteley, *The Theology of St. Paul*, p. 63. Whiteley claims to be quoting A. G. Hebert, *The Authority of the Old Testament* (London: Faber & Faber, 1947), p. 251, where we read that "the opposite of love is not hate *[sic]*; it is indifference."

83. Barth, *Church Dogmatics*, II/1, p. 394.

84. S. Erlandsson, "The Wrath of YHWH," *Tyndale Bulletin* 23 (1972): 116.

ity.[85] "Only that love which pronounces judgment on all that is not love is in the truest sense restoring and saving love."[86] Paul's injunction that love be sincere is followed by the command to hate what is evil (Rom. 12:9). A husband who did not respond to his wife's infidelity with a jealous anger would thereby demonstrate his lack of care for her.

Failure to hate evil implies a deficiency in love.[87] C. E. B. Cranfield illustrates this with a well-chosen modern example. He asks whether God could be the good and loving God if he did not react to human evil with wrath. "For indignation against wickedness is surely an essential element of human goodness in a world in which moral evil is always present. A man who knows, for example, about the injustice and cruelty of *apartheid* and is not angry at such wickedness cannot be a thoroughly good man; for his lack of wrath means a failure to care for his fellow man, a failure to love." He goes on to warn against building too much on the human analogy, for "even the very highest and purest human wrath can at the best afford but a distorted and twisted reflection of the wrath of God,"[88] a point that is amply illustrated by the history of the anti-apartheid movement. But the basic point, that lack of wrath against wickedness is a lack of caring which is a lack of love, is indisputable. "Absolute love implies absolute purity and absolute holiness: an intense burning light. . . . Unless God detests sin and evil with great loathing, He cannot be a God of Love."[89]

Indeed, P. T. Forsyth daringly states that "the love of God is not more real than the wrath of God."[90] But while this is a bold way of summarizing the point made in the previous paragraph, Forsyth was well aware that it needs qualification. Brunner insists that the wrath of God is a reality not to be denied or explained away. "But the wrath of God is not the ultimate re-

85. A. Nygren, *Agape and Eros* (London: SPCK; New York: Macmillan, 1932-39), II/1: 110f.

86. Nygren, *Agape and Eros,* I:75.

87. Lactantius notes that to love life means to hate death, to love the good means to hate the wicked (*A Treatise on the Anger of God* 5). It should, however, be noted that Lactantius's concept of love does not appear to advance beyond the concept of loving that which is worthy of love.

88. Cranfield, *A Critical and Exegetical Commentary on the Epistle to the Romans,* 1:109. Cf. R. W. Dale's comment that "it is partly because sin does not provoke our own wrath, that we do not believe that sin provokes the wrath of God" (cited in Stott, *The Cross of Christ,* p. 109).

89. D. C. K. Watson, *My God Is Real* (London: Falcon, 1970), p. 39.

90. Forsyth, *The Work of Christ,* p. 242.

ality; it is the divine reality which corresponds to sin. But it is not the essential reality of God. In Himself God is love." In the cross we see "the reality of wrath, which is yet in some way a subordinate reality, and the far more overwhelming reality of the love of God." The love of God is in fact fully understood only in the light of the cross. If God's love is seen simply as a general truth it either loses its holiness or becomes limited by it.[91]

The fallacy of those who deny the wrath of God lies in the attempt to reduce God purely to love. As Brunner notes, "the Nature of God cannot be exhaustively stated in one single word." In particular, the holiness of God must not be suppressed.[92] P. T. Forsyth has made this point forcefully with his talk of "the holy love of God."[93] Our starting point should be "the supreme holiness of God's love, rather than its pity, sympathy, or affection," this being "the watershed between the Gospel and the theological liberalism which makes religion no more than the crown of humanity."[94] "If we spoke less about God's love and more about His holiness, more about His judgment, we should say much more when we did speak of His love."[95]

Here we come to an issue that divides. Should we think of God's love and his holiness, his mercy and his wrath, as attributes that somehow need to be reconciled to one another? Barth emphatically rejects any such idea. He quotes with disapproval from Bernard's sixth sermon on the Song of Songs in which he describes mercy and judgment as the two feet of God. Bernard warns his monks not to neglect either foot. They must temper sorrow for sin with the thought of mercy, so as to avoid despair; they must temper contemplation of God's mercy with remembrance of his judgment, so as to avoid lukewarm negligence.[96] Barth objects to the "fatal idea that we can really 'kiss' God's righteousness in abstraction from His mercy."[97] Forsyth also objects to the idea that there is a "strife of attributes" in God

91. Brunner, *The Mediator*, pp. 519-21. Cf. Nygren's comment that love without judgment "is reduced to a general altruism" (*Agape and Eros*, II/1:111).

92. Brunner, *The Mediator*, pp. 281-82.

93. E.g., Forsyth, *The Work of Christ*, pp. 78-80; idem, *Positive Preaching and the Modern Mind* (London: Hodder & Stoughton, 1907), pp. 316-19, 348-54; idem, *The Justification of God* (London: Duckworth, 1916), pp. 131-32, 194-95. Temple, *Christus Veritas*, p. 257, urges that any consideration of the atonement should start with God's "holy love."

94. P. T. Forsyth, *The Cruciality of the Cross* (London: Hodder & Stoughton, 1909), p. 6.

95. Forsyth, *The Cruciality of the Cross*, p. 73.

96. *Sermon* 6.6-9, in Bernard, *Song of Songs* I (Kalamazoo, MI: Cistercian Publications, 1971), pp. 35-37.

97. Barth, *Church Dogmatics*, II/1, 380f.

between justice and mercy, stressing by contrast that God's attributes are not somehow entities separable from him.[98] R. P. C. Hanson equally rejects the idea, accusing it of "an unpleasant suggestion that God suffers from schizophrenia, and is not quite in control of himself."[99] His brother, A. T. Hanson, acknowledges that such thinking is found in the Old Testament,[100] but sees it as overcome by the recognition that God's wrath is not his attitude or feeling.

Others defend the concept. Stott takes issue with Forsyth, pointing to passages in both Old and New Testaments that acknowledge a "duality" in God and citing Brunner especially.[101] Brunner speaks freely of the duality in God.[102] It is in the cross above all that God makes both his holiness and his love known simultaneously.[103] "The objective aspect of the Atonement . . . consists in the combination of inflexible righteousness, with its penalties, and transcendent love." "The love of God breaks through the wrath of God."[104] There is a "dualism" of holiness and love.

> Only where this dualism exists, only where God is known as One who "outside Christ" is really angry, but "in Christ" is "pure love," is faith real decision and the Atonement a real turning point. Therefore the dualism of holiness and love, of revelation and concealment, of mercy and wrath cannot be dissolved, changed into one synthetic conception, without at the same time destroying the seriousness of the Biblical knowledge of God, the reality and the mystery of revelation and atonement. . . . Here arises the "dialectic" of all genuine Christian theology, which simply aims at expressing in terms of thought the indissoluble nature of this dualism.[105]

In fact the concerns of Forsyth and those of Stott and Brunner are not necessarily incompatible. In God's innermost being, his attributes are perfectly united. There is no love of God that is not holy and no holiness of God that is not loving. There is nowhere where God is love but not light,

---

98. Forsyth, *The Work of Christ*, pp. 117-18.
99. R. P. C. Hanson, *God*, pp. 45-46.
100. A. T. Hanson, *The Wrath of the Lamb*, pp. 18-20, 38, etc.
101. Stott, *The Cross of Christ*, pp. 129-32.
102. Cf. nn. 91 and 92 above.
103. Brunner, *The Mediator*, pp. 450, 470.
104. Brunner, *The Mediator*, p. 520.
105. Brunner, *The Mediator*, p. 519; cf. pp. 467-68.

and nowhere where he is light but not love. Likewise, God's love and his justice are united in his essential nature.[106] But the holy, loving God acts differently toward us in different circumstances. In his holy, loving wrath he judges us for our sins. In his holy, loving mercy he forgives our sins. It is mistaken to divide the attributes by suggesting that wrath is the manifestation of holiness or justice, but not of love. It is equally mistaken to suggest that mercy is the manifestation of love, but not of holiness or justice. But there is a clear duality in God's dealings with humanity. In salvation history, in Christ, and in Scripture we see God acting both in wrath and judgment and in mercy and forgiveness. Clearly these two differ and are in some sense contrary to one another. Yet both originate from the one holy, loving God.

Thomas Aquinas asks whether justice and mercy are found in all of God's works. He concludes that "in every one of God's works justice and mercy are found." But he also concedes that "some works are associated with justice and some with mercy when the one more forcibly appears than the other. Yet mercy appears even in the damnation of the reprobate, for though not completely relaxed the penalty is sometimes softened, and is lighter than deserved. And justice appears even in the justification of the sinner, when fault is forgiven because of the love which God himself in mercy bestows."[107] It is in line with this principle to understand Romans 3:25-26 as at least in part referring to the way in which God's justice is maintained in the justification of the unjust.[108] *The cross involves the harmonization in historical outworking of attributes that are united in the eternal nature of God.*

But while both wrath and mercy have their origins in the holy love of God, how do they relate together "where the rubber hits the road"? How

106. Kvanvig, *The Problem of Hell*, pp. 117-19, argues that both should be viewed as aspects of God's goodness. He also argues there that God's love is fundamental and that his justice and holiness are to be subordinated to it. E. TeSelle puts forward the Augustinian alternative that "justice stands in a sense *above* love, as referee or judge of its propriety" ("Justice, Love, Peace," in *Augustine Today,* ed. R. J. Neuhaus [Grand Rapids: Eerdmans, 1993], pp. 88-90). There is no need to enter that debate here.

107. Thomas Aquinas, *Summa Theologiae*, 1a.21.4 (vol. 5, pp. 81-85). The point at issue is not the correctness of Thomas's doctrine of justification but the principle that justice and mercy are found in every work of God.

108. As Cranfield, *A Critical and Exegetical Commentary on the Epistle to the Romans,* 1:211-14.

does God's wrath cohere with his love? R. P. C. Hanson rejects the idea that "God is somehow loving and angry at the same time," on the grounds that wrath is not an attitude or characteristic of God.[109] J. S. Stewart likewise rejects the idea that God's wrath means that he "for the time lays aside His love and acts like a man who has lost his temper."[110] And yet the matter is not so simply resolved. Paul tells us that while we were still sinners (and therefore under the wrath of God) God showed his love for us in Christ's death (Rom. 5:8). The juxtaposition of love and wrath is clear. As Stott puts it, God's wrath is free from personal vindictiveness and "he is sustained simultaneously with undiminished love for the offender."[111] It is also clear that wrath and mercy conflict and alternate in our experience. One who is by nature a child of wrath (Eph. 2:3) encounters the mercy of God and is saved from the coming wrath (Rom. 5:9; 1 Thess. 1:10). In this sense, for the converted sinner wrath and mercy are two distinct and non-overlapping experiences. Again, the Old Testament speaks of the mercy of God restraining and limiting his wrath.[112]

A question needs to be asked at this stage. It has been argued that God's wrath against sinners is matched by his love for them and that these two come together supremely in the cross. But to affirm that God loves the object of his wrath falls short of saying that his wrath toward that person expresses his love *for that person*. It has indeed been argued that God's love necessitates his wrath. But this has been argued from his love for righteousness rather than his love for the object of his wrath. Can it be argued that his wrath against a particular sinner is demanded by his love for that particular sinner? In answering that question, we have to distinguish between God's wrath here and now, where it can lead to repentance, and God's wrath in the final judgment, where there is no further opportunity for repentance. In the case of living human beings, wrath plays its subsidiary role in God's dealings with them, as does the law in the Lutheran dialectic of law and gospel.[113] The wrath of God serves to show us the seriousness of our sin and as such is a part of God's loving dealings with us. The situation is clearly different where the opportunity for repentance has ceased. It is less obvious how God's wrath against those who are finally lost

---

109. R. P. C. Hanson, *God*, p. 47.
110. Stewart, *A Man in Christ*, p. 218.
111. Stott, *The Cross of Christ*, p. 106.
112. Tasker, *The Biblical Doctrine of the Wrath of God*, p. 23. Cf. n. 28 above.
113. Law and wrath are linked in Rom. 4:14-15.

is an expression of his love toward them in particular. Thomas Aquinas saw such love expressed as leniency in punishment.[114] Those who see the final destiny of the lost as extinction[115] can see that as an expression of God's loving mercy.

There is no dichotomy in God's being between his mercy and his wrath, but there is a clear dichotomy between them in the way that they encounter us. Bernard was justified therefore in describing mercy and judgment as the two feet of God. They are feet that are united in the single person of their owner but that we encounter to some extent separately. The lesson that Bernard draws from this — that sorrow for sin be tempered by remembrance of God's mercy to avoid despair; that contemplation of God's mercy be tempered with remembrance of his judgment to avoid lukewarm negligence — is in harmony with the balance of the teaching of the Bible.

One further way of holding together wrath and love needs to be considered. There is a surprising consensus of opinion that God's wrath is the obverse, converse, or reverse side of his love. Wrath is but love spurned.[116] As Brunner puts it, "the wrath of God under which the idolatrous, sinfully perverted man stands is simply the divine love, which has become a force opposed to him who has turned against God. The wrath of God is the love of God, in the form in which the man who has turned away from God and turned against God, experiences it, as indeed, thanks to the holiness of God, he must and ought to experience it."[117]

How true is this? As with so many other such sayings, it is partly true.

---

114. Cf. n. 107 above.

115. Cf. N. M. de S. Cameron, ed., *Universalism and the Doctrine of Hell* (Carlisle: Paternoster; Grand Rapids: Baker, 1993), the papers from the 1991 Edinburgh Conference in Christian Dogmatics. If this view is accepted, it can be said that God's wrath is not eternal (contrary to Lactantius, *A Treatise on the Anger of God* 21) but that it has eternal consequences. Stählin, "ὀργή," in *TDNT*, 5:433-34, wrestles with this issue. Those who hold to eternal torment need to consider Jonathan Edwards's sermon on Rev. 18:20, in which he explains how the righteous forever rejoice without pity in the torments of the lost (*Select Works*, 2:245-65). Edwards clearly knew what he was talking about because the editors describe this as "the substance of two posthumous discourses"!

116. Baird, *The Justice of God*, p. 72; R. P. C. Hanson, *God*, pp. 42, 47-48; Nygren, *Agape and Eros*, I:74-75; Stewart, *A Man in Christ*, pp. 220-21; Stählin, "ὀργή," in *TDNT*, 5:425, 428; J. W. Wenham, *The Goodness of God* (Leicester: Inter-Varsity Press, 1974), p. 69. It is not being suggested that all of these writers mean the same thing by this language.

117. Brunner, *Man in Revolt*, p. 187.

Judgment is according to one's response to the love of God in Jesus Christ (John 3:16-21, 36). But why is this? It might appear that God's judgment is no more than the macabre revenge of a jilted suitor. If wrath is nothing more than rejected love, God is open to the following charge: "Why does he get so angry, then, when we just want to be left alone?"[118] But there is more to the story than simply jilted love. We are God's creatures and owe him our love and obedience. We are sinful people who have been "bought at a price" (1 Cor. 6:20). We are not autonomous beings receiving overtures of love from a neo-Marcionite God who has no more claims upon us than the romantic affections of a stranger. The love that is being spurned is the love of Creator for creature, of the One who has redeemed us at great cost. To reject such love is to turn one's back upon one's only hope and to consign oneself to wrath and judgment.

Some of the authors whom we have considered seem to feel that it is impossible for love and anger to coexist. Far more profound is P. T. Forsyth: "True love is quite capable of being angry, and must be angry and even sharp with its beloved children." "For He can be really angry only with those He loves."[119] Although A. T. Hanson insists that in the biblical teaching on God's wrath the idea of discipline is *almost* totally absent,[120] there may be some value in considering the disciplining of a child as an analogy. Suppose a child willfully and maliciously hurts another child. In what way is the disciplining of that child an expression of love? It expresses the parent's love for righteousness and detestation of cruelty. It expresses love for the victim in the form of concern for what has been done. It expresses love for the perpetrator in that it is intended as discipline. Finally, it expresses love for society in the disciplining of the child. Those who let undisciplined children loose on society show not love but lack of concern for their children and even greater lack of concern for their future victims in the rest of society.

The social implications apply also to God's wrath, which must not be understood in purely individual terms. "The love of God is not just good affections, but it can be expressed as wrath and jealousy," notes H. G. L. Peels. He continues to observe that a ruler would not be showing love for

118. Posed by Kvanvig, *The Problem of Hell*, p. 107.

119. Forsyth, *The Work of Christ*, pp. 105, 243; cf. pp. 118-19. Cf. Amos 3:2: "You only have I chosen . . . *therefore* I will punish you."

120. A. T. Hanson, *The Wrath of the Lamb*, pp. 39, 180. He sees exceptions in Ps. 6:1 and 1 Cor. 10:13.

his people if he were to allow an enemy to run roughshod over them.[121] Lactantius also emphasizes that the wrath of God is needed to maintain good order in society,[122] which is incumbent upon God if he is loving. Paul, of course, teaches that God's wrath functions in part through the organs of law and order (Rom. 13:4-5).[123] The claim that God's wrath is an expression of love is wider than the claim that it expresses love for its victim. It is also an expression of God's love for other human beings. There may be situations, such as with God's wrath against the impenitent in the final judgment, where wrath expresses love without expressing love for its object.

The love of God and the wrath of God are not ultimately in contradiction, but there is a tension between them. "The proclamation concerning the living God ultimately and finally defies a logical systematization."[124] This does not prevent us from exploring the correlation between God's wrath and his love, but it does warn us against imagining that we have completed the task.

---

121. Peels, *The Vengeance of God*, p. 293.

122. Lactantius, *A Treatise on the Anger of God* 17-18, 21, 23.

123. Cf. Stählin, "ὀργή," in *TDNT*, 5:440-41 on this passage. This implies a divine mandate for the penal activities of the state (which is not, of course, to deny that this mandate can be abused). The modern trend, therefore, of treating corporal punishment as no different from the violence of the offender or capital punishment as no different from murder is profoundly mistaken. If corporal punishment is just "hitting" and capital punishment is mere "killing," then it follows that fining offenders is mere "theft" and imprisoning them is just "kidnapping." The argument concerned is anarchistic in force and undermines all authority of the state to punish. The rejection of *this* argument against corporal and capital punishment does not, of course, imply that there are not other more coherent arguments to be considered.

124. Peels, *The Vengeance of God*, p. 294.

CHAPTER 8

Can God Love the World?

PAUL HELM

All Christians give great attention to such claims as that God is love, that God loves everyone, and that God loves the world. In this essay I shall examine aspects of such claims and particularly the interplay between the roles of natural and revealed theology in addressing them. I shall argue that considerations drawn from natural theology can help us in drawing conclusions about the intensity and distribution of the love of God.

There are various ways in which the question that forms the title of this essay might be understood.

It might be thought that the question could be quickly answered, at least by a Judeo-Christian theist. Since God *does* love the world, he *can* love it. But, as we shall see, "the world" may be understood in a rather different way from that implied in such an answer. Or the question could be understood in a quasi-psychological sense, as in, Can God *bring himself* to love the world? But I shall not be understanding the question in this sense either.

The question is also likely to call to mind in Christians some or all of the following: the exact meaning of John 3:16; the free offer of the gospel;

I am grateful to the members of the Research Seminar in the Philosophy of Religion at King's College as well as to members of the Dogmatics Conference, and especially to Dr. Patrick Richmond and Angela Helm, for helpful suggestions on an earlier draft of this essay.

168

whether the phrase "sufficient for all, efficient for the elect" is defensible on scriptural grounds; whether besides God's special grace to the church there is a general or common grace extended to all people; and the question of annihilationism and universalism.

Our question also calls to mind the problem of evil. Is there evidence that God loves the world? Can a world containing so much sin and evil be reasonably said to be loved by God? Or is the evidence mixed? And if it is mixed, what does this show us about the character of God? Even if we are able to conclude that a world containing so much evil can nevertheless have been created by God, there is the additional question of whether, if God is a God of love, he could or ought to have created and expressed his love in creating a better world than the one that he did in fact create.

This essay steers clear of all such questions. One reason is that I do not believe that at present I have anything to contribute to the further elucidation or resolution of such knotty issues. Further, such territory is well traversed and well worn; a variety of views has been canvassed, and most of these views are well known, their strengths and weaknesses well rehearsed.

Instead I intend to exercise a philosopher's privilege and investigate some more general conceptual features that lie in the background of all these debates, and to do this (again claiming a philosopher's privilege) in a particularly crude and simplistic way in order to highlight what I believe to be one of the basic issues in such debates, but doing so from a different angle than those represented by any of the questions I mentioned at the outset.

I. SOME ASSUMPTIONS

In what follows I shall start by taking "the world" distributively to mean: nothing but each human being past, present, and future. That is, for our purposes "the world" is simply a list of all individual human beings, each contingently related to the other.

This assumption is certainly questionable, as most assumptions are. For could not "the world" refer to the human species, rather than the individual members of the species? And could not evils such as decay and death be thought of as necessary for the good of the species as a whole, even though they are visited somewhat unequally on its individual members? So perhaps we should consider ourselves primarily as members of some collective, such as the human species, or a particular nation, or race, or church, or that ever-elusive "community" which politicians as well as religious leaders talk about. Perhaps we should think of the distribution of individual goods and evils as subordinate to some such collective. Perhaps God can love the world without loving every element in the world, as Augustine thought.[1]

Such an individualist approach also assumes away Leibnizianism, for example, for Leibniz held that it is impossible to think of any individual, or any class of individuals, in abstraction from all the other features of the world, including all other individuals in the world. It also assumes away all views of the world that we might roughly call "organic" — for instance, any view of the world that makes positive use of the doctrine of internal relations, albeit in a weaker sense than that of Leibniz.

So by "the world" I mean the set of particular people, individual human beings such as you and me; I shall take it for granted, at least for the time being, that while in fact we are related to other human beings, and to other individuals of countless kinds, these relations are for the most part contingent relations. What this means is that we could exist as the people we are in different circumstances, at different times and places, for example, than the ones in which we in fact find ourselves.

This, at least, is to be the assumption that forms our starting point. We shall shortly be forced to modify it, I believe, but without needing to go all the way to collectivism. Making these assumptions about the relations that hold between human beings is not to say that the existence of other human beings is not necessary for the psychological and spiritual growth of any one human being; and more importantly for the rest of our discussion, what we have already assumed is quite compatible with the idea that one of the chief ways in which the divine benevolence might be estimated is through the character of the interrelations between human beings.

God's love for the animate but nonhuman creation, and for the non-animate creation and for the spiritual world, will not be our concern. This is not to say that God does not or might not love such categories of creatures, but I choose to focus on human beings in this way to make the discussion simpler than it would otherwise be. In any case, I do not think that referring to the nonhuman creation would make much difference to the issue that I wish to discuss. In the main part of the essay I shall particularly

1. Augustine, *Confessions* VII.13.

have in mind all human beings up the time of their bodily death, though occasionally postmortem considerations will surface.

One further assumption is that I shall take the "love" of God to be his benevolence; it is not the love that is associated with admiration and loyalty, nor erotic love. Benevolence here understood I shall take to be an essential property of God, or a manifestation of an essential property. I shall leave open the question of whether such benevolence is ever deserved or merited, of whether every act of God's benevolence that human beings at present experience is also an exercise of his grace and mercy, or whether only some acts are. I think that when people claim that God is love it is love in this sense of benevolence that they have, or have chiefly, in mind.

A benevolent human person is one who wills the benefit or welfare or good of his fellows, insofar as this is within his power, and I shall assume that the benevolence of God bears some direct relationship of meaning to such human benevolence. It would be absurd to suppose that divine benevolence bore no or only little resemblance to human benevolence, but I shall not enquire further as to the similarities and differences. Nor shall I distinguish, as we sometimes do, between benevolence and beneficence. Willing and doing are, for God, if not the same thing, then very nearly so.

Further, I shall assume that God is the creator and the upholder of all that he has created, including all human life. I shall also impute to God a strong measure of control over his creation; this is to my mind one implication of seeing God as the upholder of what he has created, though I do not think that the issue of control or of its absence will enter very deeply into the discussion that is to follow.

Finally, I shall assume that divine benevolence can be measured or estimated, that it is readily identifiable. It does not matter for our purposes whether or not it can be measured exactly, but it is clearly necessary to be able to sensibly address such questions as which of two situations is or might be a greater expression of the benevolence of God and so to assume that some rough and ready ordinal measure of God's benevolence can be attempted; for instance, it is necessary that we be able to sensibly attempt to say of two situations that, other things being equal, one is a better expression of God's love than the other. A lot hangs, of course, on the other things being equal here, but I take it that if we could never in principle say that one situation is a better expression of God's love than another, then we could not sensibly discuss the love of God in relation to the world.

So much for this rather lengthy set of assumptions that forms the preface to this essay. Bearing these in mind we shall ask two questions: (1) Can God be benevolently loving to all human beings? (2) Can God be *equally* benevolent to all human beings? You will note that we are not to be concerned with whether in fact God *is* benevolently loving to all human beings but with whether he *could be*. For if he could not be, then he is not. If he could be, then whether he is or not is partly a question of what the facts are, something that falls outside the philosopher's province. Nevertheless, these questions are not wholly abstract and philosophical, for in asking questions about the love of God we shall be asking these in relation to human beings, to actual human beings, not Martians.

II. CAN GOD BE BENEVOLENTLY LOVING TO ALL HUMAN BEINGS?

I wish, somewhat unusually you may think, to approach this question as an exercise in sketching the conceptual lineaments of the relation between Creator and his human creatures, the contours that any such relation, including a relation of love, must have. I shall not be concerned with what the Christian religion or any other religion dogmatically asserts to be the relation and character of God's love to his human creation, but with sketching the possible character of such love.

So our first question is, Could God be said to benevolently uphold all human beings, notwithstanding the very varied material and other conditions in which they as a matter of fact exist? Let us pose the question more narrowly. Some individual human beings live such brief and tragic lives that we might say that all that they enjoy, if this is the correct word to use here, is a brief span of consciousness. So we might rephrase our question this way: Is conscious, sentient human life, of however short a span, itself a good, an expression of the benevolence of the Creator, such that whatever else might be true of someone who has consciousness it is reasonable to conclude that sentient life is overall upheld by divine benevolence? Is conscious, sentient life, that is to say, an outweighing good, a good that outweighs all evils? In focusing attention on conscious, sentient life I am not assuming that a benevolent God wishes above all the happiness of men and women. I make no such assumption, either here or in what follows. But conscious, sentient life seems to be important because it is a necessary condition of a worthwhile life however worthwhileness is defined. Is there a threshold of human experience such as that of enjoying a conscious, sentient life such that we can reasonably say that any person who has this experience is benevolently loved by God, no matter what else that person does or what else happens to that person?

One might maintain that there is a threshold but question whether consciousness itself is the threshold, the sort of thing that is an appropriate expression of divine benevolence. For perhaps there are different, more spiritual states the creation of which are better expressions of such benevolence, and which would form more appropriate thresholds. Perhaps there are. But I shall take it that consciousness, while not only a good in itself, is also a necessary condition of any other such spiritual state for that person; hence its centrality to our discussion. It is therefore a plausible candidate for being a threshold. Setting mere consciousness or conscious, sentient life as the threshold has the advantage of placing that threshold low enough and at a point we can all recognize.

Does it make sense to say of any individual who lives or has lived that it would have been better, *better overall as regards the divine benevolence,* if that person had not existed? Perhaps some may conclude that with respect to many individuals who have lived and died it would have been better *for those very individuals* had they not been born, that though they enjoyed a brief spell of consciousness this is outweighed by suffering that they endured during that spell. Others may regard the passing of such judgments as at worst blasphemous and at best an impertinence.

But our present concern is not with the question of whether it would have been better *for that individual* had he or she not been born, but with whether the world without that person would have been a better expression or exhibition *of divine benevolence* than, *ceteris paribus,* a world with him or her? In other words, does every birth of a conscious human being, no matter what the subsequent pre-mortem life of that human being may be, further express and so add to the increment of divine benevolence toward the world? Is the expression of divine benevolence correlated in some way with the numbers of conscious human beings who exist, for however brief a span? Or might there be a given number of human beings such that if more than that number were created the total of divine benevolence would not increase but decline? Could the law of diminishing returns apply with respect to the creation of human beings? Or is it the case that no matter to what degree existing human beings are disadvantaged by the arrival of a further human being, and assuming that such a disadvantage counts against divine benevolence, the arrival of a new human being necessarily increases the increment of those goods which are an expression of divine benevolence?

It is not obvious to me that the answer to all these questions must be "yes."

We may take an even more individualistic view of the same matter. Suppose an individual lived in a barely conscious and painful state for the few weeks of her existence, but was then transposed into unutterable divine bliss and personal fulfillment in the divine presence. Questions might be raised here about the wisdom of such an arrangement and/or about its morality. It might be wondered why a short, sharp period of conscious suffering was a necessary preliminary to the bliss. But could there be any doubt that such a person's life was overall the result of and an expression of divine benevolence? So perhaps we ought not readily to conclude that a brief human life is not an expression of divine benevolence, especially if we take into account the life beyond the grave (of which life more later).

Note that it is not being argued that bare consciousness is not an expression of divine benevolence. It may be that the very fact of consciousness is evidence that God loves that individual. On the other hand it may be said that bare consciousness could not itself be an expression of divine benevolence, but rather that it is a necessary precondition of such benevolence. On this question we will keep an open mind.

So what are we to conclude? Assuming that it is not an impertinence even to raise the question, perhaps the most we can say is that it is not obvious that the arrival in the world of another human being is not a further expression of divine benevolence, and also that it is not obvious that it is. So perhaps God could be loving to all human beings, and perhaps he is, for perhaps conscious existence for however short a time is itself an indelible expression of that love.

III. CAN GOD BE EQUALLY BENEVOLENT TO ALL?

This question is usually or often addressed in the following way: Is God's character, his benevolence in this case, such that he *must* be equally benevolent? That is, is equality built into divine benevolence such that a benevolent God must be equal in willing well-being to each of his human creatures? And is the divine benevolence, thus understood, also to be understood as effective? Are we to understand that God could not be benevolent unless each of his human creatures enjoyed his benevolence to an equal extent? Or is God's character such that he may be equally benevolent, and even that he necessarily intends to be equally benevolent, but that he is nevertheless thwarted by human sin, or human freedom, or some other factor or factors? It seems to me that each of these questions is worth discussing.

But I want to approach the issue of the love of God from another point of view, namely this: Is human life as we know it such that God *could* reasonably be said to uphold all human beings equally benevolently? I have in mind such humdrum facts as the following: that some people are male and some are female; that some are born at earlier periods of human history than others; and that the child of a pair of parents necessarily cannot be their parent. Some people live in warm climates, others in temperate ones, and so on. Some live near the sea, while others never see it. Some are intelligent, some stupid; some weak, some strong; some healthy, some diseased.

Notice that these are what we might call natural facts about people in general. In any world that is recognizably similar to our world, these differences will manifest themselves. Perhaps there are possible worlds in which there are people, though not presumably human beings, who have no parents, worlds in which everyone who lives does so for exactly the same length of time, and in which no one lives any earlier or later than any other and no one becomes diseased. But our world is not such a world, nor could it be, in the sense that it could not contain a race of people who were not recognizably similar to ourselves in at least these respects.

Perhaps there could be sentient and intelligent beings who are, strictly speaking, not members of a race but are created individually, each member similar to the others but not begotten by another member or members, motherless and fatherless like Adam and Eve. But our world is not like that; there is a human race, and it seems to be a necessary feature of being human that one has an inherited genetic structure — unless, that is, one is either Adam or Eve.

Of course, it is extremely difficult to establish what are and are not essential facts about human nature; it is easy to confuse what is uniformly true of human beings with what is necessarily true. But if having a genetic inheritance is not necessarily true of any human being we may be reasonably confident that there are some other asymmetrical properties which are essential.

Similarly, there are possible worlds in which landmasses are symmetrical, people enjoy precisely the same climate and each individual is equidistant from the sea, and people are equally strong, intelligent, and wise. But our world is not like such worlds. And as with space, so with time. Our world has one history, certain people and events occurring before others. So even if the world were radically different from the way it is, there would still be respects in which human beings were differently placed from each other, literally so. For each of us occupies a unique spatial and temporal position.

We may be able to imagine a population of individuals each indistinguishable from the other except in terms of position, and each of which simply records in its consciousness the fact of such positions. This might be a population of individuals each of whom is the subject of divine benevolence equally or indifferently in comparison with any other. But such benighted beings could hardly constitute a human race, nor would the individuals in question resemble human beings in significant ways.

Matters go deeper even than this. Each human being is an individual, with an individual consciousness and memory and an individual set of intentions. This is so even if we allow that consciousness is socially conditioned, or even socially created. And it is so even if for the moment we abstract from considerations of moral freedom and evil choice. Because I live later than Napoleon, necessarily he cannot remember the things that I remember; because he lived earlier than me, he could make plans that necessarily I cannot make; and so on. And these deep facts about human life would apply even in a universe that was like ours but was free of sin and evil. For even if we held the view, which many do hold on various theological grounds, that the distribution of goods and evils is the result of moral evil, the differences that I have been discussing would nevertheless still be present.

So is the very principle of the discernibility of non-identicals, however that principle is to be understood in detail, at odds with a uniform distribution of divine benevolence? Is the relationality that one human being necessarily has to other human beings logically incompatible with a uniformity of divine benevolence?

In raising these questions I am suggesting that even aside from the usually discussed questions of evil brought about by human choice, questions that currently tend to dominate the issue of the extension and inten-

sity of God's benevolence, there is reason to think that, in any world rele-
vantly similar to our own, God *could not* treat all people equally, and
therefore he could not distribute his benevolence with undeviating uniformity to all human creatures. And if he logically could not so distribute his
benevolence, then clearly he could not be required to do so.

IV. FOUR REPLIES

It seems to me that there are four types of reply to the line of argument
that I have been deploying. I shall call these, respectively, the *dualist option,*
the *creationist option,* the *eschatological option,* and the *objection from divine suffering.*

The Dualist Option

The dualist option is as follows. It might be granted that the public facts
about the human condition are broadly as I have expressed them, but it
may be argued that they do not matter. Such facts are irrelevant to considering the question of whether God is equally benevolent in his upholding
because what matters to God, and what are equally benevolently intended
and effected by God, are matters of the spirit. It may be objected that I have
been concerned with matters of the body but that the benevolence of God
is concerned with matters of the spirit, and these matters of the body do
not touch matters of the spirit.

This view would be, or would entail, a particularly strong form of
mind-body dualism. Ordinary mind-body dualism, as we might call it,
asserts that the body and the mind are two categorically different substances in parallel, or in an occasional relationship, or in causal interaction. The dualist option that we are considering, in order to save divine
equi-benevolence, seems to be very extreme, for it appears to assert not
only that, in usual dualist fashion, minds and bodies are categorically different, but that the mind is not, and perhaps cannot be, significantly affected by considerations arising from embodiment in a spatio-temporal
matrix. And this looks weird, strongly counterintuitive and counter-
factual. For belief, for example, is a strong component of all aspects of the
conscious life. And many of our beliefs are about, or partly about, or af-

fected by, or partly affected by, the spatio-temporal matrix in which our embodied selves are placed.

So it looks as if the dualist option could logically work but does not represent an attractive possibility. However, an ultra-dualist position is conceivable, and it might be expressed as follows.

Many of us, perhaps, will have had the experience of being in the presence of a demented old person, someone who can neither speak intelligibly nor comprehend speech. There is a strong temptation, in such situations, to suppose that these failures are akin to dumbness and deafness and that deep down a mental life continues, untroubled by the surface failures of speech and hearing, a mental life continuous with the life enjoyed when there were intelligent hearing and speech. If one were an ultra-dualist, one might surmise that we are all in the same position we are supposing the demented person to be in, and that divine benevolence is not expressed on the surfaces of our lives, but deep down — that whatever the brokenness of the surface, the depths remain intact and whole.

Ingenious and in a way relieving as such a hypothesis might be, it is of course fantastic. It is fantastic in the sense that we have no reason to think that there are such unbroken deep mental lives, and it is fantastic to suppose that if there were they, and not conscious life, would be the unique locus and focus of divine benevolence.

One might apply a similar argument to God himself, but unfortunately with similar results. For it may be said that divine benevolence is purely a matter of divine intention. Just as there are intentional theories of human ethics, so there can be intentionalist theories of the divine moral character. So it may be that God's intention is similarly benevolent to all his human creatures, but that this intention is, and remains, deep down, and that on the surface he either will not nor cannot express his equibenevolence. This may be so. But if it is so this of course reflects extremely adversely on another divine characteristic, namely divine power. It makes the ascription of both benevolence and omnipotence to God extremely implausible.

It also falls foul of another assumption that we have not so far mentioned but that seems to be extremely plausible, namely, that in order to be benevolently loved by God a human being must at some point or other be conscious or aware of the fact that he or she is benevolently loved by God. Perhaps this assumption requires the postulation of an afterlife of consciousness.

The Creationist Option

I understand that in earlier times excitement was caused by a controversy in Christian theology between the creationists and the traducianists. Creationists held that each human soul was created immediately by God at an appropriate time in the gestation of each human fetus. Traducianists held that human souls were no more or less the product of natural parental generation than were hearts and brains. It might be supposed that God ensures, if not equal benevolence, then fair benevolence, by pursuing the creationist option in the following way.

Suppose that each soul is a Reidian or Swinburnian self, the identity of which is metaphysically simple. And suppose further that God has decreed to create N such selves. We might suppose that God, recognizing the facts about necessary inequality to which we have drawn attention, allocates souls to bodies randomly, by throwing dice. As far as the creation of individual people is concerned, God permits himself to shelter behind a veil of ignorance. Then it would follow that though God foreknows that there will be an embodied soul living in good health and having a reasonable degree of intelligence, which person is embodied in this particular body, whether it is P1 or P11, say, is entirely the result of random selection.

You may think that this talk of God juggling souls and bodies is incredibly crude — and so it is. I certainly do not wish to defend either its moral or its theological propriety. Nevertheless, such a thought experiment seems to me to have two merits: it brings out in a stark way what might be involved in God's equal beneficence; and though not itself defensible, if it were defensible it would provide a clear sense in which God could be equally beneficent, or more exactly, not unfairly beneficent, in a created order that contains the significant asymmetries that our order does.

But not defending it, or regarding it as indefensible, has the following consequences, it seems to me: any relation of the soul to the body that is more unified than the dualism I have been using earlier would appear to reduce the scope for equal benevolence on the part of God. For any more unified account of the relation between soul and body, or between the spiritual and the physical, any account that makes the character of the spiritual essentially depend on that of the physical body — in respect, say, of intelligence, or moral fiber or whatever — would mean that the scope for divine equal benevolence is reduced to vanishing point.

One might meet this criticism in either or both of two ways. One might, to start with, modify the idea of the fairness in question. And one might, secondly, re-think the concept of benevolence.

One might make the notion of fairness refer not, as we have so far, to exact equality of treatment, but to a more proportional account of equality. Usually, when the differential effects of God's benevolence are considered, this is put down to the effect of human free will, or to some other explanation of the lack of causal efficacy in the divine benevolence. God holds back his benevolence, as it were, or cannot for some reason make his benevolent intentions equally efficacious for all. But there may be other possible explanations of such a differential.

Recognizing the fact that the life starting points of people differ, one might pursue this question: Could God love all people on an equal compensation principle? Or could God love all people on a case by case basis? Let us take each of these questions in turn.

First, let us consider love on an equal compensation principle. On this principle, those to whom little will be given are to be loved much, and those to whom much is given will be loved correspondingly less — the intention of such compensation, as with redistributive taxation, being to make the outcomes more equal than the starting positions. That is, one might construe benevolence as some construe justice, in terms of an equal outcome; the equality of divine benevolence would then be measured in terms of whether the outcomes of all were equal. On this view God loves all men and women equally if all end up being equally benevolently loved by God.

The problem with such an argument is not that there is a logical barrier to its occurring, but that there is no persuasive empirical evidence that it is at work, no evidence that people whose life chances are poor are generally compensated — not at least in this life, though there are plenty of cases of people responding to adversity in remarkable ways. But in general the poor are not exalted, nor are the rich sent empty away.

But perhaps, as was suggested earlier, God's goodness is known, not through the provision of bodily states, nor in conditions involving bodily states, but in interior states that are not correlated with the bodily, that neither cause nor are caused by bodily states, so that each of us enjoys equality of treatment before God irrespective of our physical particularities. The problem with this suggestion is that there is no evidence that it is true.

But perhaps we should think of such an account of divine benevolence in terms of immediate compensation. Perhaps a mite of a human being starving to death in Somalia is at the same time experiencing spiritual ecstasies — a sense of nearness to God, union with him, and all the bliss and blessing that this signifies. Perhaps. It would certainly be a marvelous thing if that were true, even more marvelous if it were universally or uniformly true for all starving human mites. But alas there is no evidence that it is true.

Some might say that even if it were true there *could* not be evidence that it was true. But I think that this would be a little hasty. Leaving aside the question of whether such ecstasies could be reported were they to occur, each of us could provide some evidence by examining his or her own case. Do you have evidence that your spiritual state compensates your bodily state in some regular and uniform way?

Let us consider, then, a second kind of proportionality. It might be argued that since each of us is in a unique metaphysical position, the divine benevolence is targeted to each of us in rather the way in which a human parent may attempt to be equally benevolent to her children, not by treating them exactly the same, but by treating them deliberately differently.

This may be the case. Certainly it is logically possible and makes good sense. But, as with the earlier kind of proportionality, there does not seem to be much empirical evidence for it; or rather, there may be much empirical evidence for it, but also much evidence against. It is hard to see how it could be plausibly argued that the human mites starving to death in Somalia are being dealt with on such a principle of proportional benevolence.

The Eschatological Option

Many have thought, and have said, that heaven will be a compensation for earthly inequalities, such that all will in the end be found to have been treated with equal benevolence by God. God's benevolence comes in two installments: the first installment in this life, the second in the life to come, with the second complementing the first. The poor are made rich in their second installment, the rich poorer, if not poor, and so on. The meek shall inherit the regenerated earth. And when the accounts are finally totted up all will be seen to have received equal rations of divine beneficence. But quite aside from the problem of why in the first place God should choose to operate an installment plan, there are problems with this; the second installment, on most views of heaven, is everlasting, and hence would necessarily be an *over*compensation for earthly riches or poverty, for beauty or ugliness.

One might argue that since heaven is unbounded in time, it necessarily compensates for any earthly ill, which is necessarily temporal, and that anyone in heaven is the object of divine benevolence equal to anyone else in heaven, no matter what their pre-mortem differences. While this may be mathematically attractive, it seems unrealistic to say that a starving Somalian mite and a well-heeled Westerner are treated equally if both enjoy heaven.

But even leaving to one side this idea of heaven as an eternity of bliss, there is still inequality between two individuals, one of whom has pain and then pleasure, the other of whom has pleasure and then pain, even if the sums of pain and pleasure that each has exactly tally.

The Objection from the Nature of Divine Suffering

Finally, let us consider the objection from the nature of divine suffering.

It may be suggested that throughout this discussion we have been construing divine benevolence too activistically, as consisting in possible plans for human benevolence that God may implement. It may be said that what is equally if not more important is to think of such benevolence passively, in terms of God's identification with suffering humanity. Then we should seek for evidence of such benevolence, not in terms of the alleviation of suffering, but in solidarity with it.

There seem to me to be at least two difficulties with this interesting suggestion. For even if we were to redefine benevolence in this way — and it is certainly plausible to suppose that it is at least an aspect of benevolence — it would not overcome the chief difficulties we have encountered. In the first place, it would not overcome the fact of the inequality, and perhaps the necessary inequality, of the human condition. Perhaps God identifies with the suffering in Somalia. Does that mean that he identifies less with the well-heeled of the West? If so, the problem of the differentiality of his love, the differences in his solidarity with suffering, remains. And second, even if we suppose such solidarity, we still need some evidence that God is actually in solidarity with the suffering in Somalia. Is there such evidence?

These points, if they are valid, seem to be equally valid against any re-definition of benevolence.

So I suggest, on the basis of these arguments, that God could not be equally benevolent to all human beings.

V. SOME CONCLUSIONS

I wish to draw some conclusions from this discussion.

The first is this: that the argument I have put forward strongly supports a more organic view of the human creation (I continue to leave to one side here the character of the non-human creation) than that suggested by mere individualism. By mere individualism I mean the view that had any person who does exist failed to exist, or been some other person, the lives of the remaining individuals would have been more or less as they are. This seems to me to be a false view, and a view whose falsity is further established by the argument above.

But even if one disliked organic or other collective views of humanity, one might still take the view that the object of God's love is the world, not because it is an organic unity, but simply in virtue of the fact that it is the one creation of God. God loves the world, his one creation, but it does not follow from this that he loves each element equally, and perhaps he cannot do so. As Aquinas put it, "God, and nature, and indeed every causal agent, does what is best overall, but not what is best in every part, except when the part is regarded in its relationship to the whole."[2]

A second conclusion is that it is implausible to put down all substantive differences in the life situations of people — the evidence provided by which we might take as evidence for divine benevolence, or the lack of it — to expressions of human free will. For if God could not in any case have created men and women equal, and if such inequality is an evil, or a sufficient condition for evil, then this is not an evil that can be put down to free will.

Another way of putting this point is as follows. In discussing the problem of evil a conventional distinction is drawn between natural and moral evil, between evil that is the result of naturally occurring forces not including human choices, and those evils for which human choices are necessary.

---

2. Thomas Aquinas, *Summa Theologiae* 1.48.2, reply 3.

But if human inequalities are evil per se, or are causally sufficient for some evils, then the distinction between these two kinds of evil becomes extremely blurred. For among the "natural" evils are inequalities of moral significance, inequalities in the character and status of persons; these evils do not require human choices for their occurrence but constrain and even determine human choices, and certainly constrain human beliefs, in a way in which earthquakes and plagues of locusts may not.

A third conclusion is that it follows that if inequality is a sufficient condition for some evils, or is per se an evil, then the "problem of evil" can be only a matter of degree. For some inequalities, and so some evils, are logically necessary given the creation of this world or anything comparable to it. The conflict between egalitarians and inegalitarians is usually a conflict over what ought to be the case, or what may be the case: are social inequalities morally permissible, and so need not be eliminated; or are they obligatory, and so morally ought not to be eliminated? If there are significant inequalities that logically cannot be eliminated, then no possible world containing human beings could express divine equi-benevolence between them, so that Judeo-Christian theists must be inegalitarians.

It may be said that while the logic of this position is sound, the fact of the matter is that the inequalities that are logically necessary are small and insignificant, and that the inequalities that do matter, that loom large in discussion of the problem of evil — the inequalities of class or race or gender or health or wealth or religion, for example — are by comparison large and significant, and that the problem of evil, certainly the problem of moral evil, is a problem that clusters exclusively around these differences. It can readily be granted that the inequalities just mentioned are significant, but it would be rash, I believe, to conclude that they are the only significant inequalities and that the inequalities of temporal or spatial location, of geography and history, as well as the inequalities of genetic inheritance, are as a consequence unimportant.

VI. A FINAL WORD

This discussion has been particularly crude and simplistic, even materialistic, you may think — the sort of thing that might well be expected from a philosopher, but not the sort of thing that amounts to a serious contribution to the subject of the love of God. Let me try to convince you otherwise on this point by drawing one significant conclusion about the love of God from what I have been trying to say.

I have been trying to sketch what the character of the love of God must be, given certain well-known facts about human nature. At the outset I said that it was not my intention to debate the usual theological questions about the extent and intensity of the divine love for sinners. But it may be that the conclusion of this essay, if sound, does have a bearing on these questions after all.

For if the benevolent love of God cannot be equally distributed, then neither can the saving love of God in Christ be equally distributed — unless of course the facts to which I have drawn attention are somehow irrelevant to how the saving love of God in Christ can be manifested. And it is hard to see how this could be, hard to see how the empirical, manifest differences among human beings have nothing whatsoever to do with the saving love of God in Christ. It seems obvious that there must be some relationship between the two. For example, either the saving love of Christ is correlated with such empirically identifiable differences, or it compensates for them, or there is some more complex relationship between them.

So the structure of the above discussion has, I suggest, that of an *a fortiori* argument. I have been arguing that some central facts about human nature and human experience forbid us to take the view that the love of God is equally experienced by all people. So this essay has been an exercise in natural theology, though, you may think, natural theology of an unusually depressing kind. But if the argument is valid then the conclusion of this piece of natural theology provides a control — a hermeneutic, if you like — for our understanding and appreciation of Christian revealed theology.

If the benevolent love of God must be unequally distributed, then *a fortiori* any other love of God must be as well. That is, if the above argument is sound, we are forbidden by it to conclude, in advance of the exegesis of a single text of Scripture, that God loves all men and women equally. It may allow us to conclude, however, that he loves all men and women unequally.

CHAPTER 9

Will the Love of God Finally Triumph?

DAVID FERGUSSON

The love of God, as it is described in the language of the Bible, produces a history. It is the history of creation, and in particular of Israel and the church. Since this is neither a static state nor a cyclical process, but a story with an anticipated ending, the love of God demands an eschatology. We cannot understand the New Testament and the message of Jesus in particular without reference to the end of history that the love of God will guarantee. It is curious, therefore, that at a time in which biblical scholars and theologians have rediscovered the centrality of eschatology for the historical Jesus and for contemporary theology,[1] the imagery of heaven and hell has become strangely remote in both preaching and the Christian consciousness, at least in the affluent West.[2]

Sociologists and historians have linked this loss of eschatological orientation to the decline in the social significance of the church. T. C. Smout applies this plausibly to the fate of Presbyterianism in Scotland.

> Christianity since the beginning had centred on the life after death. If
> the Church was vague about it, men reached their own conclusions: if

1. E.g., M. Douglas Meeks, *Origins of the Theology of Hope* (Philadelphia: Fortress, 1974).

2. Cf. Lesslie Newbigin's comparison of East and West. "In the subsequent years of ministry in England I have often been asked: 'What is the greatest difficulty you face in moving from India to England?' I have always answered: 'The disappearance of hope'" (*The Other Side of 1984* [Geneva: WCC, 1984], p. 1).

there was a God, He was good: if He was good, He would send you to heaven or at least give you a second chance if you had made a mistake; if He would give you a second chance, it could not matter tremendously if you were a bit of an agnostic here and now, or didn't go too regularly to church. God was good. It would all come right in the end. As a piece of homespun logic this had considerable strength and consistency. It caused the death of hell, the liberation of many from psychological terrors, and the cooling of much fervour among the laity. The Church of Scotland by the mid-twentieth century still gave the impression of not quite knowing what had happened, or what it should do about it. How could a Protestant religion survive in its traditional forms if God was truly Love?[3]

Whatever our verdict on this social judgment, it seems clear that for both the theologian and the preacher the traditional imagery of heaven and hell has become problematic.[4] There may be several reasons for this. The traditional doctrine of hell as everlasting punishment for those who have not owned Christ in this life has become morally problematic, particularly with reference to cultures and religions in which the name of Christ has never been articulated. The late-nineteenth-century Declaratory Acts passed by the Presbyterian churches reveal that this problem has been acutely felt for over a century in Scotland. More recently, theologians have become sensitized to the Marxist criticism that the doctrine of heaven and hell is a demobilizing strategy. It distracts men and women from attending to the improvement of material conditions in this life with the prospect of

3. T. C. Smout, *A Century of the Scottish People 1830-1950* (London: Collins, 1986), p. 195. This assessment receives some confirmation from H. R. Mackintosh's comments in 1914: "If at this moment a frank and confidential plebiscite of the English-speaking ministry were taken, the likelihood is that a considerable majority would adhere to Universalism. They may no doubt shrink from it as a dogma, but they would cherish it privately as at least a hope" ("Studies in Christian Eschatology, VII, Universal Restoration," *The Expositor* 8 [1914]: 130, cited in Richard Bauckham, "Universalism: A Historical Survey," *Themelios* 4, no. 2 [1979]: 48). The recent *Lifestyle Survey* in Scotland claims: "the most commonly held view within the Church of Scotland sample is that 'we don't know what happens after death'; and in this respect, their views are virtually identical to those of non-church members" (*Lifestyle Survey* [Edinburgh: Board of Social Responsibility, 1987], p. 28).

4. The current unease on the doctrine of hell can probably be traced back to the seventeenth century. Cf. D. P. Walker, *The Decline of Hell: Seventeenth Century Discussions of Eternal Torment* (London: Routledge and Kegan Paul, 1964).

a better and more permanent existence in the next. Moreover, biblical resources encourage the church to adopt a more critical and engaged social witness. There are signs of a greater concern with life here and now, and correspondingly less preoccupation with any life to come. This is true even of much conservative piety, which looks for health and prosperity as a sign of God's favor in this world. Edward Dowey has commented on this ironical shift in popular piety. Whereas the writers of the Scots Confession in 1560 believed that it was the ungodly who enjoyed lives of uninterrupted pleasures rather than the beleaguered and discomfited elect, these roles have now been reversed in much contemporary Christian preaching.[5]

If the time is gone when the threat of hell can corral people into church attendance and provide an effective form of social control, then perhaps the church has to learn to express the significance of God's love for human life and conduct, a significance that is reflected in the hope of the world to come. How should this be done? I wish to argue that the triumph of divine love when considered eschatologically can be cast in three possible ways, and that, because the first two are unacceptable, some version of the third requires development.

I. LIMITING THE SCOPE OF GOD'S LOVE

In much Augustinian and Reformed theology the triumph of the love of God is secured by limiting its scope. For Augustine, the number of saints, destined to make good the shortfall in the kingdom of God caused by the fall of angels, is fixed. The subsequent drama of creation and redemption brings about a resurrection to glory of a definite number of human beings. The final explanation for this salvation of some and damnation of others is the eternal decree of God. This is justified morally by appeal to the order and richness of a universe in which the grace of God redeems a portion of the human race, leaving the remainder to their hellish but righteous sentence.

---

5. "One may be permitted to doubt if the road to hell is always so smoothly paved or the life of the reborn is always so battle-scarred as pictured in Chapter XIII. Curiously, the myth of much contemporary American piety practically reverses these pictures" (Edward Dowey, *A Commentary on the Confession of 1967 and an Introduction to the "Book of Confessions"* [Philadelphia: Westminster Press, 1968], p. 182).

As the Supreme Good, [God] made good use of evil deeds, for the damnation of those whom he had justly predestined to punishment and for the salvation of those whom he had mercifully predestined to grace.[6]

At the Reformation renewed emphasis upon the sovereignty of God and the depravity of human nature brought about a recovery of these Augustinian themes.[7] For Calvin, in his more polemical work on predestination, both the love and justice of God are manifested in the execution of the eternal decrees. The love of God is manifested in the gracious redemption of the elect and the justice of God in the conviction of the reprobate. In the mystery of election God has made some vessels of wrath according to merit and others vessels of mercy according to grace.[8] Thus Calvin can grimly quote Proverbs 16:4: "The Lord has made everything for a purpose, even the wicked for the day of trouble."[9]

Without dealing at length with this theological scheme, it is not difficult to see why it has occasioned much criticism. The determination of one's final destiny by a hidden and inscrutable decree of God undermines the intended comfort of the doctrine of predestination. Instead of providing pastoral assurance it leads inexorably to fear and uncertainty. Behind the grace of Christ toward sinners lurks uncertainty about the identity of those who are finally destined to be the recipients of that grace. This scheme appears also to render the love of God arbitrary, thus raising doubts about whether the essence of God can properly be described as love. It is at odds with the plain sense of Scripture that witnesses to God's love for all people in Jesus Christ. And it raises a difficult moral question about the character of God in so limiting the scope of his grace. We might argue that, since the condemnation of all is just, the deliverance of some merely tempers that justice with mercy, and that in any case divine justice is not to be measured by human justice (a line of defense employed by both Augustine and Calvin). Yet this only compounds the problem, as the following illustration of Stephen Davis reveals:

6. Augustine, *Enchiridion* 36, in *Library of Christian Classics,* vol. 2 (London: SCM, 1955), p. 399.

7. Yet their presence in late-medieval thought cannot now be overlooked. Cf. Heiko Oberman, *The Dawn of the Reformation* (Edinburgh: T. & T. Clark, 1986).

8. E.g., *Concerning the Eternal Predestination of God,* ed. J. K. S. Reid (Cambridge: Clark & Co, 1961), p. 126.

9. John Calvin, *Institutes* 3.23.6.

Suppose I discover that my two sons are both equally guilty of some wrong — say they both trampled some of my wife's beloved roses in the back yard. And suppose I say to one of them: "You are guilty and your punishment is that you will be confined to your room." And suppose I say to the other one: "You are equally guilty, but as a gift of love, I'm going to let you go without punishment." Surely it is obvious on the face of it that I have been unfair.[10]

II. UNIVERSALIZING THE SCOPE

If one locates the defect of this theological scheme in its limitation of the scope of God's love, then one might remedy this defect by universalizing that scope. This, in effect, is what happens in Karl Barth's modification of Calvin's doctrine of election through its greater Christological concentration. Jesus Christ is not merely the one through whom the divine decree is executed; he is also the one through whom that decree is framed. Included in the election of the Son is the election of all human beings for whom Christ lived and died. Having borne and cancelled our reprobation on the cross, Christ lives as the one in whom all are elect. Election is not a mixed message of joy and terror but a message of unequivocal celebration for all human beings. It is not predicated on the observation that some believe while others show a blithe disregard for the gospel. It is derived solely from the church's proclamation of Christ as the friend of sinners. It thus places pastoral assurance on a firmer theological foundation.

It is not a mixed message of joy and terror, salvation and damnation. Originally and finally it is not dialectical but non-dialectical. It does not proclaim in the same breath both good and evil, both help and destruction, both life and death. . . . In substance, therefore, the first and last word is Yes and not No.[11]

Although this doctrine of election is set out in *Church Dogmatics* II/2, the way had already been prepared for it by the discussion of the divine attributes in II/1. Here the grace and mercy of God are primary and are to be

10. Stephen Davis, "Universalism, Hell and the Fate of the Ignorant," *Modern Theology* 6, no. 2 (1990): 181.
11. Karl Barth, *Church Dogmatics* (Edinburgh: T. & T. Clark, 1956-75), II/2, pp. 12-13.

understood as including the divine holiness and righteousness. There is thus no prospect in Barth of a divorce between love and justice in God's character. Holiness and righteousness determine the ways in which it is appropriate to think of God's love as this has been revealed in the Old and New Testaments. Divine holiness is an aspect of God's transcendence over the creation in respect of which divine love bears the character of sheer grace when it is offered to the creature.[12] Divine righteousness is manifested in the covenant relationship through which God's forgiveness and his demand for penitence, praise, and obedience are revealed. Our understanding of what human justice entails derives from a knowledge of God's action in the life of his people.[13]

The eschatological consequence of this in Barth's theology is not entirely clear. It raises the prospect that the final number of God's people may be far greater than we might imagine. Barth's doctrine moves in a universalist direction, yet he denies that he is thereby committed to affirming an *apokatastasis*, a universal restoration. Yet how can universalism finally be avoided if both the sovereignty and universal scope of God's love have already been enacted once for all in Jesus Christ? Barth's strange answer is that we cannot impose a closure on God's sovereign freedom by postulating an *apokatastasis*. We cannot as it were tie God's hands in this way. Neither can we do so by explicitly denying universalism.

> It is His concern what is to be the final extent of the circle. If we are to respect the freedom of divine grace, we cannot venture the statement that it must and will finally be coincident with the world of man as such (as in the doctrine of the so-called apokatastasis). No such right or necessity can legitimately be deduced. Just as the gracious God does not need to elect or call any single man, so He does not need to elect or call all mankind. His election and calling do not give rise to any historical metaphysics, but only to the necessity of attesting them on the ground that they have taken place in Jesus Christ and His community. But, again, in grateful recognition of the grace of the divine freedom we cannot venture the opposite statement that there cannot and will not be this final opening up and enlargement of the circle of election and call-

---

12. Cf. Barth, *Church Dogmatics*, II/1, p. 360.
13. Barth, *Church Dogmatics*, II/1, p. 384. This is discussed by W. Pannenberg, *Systematic Theology*, vol. 1 (Edinburgh: T. & T. Clark, 1993), pp. 432ff. Cf. Gerhard Von Rad, *Old Testament Theology*, vol. 1 (London: SCM, 1965), pp. 370ff.

ing. Neither as the election of Jesus Christ, the election of His community, nor the election of the individual do we know the divine election of
grace as anything other than a decision of His loving-kindness.[14]

There is something odd in this denial of an *apokatastasis.* To be sure, God
does not *need* to elect any human being, but Barth has already claimed that
God's freedom is exercised in love and is enacted in the election of all people in the person and work of Christ. G. C. Berkouwer comments on this
theological maneuver:

> In view of Barth's emphasis on the factuality of Christ's rejection, it is
> not possible to close the door to the apokatastasis doctrine by pointing
> to the fact that the Bible speaks of rejection as well as election and then
> entrust everything *eschatologically* to the hand of God. Did not the hand
> of God become visible in His works, and specifically in the one central
> "modus" of His work in Jesus Christ, in election as the decretum
> *concretum,* in the triumph of grace?[15]

Defenders of Barth's consistency on this matter have pointed to his
"actualism."[16] In the light of Barth's understanding of eternity, the divine
decree is perceived as constantly actualized in the present while also possessing a past and future dimension. God's action on creation thus pre-
cedes, accompanies, and succeeds every human act. In this respect election
is contemporaneous rather than an event in the past that determines the
shape of the future. This activity of the eternal God has a Trinitarian character. Thus John Colwell comments:

---

14. Barth, *Church Dogmatics* II/2, p. 418.

15. G. C. Berkouwer, *The Triumph of Grace in the Theology of Karl Barth* (Grand
Rapids: Eerdmans, 1956), p. 115. For a similar criticism of Barth's teaching, though one that
leads in a different direction, see Emil Brunner, *The Christian Doctrine of God,* vol. 1 (London: Lutterworth, 1949), pp. 346ff.

16. George Hunsinger describes actualism in the following way: "Barth's theology of
active relations is therefore a theology which stresses the sovereignty of grace, the incapacity
of the creature, and the miraculous history whereby grace grants what the creature lacks for
the sake of love and freedom. . . . The church, the inspiration of scripture, faith and all other
creaturely realities in their relationship to God are always understood as events. They are not
self-initiating and self-sustaining. They are not grounded in a neutral, ahistorical, or ontological relationship to God independent of the event of grace" (*How to Read Karl Barth* [Ox-
ford University Press, 1991], p. 31).

[E]lection can be perceived as a living and thoroughly Trinitarian event. The primal decision of the Father does not preclude but includes the actualization of that decision in the life, death and resurrection of the Son. Similarly the decision of the Father as it is actualised in the Son does not preclude but includes the real event of the participation of men and women in that decision through the power of the Holy Spirit. In the authentic temporality which is God's eternity the faith, hope and love of individual men and women are genuinely comprehended within the event of election.[17]

Universalism can be avoided, it is argued, by claiming that the final outcome of human persons vis-à-vis Jesus Christ depends upon the free and future activity of God the Holy Spirit. With respect to those apparently outside the circle of the church, "we may no more presume upon the ultimate finality of their rejection (limiting God's grace) than we are permitted to presume upon their ultimate salvation (limiting God's freedom)."[18] As an exposition of Barth, I have no quarrel with this argument. It seems to me to provide a powerful response to the charge of Christomonism — the view that the weight attached to Christ's work evacuates the rest of history of all significance — yet I share Berkouwer's skepticism as to whether it dispels the problem of universalism. If we are not permitted to affirm universalism because it restricts the sovereign freedom of God, a deep-seated tension emerges between this latest invocation of divine freedom and the earlier description in *Church Dogmatics* II/1.

For Barth, the freedom of God characterizes the way in which God loves us both in his transcendence and in his immanence. Divine freedom is not caprice but freedom, from cosmic processes, to be the eternal God of love. And this freedom is consonant with the love of God revealed in Jesus, even when considered eschatologically.

There is no caprice about the freedom of God. The faithfulness which he evinces and proves in His freedom with regard to His creation is His own faithfulness. It cannot, therefore, be reduced to the level of the regularity

17. John Colwell, "The Contemporaneity of the Divine Decision," in *Universalism and the Doctrine of Hell*, ed. Nigel M. de S. Cameron (Edinburgh: Rutherford House, 1992), p. 158. For another impressive attempt to rescue Barth from the charge of this inconsistency see J. D. Bettis, "Is Karl Barth a Universalist?" *Scottish Journal of Theology* 20 (1967): 423-36.

18. Colwell, "The Contemporaneity of the Divine Decision," p. 157.

of a cosmic process. But it is not on this account concealed from us so that as a matter of fact and in practice we do not know to whom and to what we are clinging when we embrace and apprehend by faith this divine loyalty, when we are summoned by it, and consoled by it, and in turn invoke it. But what it purposes and wills is sure, as is the fact that in all its forms it is true steadfastness, responsible dealing and no irresponsible game. The fact is sure that God constantly turns to us, whether He seems near or far, whether He speaks to us in silence and in secret or whether He addresses us openly, whether He blesses us or punishes us, kills or makes alive. The fact is sure that He is none other than the Creator, the Lord of the Church, the Ruler of our hearts and consciences, the Judge at the last day, the same Lord to me and thee and to his angels and archangels, the same yesterday, today and for ever, here and now and in the remotest lands and times, ever diversely manifested in His freedom, yet ever the same, never and nowhere a different God. But we are sure of this fact only because God is Jesus Christ and Jesus Christ is God.[19]

The denial of universalism in the interests of divine freedom is problematic in light of such passages. The difficulty of avoiding universalism in Barthian theology arises, I would suggest, not from any defect in its account of divine freedom but in the absence of an adequate account of the role of human freedom in unbelief. Barth has much to say about the linkage between what God has done and what human beings are thereby called to do. The space devoted to ethical activity in the *Church Dogmatics* is often ignored in this context. This gives a significance to human conduct as demanded and enabled by divine action. Yet the possibility that a human being might freely reject his or her election is hinted at only obliquely by the later Barth,[20] largely, I suspect, because he cannot contemplate an ac-

---

19. Barth, *Church Dogmatics*, II/1, p. 318.

20. In IV/3 at 70.3, "The Condemnation of Man," Barth comes closest to arguing that human beings can finally refuse their election: "To lie is to try to substitute for the election of man fulfilled by God a rejection which is not God's will for him and which according to God's Word is averted by His act. . . . The lying man as such, set in the situation corresponding to his imaginations and pretensions, can only be the man who is judged and condemned by God and is therefore lost" (pp. 464-65). Yet in the final analysis this fear seems to be overcome by a stronger hope in Barth: "If we are certainly forbidden to count on [an apokatastasis or universal reconciliation] as though we had a claim to it, as though it were not supremely the work of God to which man can have no possible claim, we are surely commanded the more definitely to hope and pray for it as we may do already on this side of

count of human freedom that is not in concert with divine sovereignty. The problem of universalism in Barth might be elucidated not so much by reference to his doctrine of eternity in II/1 or election in II/2 but in his treatment of human freedom in III/3. Here, despite the insistence on human freedom as enabled and guaranteed by divine sovereignty, little scope is given to the possibility that divine sovereignty might be exercised by the gift of a radical freedom that enables the creature absurdly to reject his or her election in Jesus Christ. For Barth, as also for Calvin, the secondary causes of creaturely activity are subordinate to the primary cause of God's will. Although Barth, in contradistinction to Calvin, is unequivocal in affirming that the supremacy of the *causa prima* is love, this makes little difference to the scope assigned to human freedom, as a *causa secunda*.[21] Human autonomy is generally excluded by Barth because of its inevitable association with a synergism or semi-Pelagianism that will compromise the sovereign grace of God.[22]

In the interests of securing divine sovereignty, Barth has something resembling a compatibilist account of freedom in which human freedom is harnessed to the divine intention. What is required is a stronger account of freedom in which the human creature is granted space in which to accept or reject divine love. This freedom should itself be seen as a gift of divine love. Thus Nigel Biggar has rightly commented:

> At this point Barth's understanding of the lordship of God's grace lapses into incoherence. For he makes it perfectly clear that what the gracious God seeks is the free, glad, spontaneous, voluntary co-operation of his

---

this final possibility, i.e. to hope and pray cautiously and yet distinctly that, in spite of everything which may seem quite conclusively to proclaim the opposite, His compassion should not fail, and that in accordance with His mercy which is 'new every morning' He 'will not cast off for ever'" (p. 478). Passages such as this disconfirm the view that Barth's theology is suspended at a point equidistant from limited atonement and universalism. The leaning of his thought is clearly in the latter direction.

21. "His *causare* consists, and consists only, in the fact that He bends their activity to the execution of His own will which is His will of grace, subordinating their operations to the specific operation which constitutes the history of the covenant of grace" (Barth, *Church Dogmatics*, III/3, p. 105).

22. "Is there any humanity more free or autonomous or perfect than that of the men after God's own heart who according to their own confession experience the divine activity towards them without any will or response at all on their part?" (Barth, *Church Dogmatics*, III/3, p. 147).

creatures. But in arguing that this freedom for God is something that all human creatures must ultimately enjoy, Barth seems to propose a form of "compatibilist" account; namely, that human beings are determined to choose freely what is right. This yields a notion of human freedom that is more apparent than real, and it raises questions about the graciousness of a grace that does not concede to the beloved the freedom to turn away permanently. It is true, of course, that the freedom to reject the liberating grace of God is the freedom to enter voluntarily into bondage. But if the ultimate spiritual and moral commitments of human beings are to retain their dignity and weight, then it is just such a paradoxical freedom that they must possess.[23]

Without some such appeal to a stronger notion of human freedom before God, I can see no way in which Christian theology can avoid either the Augustinian disjunction of divine love and justice on the one side, or the incipient universalism of Barth's doctrine of universal predestination in Christ on the other. Only a theology that recognizes the freedom finally to rebel against God can avoid the determinism of either double predestination or universalism.

III. AGAINST UNIVERSALISM

Before exploring what this possibility could look like, we might ask what is wrong with universalism in any case. The burgeoning literature on this subject suggests that seventeenth-century disputes between predestinarians and Arminians have now been transposed into late-twentieth-century disputes between separationists and universalists. It is not surprising, therefore, that even some of the mediating proposals put forward by Molinists have been applied to recent debates over universalism.[24]

One of the more perplexing aspects of the current controversy is the way in which critics of the universalist case concede that it would be nice if

23. Nigel Biggar, *The Hastening That Waits: Karl Barth's Ethics* (Oxford: Clarendon Press, 1993), pp. 5-6.
24. Thus William Lane Craig has drawn upon the concept of divine middle knowledge to resolve the problem of a world in which the ignorant appear to be damned. See his "'No Other Name': A Middle Knowledge Perspective on the Exclusivity of Salvation Through Christ," *Faith and Philosophy* 6, no. 2 (1989): 172-88.

it were true. Thus Stephen Davis in a measured assessment of the issues can say unashamedly, "Let me confess that I would deeply like universalism to be true. Like all [sic!] Christians, I would find it wonderfully comforting to believe that all people will be citizens of the kingdom of God."[25] And William Lane Craig in an article that scarcely yields an inch to the universalist case surprisingly remarks, "No orthodox Christian likes the doctrine of hell or delights in anyone's condemnation. I truly wish that universalism were true, but it is not."[26]

Such remarks are puzzling. Are we saying that God's final scheme is undesirable? Are we even suggesting that our own moral preferences are somehow better than God's? Can we claim to be evangelical if we hold that it would be good if universalism were true while also lamenting wistfully that this is not what God has on offer? There is a good dominical response to this: "If you then, who are evil, know how to give good gifts to your children, how much more will your Father who is in heaven give good things to those who ask him" (Matt. 7:11).

Perhaps the principal attraction of universalism is its ability to present a vision of cosmic fulfillment in which God executes justice, not only for human beings whose lives have been maimed by nature or society, but also for the whole creation. The redeemed community is not a small gathering of the elect plucked from a world rushing headlong to damnation. It is a universal community into which God can gather those whose earthly existence lacked, perhaps through no fault of their own, the physical, social, and religious well-being that he wills for us. The universalist can articulate the hope of "festivals at which the poor man/Is king and the consumptive is/Healed; mirrors in which the blind look/At themselves and love looks at them/Back; and industry is for mending/The bent bones and minds fractured/By life."[27]

Universalism should not be tempered therefore until its profound attractions are understood. We might try to avoid it by proposing that the grace of God is offered to all in Christ but, for those who reject it, God's scheme of justice demands eternal punishment or at least annihilation. A good deal of support for this position can be found in the New Testament, and it probably holds sway among many Christians. Nonetheless, its theo-

25. Davis, "Universalism, Hell and the Fate of the Ignorant," p. 178.
26. Craig, "'No Other Name,'" p. 186.
27. R. S. Thomas, "The Kingdom," *Later Poems 1972-1982* (London: Papermac, 1984), p. 35.

logical difficulties lead me to the conclusion that it requires some emendation if it is to satisfy as an alternative to universalism. Its apparent separation of divine mercy from a system of divine punishment reintroduces into the doctrine of God a hiatus between God's love and justice. If love is the eternal essence of God, and the Father's desire is thus for the home-coming of every prodigal child, how can a temporal limitation be placed upon this desire? Does God's desire for our well-being cease at death or even in hell? (It is this thought that makes hell at most a purgatorial institution in universalist thought from Origen to John Hick.)[28] If God's love and justice are to remain integrated, then we must think of rejection as itself a function of God's love.

A second difficulty with this position is its assumption that a free decision for Christ can be made over the course of a lifetime. I doubt whether this can be the case for all people or perhaps even for the majority. The problem of those who have lived outside the sphere of Christian preaching has received much attention in the literature. Solutions range from positing divine judgment to common grace and general revelation, to the possibility of a postmortem encounter with Christ.[29] We are in the realms of speculation here, though such speculation involves significant pastoral and theological issues. Less attention has been given to those who have rejected a corrupt form of Christianity, or those whose life circumstances have been so heavily stacked against them that the scope for genuine responsible choices has been severely restricted. Most of us who have conducted funeral services for those who have lived apparently ignoble lives are content merely to commend them to the mercy of God rather than to assume that their eternal fate is catastrophic. Is there a theology that can sustain this hope without lapsing into a complacent universalism?

I take it that the New Testament comes down fairly decisively against universalism.[30] To argue the contrary requires implausibly both a very lit-

28. Cf. Richard Bauckham, "Universalism: A Historical Survey," *Themelios* 4, no. 2 (1979): 48-54.

29. This latter option has been gaining ground in recent Protestant theology. Cf. George Lindbeck, "Fides ex auditu and the Salvation of Non-Christians," in *The Gospel and the Ambiguity of the Church*, ed. Vilmos Vatja (Philadelphia: Fortress, 1974), pp. 92-123. Cf. Davis, "Universalism, Hell and the Fate of the Ignorant."

30. For a robust statement of this view see I. H. Marshall, "Does the New Testament Teach Universal Salvation?" in *Christ in Our Place*, ed. T. A. Hart (Exeter: Paternoster, 1989), pp. 313-28.

eral reading of passages such as Romans 5:11, 1 Corinthians 15:22, and Colossians 1:20 and the demythologizing of many more separationist texts. The insistence upon an inexorable salvation that will come about in distant eons seems strangely at odds with the compelling call of Jesus to repent for the time is at hand. The New Testament witness is one reason in particular why one might reject universalism without thereby delimiting the scope or duration of God's love, or denying the cosmic vision that it articulates.

Universalism appears to be committed to a theology that is as deterministic and destructive of human freedom as the doctrine of double predestination in hyper-Calvinism. In particular, it does not allow any human being the freedom finally to say "no" to God. Yet without this possibility can we really be said to have the freedom finally to say "yes" to God? John Hick's argument for God as a cosmic therapist who will assist all his creatures in attaining spiritual health seems to break down at this juncture. It presupposes that all persons will either submit voluntarily to or be administered coercively a para-eschatological course of therapeutic treatment. That this implies a diminution of the significance of freedom is a point well made by Grace Jantzen:

> If I perpetually choose selfishness and distrust and dishonesty, and my character is formed by these choices, it seems perverse to say that eventually these choices will be reversed and I will attain the same moral perfection as I would have if I had all along chosen integrity and compassion. Part of what it means to be free is that our choices have consequences; it is playing much too lightly with the responsibility of freedom to suggest that these consequences, at least in their effects upon ourselves, are always reversible, even if only in the endless life to come.[31]

If universalism is to be rejected without compromising the love of God, then it must be in terms of a negative use of that freedom which is itself a gift of divine love. God does not wish our love of him to be coerced. Were it so, it would not truly be love, for love must be freely given and received. The condition of our loving God, therefore, is the possibility that some may realize the possibility of rejecting him. This freedom is not out-

31. Grace Jantzen, "Do We Need Immortality?" *Modern Theology* 1 (1984): 40. I owe this reference to R. R. Cook, "Is Universalism an Implication of the Notion of Post-Mortem Evangelism?" *Tyndale Bulletin* 45, no. 2 (1994): 404.

side the providence of God. It is a freedom in which he concurs. When confronted by the presence of God our ability to respond must be effected by the Holy Spirit, but this does not imply that the response must always be positive. The necessary condition of the freedom bestowed by the love of God, therefore, is the possibility of our rejecting him. This is an argument stressed in recent Catholic theology.

> If the possibility of heaven is rooted in a free act of love whereby the human person accepts and responds to the grace of God, the possibility of hell is rooted in the very same freedom. If we are not free to reject, then neither are we free to accept. . . . The affirmation of the possibility of hell is, therefore, a necessary conclusion from this understanding of human freedom. This is not only a question of the meaning of freedom in the moment of death. It draws our attention to the moral seriousness of all the free decisions of human life as well. Thus, as Ratzinger argues, the real intent of the doctrine of hell is to underscore the seriousness of human existence and human action. If we view our lives as an opportunity for endless revisions and changes of mind, we will be far less serious about the moral character of our decisions than we would be if we lived in the light of the real possibility of final failure.[32]

Yet this must not lead to a synergism in which we become equal partners with God. To accept God's gracious invitation to sit at his table is to recognize one's need, a recognition that by its nature is an acknowledgment of our poverty. The Bible tends to explain why some say "no" to Christ — I have purchased a field, I have bought five yoke of oxen, I have married a wife — but sees little need to explain why others leave their nets and follow him. It is as if the gracious call of Jesus is the only explanation necessary. There is no symmetry between acceptance and rejection, and no sense in which the trust we show is of equal weight to God's mercy. Even unbelief is a condition provoked by the love of God. This libertarian notion of freedom must find a place in one's theological system, but perhaps only as an addendum to explain the possibility of one's rejecting God.

It is this asymmetry between faith and unfaith that should prevent us from lapsing into a semi-Pelagianism or psychologism of belief. Human freedom is not to be invoked as an explanation for our redemption; the

---

32. Zachary Hayes, *Vision of a Future: A Study of Christian Eschatology* (Wilmington: Michael Glazier, 1989), pp. 187-88.

love of God in Christ and the influence of the Holy Spirit are all-sufficient. To isolate our acceptance of grace is to assign it a significance it does not deserve.[33] The appeal to human freedom as an explanatory condition is valid only in the asymmetrical case of unbelief. Here we are confronted by a possibility that has no explanation beyond an absurd use of the freedom that God grants us as human persons. Without some such appeal to deliberate human rejection of God, we can explain the possibility of unbelief only in terms of ignorance or a divine decree. Neither alternative can be consistent with the love of God declared in Scripture.[34]

Anthony Burgess once remarked that he believed in hell but did not think anyone was there. Is it possible on the above scenario that everyone might in the long run freely choose God? It is possible, and one may hope that the heavenly city will be much more populous than the size of the church might suggest. If one can hope in God's love then there is reason for some confidence regarding the destiny not only of ourselves and our loved ones but also of our ancestors who predate us perhaps by millions of years. Yet the possibility of freedom being eternally misused cannot be discounted and should in any event caution us against too complacent a view of our own destiny. If choices are genuine only when made in the full knowledge of God's love in Christ, it is in the church that the burden of human responsibility is greatest.

How can this be turned into an effective eschatological message for the times in which we live? How can the Christian life continue to be suffused with an eschatological hope in societies that are increasingly fragmented and comprise individuals whose primary goals relate to private success and comfort for this life only? Even the enterprise of death is now de-

---

33. While my position has some similarities to the Wesleyan account of human responsibility created by prevenient grace, I do not wish to place any emphasis upon belief as a free act. This can lead to a questionable psychologism of faith in which the focus of theology and preaching is unhelpfully directed to the inner life of the believer, and thus away from Christ, the one who has kept the faith for us. For an excellent exposition of Wesley's account see Thomas C. Oden, *John Wesley's Scriptural Christianity: A Plain Exposition of His Teaching on Christian Doctrine* (Grand Rapids: Zondervan, 1994). I am grateful to Tom Noble for this reference on the Wesleyan position.

34. This is formally similar to the moral phenomenon of the weakness of the will (*akrasia*). Some philosophers, in perceiving the absurdity of responsibly choosing what one knows to be wrong and harmful, have redescribed the phenomenon in terms of sheer ignorance. I do not view this as an option for Christian theology, for the language of confession typically implies that we choose what we know to be wrong.

scribed in postmodern terms, as individuals insist upon being allowed to die and to grieve in ways of their own choosing.[35]

One of the most valuable functions that eschatology can perform is to recall the extent to which a redeemed life is communal. It is life in fellowship with God, with other people, and in a new creation. The Christian doctrine of the resurrection of the body is better placed than a theory of the immortality of the soul to point to this hope of a new community. An eschatology needs to express the ways in which our lives are bound up with those of our neighbors and with creation as a whole and involve decisions and projects of eternal significance. By so doing the eschatological vision of the kingdom of God can furnish us with a sense of the permanence and grandeur of God's love. The possibility that we may inexplicably exclude ourselves from this ultimate community is a condition of the significance of our God-given freedom. It gives to our time here and now a momentous weight. At its best, this vision should energize rather than distract us from the tasks of the present and cause us ever hereafter to trust in God's unending love.[36]

35. This is analyzed sociologically by Tony Walter, *The Revival of Death* (London: Routledge, 1994).

36. Despite my earlier remarks on Barth, I find in his writings an overwhelming sense of the importance of the time given to us: "The time in which we live is our place. It may be a modest place, but it is ours. As such, it is our place in the cosmos and in history, but also in relation to the particularity of the divine *opus proprium* which awaits us, to the calling, covenant and salvation of God, to Jesus Christ who became man for us. . . . The command of God summons him [i.e., us] to be wholly and exclusively the man he can be in this place and this place alone. It thus lifts him out of the stalls and sets him, not behind the stage, but on it, to appear at once and well or badly to say his little piece as appointed" (Barth, *Church Dogmatics*, III/4, p. 579).

CHAPTER 10

Postscript: The Love of God —
A Sermon on Hosea 11

ROY CLEMENTS

I. INTRODUCTION

I don't know if you're familiar with Nanette Newman's compilation of juvenile reflections entitled *Children's Thoughts on Love*. Some of the contributions are quite hilarious. Take the earnest gratitude of Zoe, for instance: "I love my teacher because she gives me a good education." That's education spelt "ejukashun." Not as good as you think, Zoe.

Other offers are strangely profound. Take this one from Norman, aged 7: "Babies need to be loved by their mothers in case everyone hates them when they grow up." There's a Freudian psychiatrist in the making, I'll be bound.

But the thing that startles you most forcefully in Nanette Newman's collection is how often the pathos of family breakdown seeps through rather quietly in the unrepressed candor of these young authors, often with quite moving results.

Like this confession from Jean, aged 7: "My Daddy went away and we have to keep remembering to love him."

Or Anne, aged 8: "My Mummy and Daddy are in love most of the time, but when I go to bed they shout a lot."

"Mummy says that Daddy does love me," affirms David, aged 7, "but he is very busy at work."

Or perhaps most poignant of all, Paul, aged 7: "I love my mother because I have a photograph of her and she sends me presents."

If these kinds of sentiments were typical of children's experiences of love in the late twentieth century then one has the feeling that love is doomed to becoming a pretty superficial word in the early twenty-first century. Indeed the signs are that it is already beginning to happen — people are being cynical about love. Stephen Turner catches the contemporary mood rather well in a telling little poem entitled "Declaration of Intent":

She said she'd love me for eternity,
But managed to reduce it to 8 months for good behaviour.
She said we fitted together like a hand in a glove,
But then the hot weather came and such accessories
        were not needed.
She said the future was ours,
But the house deed was made out in her name.
She said I was the only one who understood her completely,
And then she left me.
She said she knew I'd understand completely.

"They lived happily ever after" may be the way fairy tales and romantic stories end, but in real life the divorce rate now exceeds 50 percent — statistics are no longer on the side of "they lived happily ever after."

Love has become at best an ephemeral will-o'-the-wisp, a sentimental measles that one catches and then recovers from.

All of which is having tragic consequences, and not only on young children who are the innocent victims of emotional breakdowns, as Nanette Newman's book indicates. I want to suggest that it's also having a rather serious effect on the spiritual life of Western society. For a society that is no longer understanding or believing in love is in my view also going to have a hard job understanding or believing in God, or at least the God of the Bible. Love is, according to John, an indispensable condition of valid and practical theology.

It is, of course, possible to misrepresent God by failing to do justice to his transcendence. "To whom will you compare God?" asks the prophet Isaiah, and the challenge goes unanswered because God is by definition unique — the incomparable one.

Four hundred years ago Martin Luther complained that Erasmus had failed to do justice to this ineffable mystery that is God. "Your thoughts of

God are too human," he complained. And early in the twentieth century Karl Barth issued a rather similar warning to the liberal theologians of his own day. God is wholly other, utterly different from everything with which we are familiar.

In both cases, I guess, the remark was justified; we all too easily reduce God to some kind of heavenly Santa Claus figure, a pathetic projection of our own longings for parental comfort and security. And talk of the love of God can easily fall into the trap of that sort of anthropomorphic sentimentality.

But it is possible to go too far in that direction of emphasis on the divine transcendence. Indeed, it seems to me that the Barthian school did go too far, so stressing the otherness of God that in time it seemed to be almost impossible to say anything of God at all of a propositional nature.

Well, clearly the apostle John doesn't go that far. He's quite prepared to articulate a propositional truth about God using vocabulary of human experience: "God is love. Whoever lives in love lives in God, and God in him" (1 John 4:16b). John certainly doesn't intend to identify God with a mystical force behind the universe like some nineteenth-century pantheist poet. Still less is he advocating tantric yoga like some hippie guru of the 1960s.

No, when John says God is love, he is seeking to make an objectively true statement about the character of the personal creator God of the Bible. And in so doing he is surely also implying that if it is possible, like Erasmus, to have thoughts of God that are too human, it is also possible, like Barth, to have thoughts of God that are not human enough.

To give him credit, Karl Barth recognized that imbalance in his theology, and later in his life he publicly repented of it in a rather famous lecture he gave, significantly entitled "The Humanity of God."

It is inevitable, of course, that we have to draw on our human experience for the metaphors we use in order to speak of God in our dogmatics. This is not anthropomorphic idolatry; it is the precondition of any meaningful revelation of God that can be grasped by the human mind. God himself, in fact, according to Christian orthodoxy, in his inspired word invites such analogies again and again and again — analogies to our human experience. He accommodates himself to it.

And therefore, whatever else may be enshrined in that remarkable propositional statement of John that God is love, at the very least surely the apostle is implying that of all the facets of our human experience upon which we must necessarily draw for our vocabulary, the vocabulary upon which we construct our theology, none is more important — even crucial — than the human experience of love.

The congruence between God and his divine image in human beings is never more closely defined than in the semantic associations of that word "love."

Our world without love must be, in a very real sense, a godless world. For "God is love. Whoever lives in love lives in God, and God in him" (1 John 4:16b). Perhaps that is what Dostoyevsky meant when he defined hell as the suffering of being unable to love.

One person understood that indispensable correlation between the human experience of love and a true knowing of God, and understood it long before John articulated it in his first letter. I speak of Hosea, the eighth-century prophet of Israel.

Now no one could accuse Hosea of encouraging a sentimental notion of God in his compatriots. No, his God is lofty and awesome. In fact there are passages in Hosea that rival the ferocity of his contemporary Amos in the belligerency in their description of the divine judgment.

But there is something else in Hosea too, something distinctively his own. And, significantly, that idiosyncrasy in Hosea is very much associated with Hosea's own love life. For Hosea was a man with his own tale of marital unhappiness to tell. Under divine direction he had taken to wife the prostitute Gomer, and this union did not result in any renunciation of her lifestyle. On the contrary, in one tragic passage in Hosea 3, we seem to find the prophet in the humiliating situation of having to compensate the latest gigolo in Gomer's life for the loss of his own wife's sexual services.

"Love her," the Lord told him. With extraordinary emphasis he repeats it: love her even though she is an adulteress. Love her as the Lord loves the Israelites, even though they commit adultery, too, by their devotion to pagan idols. So the heartbreak and trauma of this torturous marriage becomes a kind of dramatized prophecy. Under the inspiration of God, Hosea's experience of unrequited and abused love informs his theology. So again John would later perhaps put it in learning the meaning of love. He also knew what it meant to know God. For God is love, and only those who live in love can know him.

Nowhere does Hosea demonstrate the depth of the theological sensitivity that the struggle to love Gomer gave him more meaningfully than in chapter 11. Though this passage is comparatively little known, I regard it as one of the jewels in the Bible, for in it we see portrayed in a remarkable and vivid way what the love of God means to God himself.

Of course it is true that God is not like us: "I am God and not man — the Holy One among you" (11:9). There's a transcendent God, and woe betide us if we ever forget it. Yet paradoxically Hosea insists that there is one very fundamental and important way in which God is like us. He loves, and loves in a way that we human beings can understand and experience. And because he loves, he feels. He can be hurt. He can suffer.

As confidently as we may speak of the majesty of God, Hosea would have us know in this passage that we can speak just as confidently of the passion of God.

It is this aspect of the divine passion that I would like you to think about with me for a little while, lest through neglecting it, our thoughts of God, though adequately transcendent, may nevertheless be too cold, too detached. We can certainly err like Erasmus by having thoughts of God that are too human, but we can err also by having thoughts of him that are not human enough.

Follow with me then in this passage of Hosea 11 the story of the love of God: the hurt love first of all, the wounded love of verses 1-4; the angry love, the wounded indignation of verses 5-7; and in verses 8 and 9 the passionate tension between these two things, the passionate love.

II. WOUNDED LOVE (HOSEA 11:1-4)

We'll start with the wounded feelings of the early verses: "When Israel was a child, I loved him, and out of Egypt I called my son. But the more I called Israel, the further they went from me" (vv. 1-2a). With considerable theological originality Hosea is portraying God here in soliloquy. God isn't addressing anybody; he's talking to himself. This, of course, is always a dramatic device by which an author is trying to open a window into the mind of the person concerned. So here Hosea is bold enough to open for us the mind of God, God's inner thoughts. Dare we say, God's feelings?

What do we find when we peep through that audacious window? Do we find the stern impartiality of an omniscient judge? Do we find the aloof dignity of an omnipotent sovereign? No. Astonishingly, in this passage the prophet tells us that what we find when we look through that window at the heart of God is a broken heart, the broken heart of a deserted parent:

"When Israel was a child, I loved him, and out of Egypt I called my son. But the more I called Israel, the further they went from me. They sacrificed to Baals and they burned incense to images" (vv. 1-2). It is rather characteristic of Hosea to depict God looking back to the good old days of the exodus when Israel first came out of Egypt. But this particular piece of divine nostalgia exceeds any other in its poignancy. Can't you hear the generosity of God's electing love here: "When Israel was a child"? It's a picture of a man finding an orphaned baby boy and cherishing him. So enchanted with him is he that he redeems him from the slavery in which he is born and adopts him as his very own child. "My son," he calls him. Nowhere is the graciousness of God's choice of Israel described in more moving terms.

In verse 3 Hosea moves on to describe the tenderness of God's parental love and instruction: "It was I who taught Ephraim to walk, taking them by the arms; but they did not realize that it was I who healed them. I led them with cords of human kindness, with ties of love; I lifted the yoke from their neck and bent down to feed them" (vv. 3-4). So the picture continues of a father who is gently nursing his child through those precious early years, supporting him by his arms while he makes those first faltering steps, applying the salve onto those bumps and bruises that every toddler inflicts upon himself. It is hard to imagine God's dealings with Israel ever being described in terms of greater affection.

Some scholars believe that when we get to verse 4 Hosea's metaphor changes to that of a pet or animal being looked after by a humane master. That's how the NIV interprets it. But I am strongly attracted to the view of those who have revocalized the consonants of the Hebrew word translated "yoke" in verse 4 so that it reads "baby" instead. Understood that way, it is possible to render the text as, for instance, the NEB does, as a continuation of the parable of the infant and the parent: "I harnessed them in leading reins. I lifted them like a little baby to my cheek. I bent down to feed them."

Whichever way we take it, it is a thrilling picture of God's care for his people, his condescension — king of the earth, but bending down to guide them, to comfort them, to feed them. It is a beautiful picture. Not even in the New Testament, I suggest, is God's love described in more moving terms than these: as a generous, gentle, devoted parent.

Yet in spite of all this fatherly goodness, what had this much loved infant grown into? An inconsiderate, surly, rebellious lout. "They didn't know I was the one who healed them," complains God. Perhaps some of us are parents of teenagers; we don't need these words to understand the pathos that lies behind them. We know what Hosea is talking about from personal experience, perhaps. We know what it's like to be slapped in the face by our own children. But is it not an extraordinary thing to discover that God knows what that is like too? Perhaps there's some comfort here for some of us who feel rejected by those we love: by our children or by our parents; by a wife or a husband. God in that situation does not offer us mere patronizing pity. He knows how hurt we have been, for he is no stranger to such heartbreak himself, nor to the violent emotional response that such heartbreak kindles.

III. ANGRY LOVE (HOSEA 11:5-7)

From the wounded feelings of verses 1 to 4 we go on to the angry love of verses 5 to 7: "Will they not return to Egypt and will not Assyria rule over them because they refuse to repent? Swords will flash in their cities, will destroy the bars of their gates, and put an end to their plans. My people are determined to turn from me. Even if they call to the Most High, he will by no means exalt them."

Now there are unfortunately some difficulties unraveling the Hebrew in this particular text, particularly in verse 7. But the general thrust of these three verses is plain, even if some of the details are not. God's immediate reaction to Israel's insult is to be furious with her. "I've treated her with a velvet glove all these years," he says; "now she's going to get a taste of the iron fist. After all, bondage in Egypt is where I found her; if she appreciates so little all I've done for her, let her go back to it. If she thinks so little of my fatherly love, let her see if she prefers a tyrant's word instead. If she thinks pagan gods better than me, let her try a little pagan hospitality. She said no to me once too often. I've been calling her for centuries and she has refused to repent. Now it's my turn to play deaf. She'll discover I can be just as obstinately unresponsive as she is when I want to be. Even if they call to the Most High, he will by no means exalt them."

We know from history that this was no empty threat. Hosea's words were almost certainly spoken on the very brink of national catastrophe for Israel. Within a few years Israel would be swallowed up by the Assyrian invasion. The violence of war would indeed devastate these proud cities, and all Israel's dreams of future prosperity would be shattered just as Hosea predicts. So the anger of which he speaks here is no mere literary device designed to promote audience shock. It was a real anger, and it issued in a real judgment.

That is important, isn't it, when we think of the love of God. People so often these days want to argue that the Bible isn't serious in attributing anger to God, that it's just a metaphor, an anthropomorphism, a way of speaking about God as if he were human, which of course he isn't. We're no more to imagine God being truly angry than to imagine him really having a mouth or a hand. Well, Hosea is certainly using metaphor in this chapter, but he would have us know that if our picture of God is too sophisticatedly superhuman to be capable of real anger, we have gone too far. The real God who revealed himself in the history of Israel was angry with her sin and took formidable action against her because of it. The thousands of Israelites who perished in the Assyrian conquest were left in no doubt about that. It is naive to think that God cannot be hurt by the insult of our sin, and it is just as naive to think that he is not infuriated by the insult of our sin.

Actually, of course, once again, when we are honest with our own feelings and experience we understand that perfectly well. People constantly will ask you, of course, how can a God of love judge anybody? But you might as well ask how could a God, who loved this people as much as verses 1 to 4 clearly indicate Yahweh loved Israel, destroy that people by enemy invasion? What sort of father is this? The answer, of course, is that anger is not incompatible with love, and every parent knows it. In fact, we are far more angry at the abuse and insults of those we love than of those for whom we care nothing. It is angry love we see here. It was precisely because he loved Israel so much that we read, "Swords will flash in their cities." This is still the covenant God, and it is the curse of the covenant that he is invoking. We must not think that there is no penalty for the ingratitude and rebellion of our human sin.

IV. PASSIONATE LOVE (HOSEA 11:8-9)

Yet, of course, that still isn't the end of the story, which brings us to verses 8 and 9. We've seen the wounded love of verses 1 to 4 and the angry love of verses 5 to 7; now we see the passionate love of verses 8 and 9, as the wound and the outrage battle in the heart of God. "How can I give you up,

Ephraim? How can I hand you over, Israel? How can I treat you like Admah? How can I make you like Zeboiim? My heart is changed within me. All my compassion is aroused. I will not carry out my fierce anger, nor will I devastate Ephraim, for I am God and not man, the holy one among you. I will not come in wrath." I believe these have to be some of the most remarkable verses in the whole of the Old Testament. We have said that Hosea has composed here soliloquy, opening a window into the inner feelings of God. But who would have dared to think that the prophet would depict those feelings in such a state of seething conflict, of contradiction? These trenchant rhetorical questions of verse 8 seem to suggest confusion and uncertainty in God's intention. He can't make up his mind. He is utterly distraught, like an anguished parent; he wants to beat his disobedient child and hug him simultaneously. Admah and Zeboiim were cities of the plain that perished with Sodom and Gomorrah, according to Jewish tradition, so clearly God's anger here is so severe that the total annihilation of his people is within the compass of his mind, and yet no sooner has his righteous indignation commended such an act of judicial retribution than his love revolts against the prospect and insists that such a course of action is unthinkable. Isn't that an extraordinary picture?

Can God really be as human as this? Can he really feel as inwardly torn as this? Can his passion confuse him as so often our passions confuse us? And how are we to interpret the apparent resolution of this confusion that God seems to achieve in verse 9, when he says, "I will not carry out my fierce anger, nor will I turn and devastate Ephraim, for I am God and not man, the holy one among you. I will not come in wrath"? Isn't that ironic? All through this chapter, Hosea has been employing the most outrageous anthropomorphic language, likening God to a man again and again and again. Now he tells us that Israel's only hope lies in the inadequacies of such language. It is precisely because God is unlike man that mercy has any chance at all, he says. It is a very provocative thought. It reminds me of one who protested, "Lord, who then can be saved?" and who received in reply, "With men it is impossible, but not with God. All things are possible with God." Taken at a human level, there is no way out of the emotional impasse into which God's love for his people has projected him. He cannot deny the injury to his love; Israel's sin must be punished. But neither can he deny the mercy that his love commends; Israel's sin must be pardoned. Hosea insists that, though there seems to be no human solution to that passionate dilemma, there is a divine one. Because God is God and not man, he will find a way. He is determined about that. Mere human beings might find themselves paralyzed, rendered helpless by these conflicting emotions; but God, because he is God, is able to feel and yet is not in bondage to those feelings. By an act of sovereign choice, he can cut through that Gordian knot of agonizing alternatives and create hope out of despair — at least that is Hosea's conviction. Where sin abounds, he is convinced that grace will abound all the more. "I will not come in wrath."

Inevitably when we read these verses we want to ask, when? how? In the immediate, of course, Hosea seems to see some solution in a restoration following the Assyrian conquest to which verses 10 and 11 address themselves. But am I not speaking the truth when I say that, for any Christian reader, there is a much deeper answer to that question as to when and how this prophecy of Hosea was fulfilled? I give it to you in one word — in Jesus. Look at Jesus, see him hanging on the cross, and there you see the passionate love of God. This is how we know what love is, says John. Jesus Christ laid down his life for us. "This is love, not that we loved God, but that he loved us and sent his Son as the atoning sacrifice for our sins" (1 John 4:10). When John says that God is love, of course, he does not mean, any more than Hosea meant, that judgment is unreal, that it is an empty threat. No, the wrath of God is real. God is angry; John knew that as well as Hosea. Yet John never writes that God is wrath in the same way he writes that God is love. That is interesting for our dogmatics, isn't it? For wrath, as Luther puts it, is "God's strange work." It is alien to his essential character. God's wrath is a response called into existence by the phenomena of our sin. But God's love, on the other hand, is an eternal energy burning within the Godhead. There was a time when there was no sin in the eye of God for him to hate. But there never was a time when there was no Son in the heart of God for him to love. And, says John, it was that very Son he sent into the world to work out the passion that Hosea's prophetic insight, many centuries before, discerned must somewhere find resolution in this broken and sin-sick world.

You want to see the love of God, wounded by the insult of your sin? Then, says John, look at the cross, see it written there in the passion of Jesus. You want to see the love of God angered by your sin? Look at the cross, see it written there in the passion of Jesus. You want to see how much God loves you in spite of that sin? Look at the cross, see it written there in the passion of Jesus. The very shape of the cross, it seems to me, symbolizes this passionate collision of contradictory emotions of which Hosea speaks.

There, the divine love, in all its anger and its compassion, meets in one momentous catharsis.

Hosea was right, wasn't he? There was no human solution to this divine dilemma that our sin poses. How could God be just and overlook our sin? How could he be love and punish us for it? God is not man, however, and in his wisdom he found a way — a way that neither compromised his righteousness nor denied his mercy. And we see that worked out in the cross. "This is how we know what love is. God sent his Son into the world as the atoning sacrifice for our sin." Do you see what I mean then when I say that, while undoubtedly it is possible to have thoughts of God that are too human, it is also possible to have thoughts of God that are not human enough? God is human enough to be hurt by our sin, human enough to be angered by our sin, human enough to suffer for our sins — and this, says John, is what we mean when we say, "God is love."

We could spend a great deal of time drawing out what the implications of such a message of love ought to be for a world like ours. Let me just say two things. It does seem to me that this distinctive biblical doctrine of a loving God who suffers because he loves is the very thing our sad world needs to hear, if ever the fractures in our families and marriages are going to stand any chance of being repaired, and if those appalling statistics of marital breakdown are ever to be reversed. What has happened, of course, in recent years, is that a world has grown up around us that is frightened of pain. That is why people dare not love in the way that the Bible requires them to love: for better, for worse, till death does us part. This is why they find such a commitment daunting; they don't want to be hurt. They have seen people hurt by loving in an unreserved way, and they shy away from it. But you see, to know what love really is inevitably means taking the risk of being hurt, and until our community learns that again and is willing to take that risk again, then marriage contracts are going to be very ephemeral and increasingly unpopular.

Sadly, we live in a world that expects to be surrounded from birth to death in a kind of cozy glow of painlessness, of analgesia. Everything must be done for our benefit, for our self-fulfillment; narcissism is our characteristic neurosis. We have replaced *agape* love, which suffers, with our own form of *eros,* a love that selfishly desires and wants and needs, but pays no price of pain for its desire; and the danger is, of course, that we in the church, instead of identifying this appalling blunder in the very nature and definition of love that our society is committing, will simply collude with it, surrender to it, just as in Hosea's day the false prophets surrendered to the sensuality of Baal. Just as in John's day the heretics surrendered to the sensuality of the Gnostics, so it seems to me that we are in grave danger of abandoning this costly love that suffers for a different kind of Christian love altogether — an anemic, sensual, cheap kind of *eros*. Rollo May, the American psychiatrist, argues that the popularity of many religious cults today is that people are looking for an *eros* experience of God. They want an experience that fulfills them. They aren't looking for love that might cause them pain. Suffering is not on their agenda at all, and when it comes they feel cheated.

People can very easily think they are experiencing Christian love when in fact they are being seduced by pagan *eros*, not Christian *agape* at all. Small wonder that the love of God is conceived in such self-indulgent and emotional terms today. Small wonder that suffering seems such an un-thinkable contradiction to the Christian message, that the clamor for heal-ing is so obsessive. Small wonder that the latest craze is for laughter. Small wonder that the cross is so little understood and so inadequately preached upon. Small wonder that people find it so hard to distinguish anything re-ally unique about Christianity within the pluralistic confusion of our multi-faith society. And that brings me to the second aspect of application I want to suggest to you.

It seems to me that once the distinctiveness of this God of suffering love is obscured, it is all too easy to reduce Christianity to just one more of the 57 Heinz–made varieties of the religious experiences with which the world is cluttered. What do we have to say that is different from any other religion, if you strip from our religion this God of suffering love? I remem-ber when I lived in Africa, hearing a very wise — quite simple, but very wise — African trying to deal with this very subject in his own congrega-tion. It was a congregation where African traditional religion was popular, where Marxism was being flirted with by the educated youngsters, where Islam was a constant threat, not far away, and where, of course, Christian-ity was seeking to retain its toehold in that really very young situation and missionary outreach. And this pastor was trying to encourage his people with the thought that they should be Christians, that they should eschew these other alternatives that were beckoning them. In order to make his point, he told a story. I'll tell it to you.

It's the story of an African village, a very simple, typical African vil-lage, in which one night there was a fire in one of the small dwellings. It was made only of straw and stuff and very quickly burnt to the ground, and all inside this little hut, being asleep when the fire broke out, perished in the darkness of the night, with the exception of one small boy child. In this dark night as the fire was just taking hold, some unknown member of the tribe dashed into the fire and pulled this little child to safety before the whole thing went up in a conflagration and nobody else could be saved. This little child emerged unscathed. When dawn came, the elders of the tribe were confronted with a difficult problem. The man who had rescued the child had disappeared, the child was just left lying on the ground, and they had to decide what to do with him. They thought that it was a great sign of divine providence that this little child had been preserved, and they began to dispute about who within the tribe should have the privilege and honor, not to say responsibility, of raising this child so favored by God. Well, of course, those who were wealthy, those who felt that their wives were particularly good mothers, things of that sort, all brought in evidence before the elders' court. Finally a man stood up, a comparatively insignificant member of the tribe, and insisted that he had a superior claim to all the others for the care and the adoption of this boy child. Why, they asked, what right have you got to have him? You are not wealthy. You are not important. So he showed them his hands. They were burned. He had been the one who had rescued the child. What greater evidence of love and devotion for that child could they ask for than that? Who could possibly have a superior claim than he?

And this old African pastor, I remember, leaned over his pulpit and said, "Oh, I don't dispute that the old gods and our forefathers have wisdom and power. I don't dispute that Muhammad has taught many great and noble things. I don't dispute that Marxism has much to offer a colonial people like us." But he said, "I must follow Jesus because he alone has scars in his hands, scars acquired because he loved us and suffered for the sake of that love." Of whom else could that be said? Of whom else in the whole range of human philosophy and religion could that be said? Yes, you can have thoughts of God that are too human; but when the Bible tells us that God is love, it is surely telling us that it is also possible to have thoughts of God that are just not human enough. For our God, uniquely in this world of faiths, loves and suffers because he loves.

Contributors

LEWIS AYRES, Candler School of Theology, Emory University

GARY D. BADCOCK, Huron University College, London, Ontario

ROY CLEMENTS, formerly Pastor, Eden Baptist Church, Cambridge

DAVID FERGUSSON, University of Edinburgh

GEOFFREY GROGAN, Principal Emeritus, Glasgow Bible College

TREVOR HART, University of St Andrews

PAUL HELM, King's College, London

TONY LANE, London Bible College

ALAN J. TORRANCE, University of St Andrews

KEVIN J. VANHOOZER, Trinity Evangelical Divinity School